"I wouldn't trade this experience for anything."

Imagine yourself living in a houseboat on the Amazon, studying the Brazilian ecosystems, speaking Portuguese, and sighting pink river dolphins as you prepare for bed. That's part of what you could expect from the **Antioch College Brazilian Ecosystems program.**

"It was the best semester you could do without going to the moon."

Even the greatest wanderlust will be sated after traveling for five months to these nine spectacular countries: Switzerland, Greece, Israel, Egypt, India, Nepal, Hong Kong, China, and South Korea. From the Taj Mahal to the Pyramids to Tiananmen Square, history comes to life on the **St. Olaf College Global Semester.**

"I woke up several times at night to the roaring of lions."

Or perhaps communing with the elephants, zebras, and antelopes of the Serengeti is more to your taste. At the **School for Field Studies Kenya program** you'll learn about wildlife management and environmental policy while giraffes munch at the trees in the background.

From meditating underneath the Bodhi tree with Buddhist masters in India to climbing Mount Sinai, from sailing a 125-foot schooner in the Caribbean to listening to an Aboriginal elder tell stories around a campfire, *The Student's Guide to the Best Study Abroad Programs* has something for everyone.

THE STUDENT'S GUIDE TO THE BEST STUDY ABROAD PROGRAMS

GREG TANNEN
AND
CHARLEY WINKLER

WALKABOUT

POCKET BOOKS
New York   London   Toronto   Sydney   Tokyo   Singapore

An *Original* Publication of POCKET BOOKS

POCKET BOOKS, a division of Simon & Schuster Inc.
1230 Avenue of the Americas, New York, NY 10020

Library of Congress Cataloging-in-Publication Data

Tannen, Greg.
    The student's guide to the best study abroad programs / by Greg Tannen and Charley Winkler.
        p.   cm.
    ISBN 0-671-55027-6
    1. Foreign study—Handbooks, manuals, etc.   2. American students—Foreign countries—Handbooks, manuals, etc.   I. Tannen, Greg.
II. Title.
LB2376.W55   1996
370.19'6—dc20
                                                                95-49169
                                                                CIP

First Pocket Books trade paperback printing June 1996

10 9 8 7 6 5 4 3 2 1

Cover design by Lisa Litwack
Front cover illustration by Theresa Smith

Text design by Stanley S. Drate/Folio Graphics Co., Inc.

Printed in the U.S.A.

WALKABOUT —an Australian Aboriginal (or Koori) term for self-discovery. Traditionally, members of the Koori culture take a few weeks, months, or even years out of their normal day-to-day life and go "walkabout" in the outback. It is a quest for knowledge of self, the world, and the relationship between the two.

ACKNOWLEDGMENTS

This book simply could not have been written if it wasn't for the support, suggestions, and critique of our families—to the Tannen Clan and the Winkler Tribe we offer our eternal thanks. Thanks also to Laura Albritton and Michele Rubin, Dan Shine for ego massaging, Christie Cockram for overseas support, and Martina Mitchell and George Marsden for our Pueblo getaways. Special thanks to Steve Tannen for drinks, chili dinners, ideas, never-ending enthusiasm, and unpaid work to boot, and to Peter Tannen for sagely advice. Of course, a big thank-you to our editor, Amy Einhorn, who made this all finally possible.

CONTENTS

THE TOP 25

(in no particular order):

THE 2ND 25

(in no particular order):

THE TOP 25
(in no particular order)

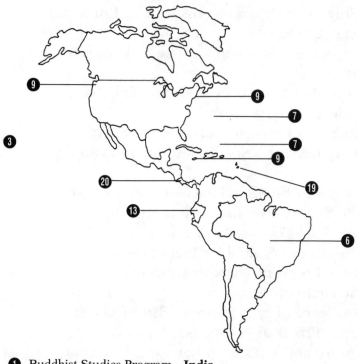

1. Buddhist Studies Program—**India**
2. Harlaxton College—**Great Britain**
3. Semester at Sea—**Global**
4. Arts in Context—**Great Britain**
4. Arts in Context—**Italy**
5. Charles University—**Czech Republic**
6. Brazilian Ecosystems—**Brazil**
7. Sea Semester—**Atlantic Ocean**
7. Sea Semester—**Caribbean Sea**
8. Edinburgh Program—**Scotland**
9. Marine Biology Program—**Washington**
9. Marine Biology Program—**Jamaica**
9. Marine Biology Program—**Massachusetts**
10. Women's Studies—**Poland**
10. Women's Studies—**Germany**
10. Women's Studies—**The Netherlands**
10. Women's Studies—**Great Britain**

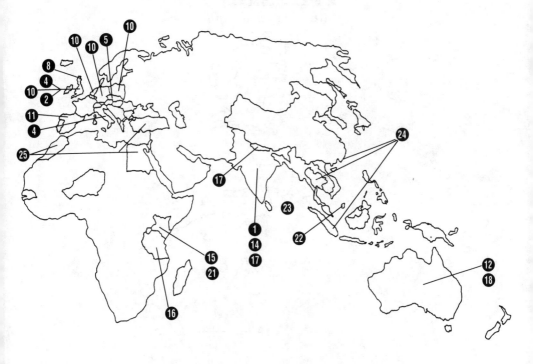

⑪ Semester in Seville—**Spain**

⑫ Australia Natural and Human Environment—**Australia**

⑬ Ecuador Comparative Ecology—**Ecuador**

⑭ India Program—**India**

⑮ Kenya Coastal Studies—**Kenya**

⑯ Tanzania Wildlife Ecology and Conservation—**Tanzania**

⑰ Tibetan Studies—**India**

⑰ Tibetan Studies—**Nepal**

⑱ Tropical Rain Forest Management—**Australia**

⑲ Marine Resource Management—**British West Indies**

⑳ Studies in Sustainable Development—**Costa Rica**

㉑ Wildlife Ecology and Management—**Kenya**

㉒ Island Management Studies—**Palau**

㉓ Global Semester—**Global**

㉔ Term in Asia—**Indonesia, Hong Kong, Thailand**

㉕ Term in the Middle East—**Morocco, Turkey, Israel, Egypt**

THE 2ND 25

(in no particular order)

1. American University in Buenos Aires—**Argentina**
2. The Czech Program—**Czech Republic**
3. The Russia Program—**Russia**
4. Parliamentary Internship Program—**Ireland**
5. Semester Programs in Peace Studies—**Austria**
6. Niamey, Niger Program—**Niger**
7. University of Otago—**New Zealand**
8. Hanoi University Program—**Viet Nam**
9. IKIP Malang Program—**Indonesia**
10. DiS—**Denmark**
11. ACM/GLCA Japan Program—**Japan**
12. IAS Beijing Program—**People's Republic of China**
13. IAS Singapore Program—**Singapore**

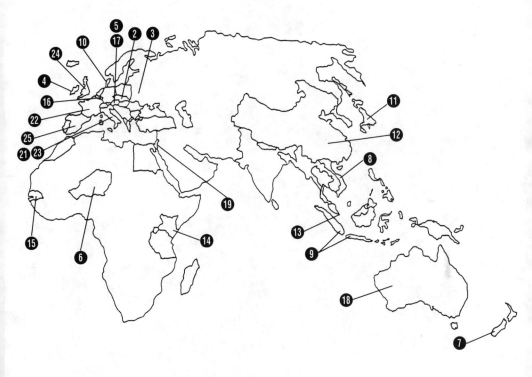

INTRODUCTION:

A Few Opening Words

We want to open up this book by repeating a phrase that was said over and over to us while we interviewed hundreds of students who had participated in semester abroad programs in the academic years of 1993, 1994, and 1995:

"My time abroad was the best thing I have done in my entire life."

Semesters abroad can be *incredible* experiences, and this book is about the most extraordinary programs that we could find—the ones that had a little extra *something* to offer. Whether this means that you're aboard a ship that goes around the world and visits nine countries, or that you're studying Buddhism in the town where the Buddha attained enlightenment, the programs that you'll find in this book are the ones that made us pause in our research open-mouthed and go, "Wow."

However great a semester abroad *can* be, until now choosing a program was really a shot in the dark—maybe it will be wonderful, maybe it will be completely wrong for you. The only available books out there on semesters abroad consisted solely of names and addresses and perhaps a 2-line description of the academic focus. These books tell you nothing more than what you could get from a brochure, or a study abroad office. The study abroad offices are frustrating sources of information because they can't tell you what you really want to know—how the program *is*. They can't tell you, because they've never been on them. The big 1,500-page study abroad directories don't tell you this either, but they *are* useful to prop up the sofa in your apartment, which is what we did.

However, *The Student's Guide to the Best Study Abroad Programs* was written by interviewing students who had just finished the actual programs. These are the only people who can tell you how good a program *really* is: what was great about it, what was horrible, how the academics were, how the social life was, what the program is *all about*. There are really no other authorities on the programs. We are not Semester Abroad Gods. We're simply people who have done a lot of research, a lot of interviews, and, somewhere along the line, had to pick and choose. The programs in this book are the ones that impressed us the most.

While there are over a thousand semester abroad programs, the screening process was actually not as hard as it may seem. For instance, if a program places you in a room with a bunch of other Americans, houses you with other Americans, and leaves it at that, it's not in this book. However, if a program tries to integrate you into the culture, places you in a homestay, offers language study, and gives you weekend field trips to boot, then it definitely made our list for programs to investigate.

We called the programs themselves, read all of their material available, scoured all other information we could find on them, and interviewed past students in-depth. If a program passed these tests and still impressed us, we included it in the book. Of course, these are programs that impressed *us*—they won't necessarily impress everyone. We're as biased as everyone else is (although we try damn hard not to be).

We also wanted to write this book to let students know about the diversity of options open to them. The scope of topics for a semester abroad is staggering—from studying wildlife ecology and conservation in Tanzania, to studying marine biology at sites on the Pacific, Atlantic, and the Caribbean Sea. If you want it, it's probably out there. In this book, we tried to review programs that not only were at a variety of locations, but also covered a variety of topics.

You can count on the programs reviewed in this book; we researched them and they get our stamp of approval. However, we offer no visions of perfection: if the food is lousy on a program, we'll tell you. In the Top 25, we'll tell you what the students thought: their impressions, experiences, advice, observations of what's wrong with the program, and their suggestions of how to fix it.

We'll also talk about:

Financial aid	Faculty
Living conditions	Typical days
Free time	Personal expenses
Extra costs	Academics
Social life	Homestays
Preparation	Structure of program
Male/female ratio	Environment

Except where noted, all prices include housing, tuition, and meals. We also have a second listing of 25 programs. Although not our top picks, these are excellent and solid semester abroad programs. These reviews are much shorter, and generally just try to sketch a program to give you an idea of what it is all about. There are a limited amount of student opinions. Again, except where noted, all prices include housing, tuition, and meals.

There are hundreds of other programs out there that we have not reviewed, and for these we have an appendix. The appendix has an assorted listing of nationally accepted study abroad programs. It is not a complete listing—there are over 1,300 study abroad programs available out there. We have included only a variety of programs in order to offer a diverse look at the study abroad field. We've arranged the appendix by country, and all information is accurate for 1995. Except where noted, all prices are for out-of-state, out-of-organization students, and include tuition, housing, and meals.

Note About Semesters Abroad

In general, most semesters abroad can be wonderful experiences. But just because they aren't reviewed in this book does not mean that there is something *wrong* with them. Almost all of the programs that we looked at, but did *not* review, seemed to be solid, well-run programs.

This is an important point: it is an incredible experience in itself just to be somewhere else. However, if a program "only" puts you in the middle of Germany, studying at a German university, it probably didn't make it into our publication—although nearly every person we talked to who went on such programs had (again) the best time in their lives.

We also did not include programs in which the academics seemed almost an afterthought. For example, studying French on the French Riviera, living in studio apartments with only mornings devoted to classwork. Without strong academics, abroad programs simply become long vacations instead of overseas study. Any tourist can visit all of the sites of a country, or observe the different customs. But a good abroad program will explain the significance of what the students are seeing—its history, its meaning, its importance.

The point is this—there are a lot of programs out there that we did not review, and if you don't find any programs in this book that pique your interest, you need to look into other programs. However, there is no sane reason to dole out the big bucks and get yourself immersed in a foreign culture if you are just going to eat Big Macs and hang around the dorms with people from Ohio. To avoid programs like this you need to . . .

Do Your Own Research

If you are looking at a program that we did not review in this book, there are a lot of things that you need to think about, and a whole lot of things you need to research. Here are a few guidelines, just to help you in finding out what your program is *really* about. (God knows that *we* could have used something like this. . . .)

Make a target list of the specific things that you want to cover, for example:

- Host country
- Curriculum, curriculum intensity
- Language requirements
- COST!!
- Duration

WILL THE CREDITS TRANSFER?! *Everyone* needs to make sure that their credits transfer, even with programs reviewed in this book. This can be a real brick wall while trying to get into a program that appeals to you. The problem is that it may not appeal to your home campus registrar! To you, it may be seventy days in the Alaskan wilderness learning field biology firsthand, but your administrators may look at the required rock climbing/sea kayaking course and hand you three gym credits for the entire program (true story)!

A little self-scrutiny before deciding on a particular program isn't a bad idea, either. Are you the type of person who enjoys jumping into the pool, or do you need to do it inch by inch, to get used to the water? Do you find an unfamiliar environment uncomfortable—not knowing the customs, the cities, not to mention the language? Do you want complete freedom to romp through a country, or would you like more structure and orientation? Think about all of these questions before you go.

RESEARCH ALL POTENTIAL SEMESTERS ABROAD THOROUGHLY. There is a fairly diverse listing of nationally accepted abroad programs in the Appendix in the back of the book. If any pique your interest, call them up and ask for all of their publications, as well as a way to contact recent past participants. You can only get a true feeling for a program by talking with people who have been there. This book is a useful guide for that. Look at the way that we've reviewed programs, and use that as a guide for your own research: How were the academics? Were they a joke or an impossibility? Are there any requirements? Is it a big-party program? Where did you live and how were the conditions? What were some of the things you can do outside of the program? And so on.

Most people are so enthusiastic about their programs that they'll be as helpful as they can possibly be.

A Little Advice About Traveling Abroad

If you're starting to really get interested in going abroad, the next step is get beyond, "Oh! Africa! I'm going!", and think about everything the trip really implies. Traveling overseas can be a wonderful, exciting, enlightening experience. . . . It can also be dangerous, frightening, and depressing. Although we really do feel that practically everyone should study overseas, we do not want to paint a false picture. It can be tough. Women in particular can have a hard time with harassment, especially in third world countries. Motorcycle accidents happen. Students get sick from drinking the water. AIDS is prevalent in many countries.

Our best advice is the advice the students unanimously gave—go *prepared*. Almost every student we talked to strongly suggested reading up on the host country to have a better idea of what to expect—to know the country's customs, dangers, and delights— beforehand. Also, listen to the advice from the programs themselves—they know what they're talking about and are telling you what to do and what not to do for your own safety. Calling up the State Department is not a bad idea either, to get tips on traveling and updates on the political, economic, and social status of the country you're going to. These sources are far better equipped to give you advice than we are, and they're there for your use. So use them.

An Academic Sermon and the End of the Introduction

To all of those concerned parents, stuffy administrators, and curious students: Academics in programs that go overseas are generally less focused on textbook learning than the average American university or college. Instead (and this is how we feel it should be), they allow students a lighter course load in order for them to experience a culture firsthand. As one of our interviewees put it, "You can't smell India from a textbook, you wouldn't know a Russian tundra from a picture." Even programs focused specifically on a particular academic subject are usually supplemented with "hands-on" field research, getting the student out of the library and into the world. The best way to learn, clearly, is by doing. As some wise person said, "True learning does not come from books, true learning comes from experience."

And lastly, although we have tried very hard to make sure all of the information in this book is as accurate as possible, things change. Faculty resign or are replaced, prices go up or down, new locations are chosen, entire programs are canceled. Don't use this book, or any book for that matter, as a *complete* authority on semesters abroad. Find programs that sound interesting to you, research them thoroughly, take the ones that stand out, and make your own "Best Of."

And our final bit of advice to all of you who are thinking about going on a semester abroad—Do it! It will be the time of your life.

THE
TOP
25

BUDDHIST STUDIES PROGRAM

LOCATION: Bodh Gaya, India

HOST SCHOOL: Antioch College

DESCRIPTION: A four-month stay in a Buddhist monastery in India, studying, learning, and experiencing Buddhism. Course focus includes culture, history and philosophy of Buddhism, meditation, and language study.

DURATION: Semester

COST: $9,700 (airfare to London not included)

FINANCIAL AID: None. Federal loans and scholarships may be used.

PREREQUISITES: None

COURSE FULFILLMENT: Religion and Philosophy

NO. OF STUDENTS: 30   M/F RATIO: 4/3

HOUSING: Housed in a Buddhist monastery

COMPUTERS: Not provided. Personal computers not suggested or needed.

CONTACT INFORMATION
Robert Pryor
Program Director
Brazilian Ecosystems
Antioch College
Yellow Springs, OH 45387
Phone: (800) 874-7986
Fax: (513) 767-6469
E-mail: jraw@college.antioch.edu
WWW: http://192.161.123.121:125/academic.html

Overview

"You put on Buddhist lenses to see the world through."

If you want to study Buddhism, what better place could there be than Bodh Gaya? It was here that the Indian Prince Siddhartha Gautama attained enlightenment under the Bodhi tree and became the Buddha. For two and a half millennia since then, Buddhist pilgrims of all traditions have come to Bodh Gaya, returning to the fount, as it were.

This is the setting for Antioch's Buddhist studies program. For the past fifteen years, roughly thirty students from a broad range of well-established universities and colleges have traveled to the northern reaches of India each year to examine firsthand the Buddhist way of life and its religious philosophies. The program, which lasts from September to December, is designed to give students as many different views of Buddhism as possible, while having them practically *live* the knowledge they gain from textbooks, lectures, and discussions.

To Americans, Indian society and culture delivers a healthy dose of culture shock. The children cling to you, the people stare at you, and cows have the right of way. To prepare you, the program begins with a three-day orientation period in London. There you have the benefit of meeting the group, getting an initial perspective on India, and having a bit of time to "take a deep breath." The next step is three days in New Delhi. Here the structure is relaxed so that you have free time to walk around and soak in the new sounds, sights, and smells. You regroup occasionally for lectures and discussions about what was new, different, and disturbing. The only way to describe the tremendous job that Antioch does, not only with the orientation but with the program as a whole, is to say that they allow you to explore on your own, while always being there for you if you need help, advice, or a shoulder. As one student said, "They give structure to a completely unstructured environment."

You then move on to Bodh Gaya, where you stay in the Burmese Vihar ("monastery") that's to be your home for the next nine weeks. Here you concentrate on academics (language study—Tibetan or Hindi—and one core course), meditation techniques (Vipassana, Zazen, and Dzogchen), and a commitment to the Buddhist way of life, with a generous amount of time left over for your own explorations and experiences.

The next step, considered a highlight of the program by most students, is the three-week independent research project. During this time, you may conduct your research at the monastery itself, or you may leave Bodh Gaya to investigate and report on a topic that you have selected with the help of the faculty and staff at the monastery.

The last week is spent back in Bodh Gaya writing and finalizing these projects.

Environment

"The cow shit kept the mosquitoes away."

INDIA

India is, by far, one of the more spiritual, enlightening, and culturally preserved countries in the world. There are many great, wondrous things to experience; yet there are, of course, difficulties that you will encounter as a new inductee to Indian life.

In particular, the poverty there is simply a grave reality, and every westerner has to deal with it at some point. One student, familiar with the panhandling in New York City, was shocked at the number of old women and children who implored him for money. However, most of the students that we talked to never felt themselves in danger in any of the bizarre circumstances they found themselves.

There are also the day-to-day occurrences that may drive you crazy. The pace of India marches to its own drummer, and it's a drummer more in the style of Keith Moon (not really keeping a beat *per se*, but kind of keeping many different ones all at once). On the one hand, your tri-shaw driver may seem to be in a death-defying hurry to get you to your destination, while your time spent at the post office may challenge the patience of even the most enlightened person.

BODH GAYA

Bodh Gaya is a small town, around 10,000 people, but "big enough so you don't know everybody, and you are never bored." Descriptions range from "a remarkably peaceful place with a lot of town unity," "hot, dirty, and crowded," "great and clean by Indian standards," a place with "a cosmopolitan outlook in a very rural place in the middle of nowhere," to "a vibrant town where the people are extremely friendly."

It's a unique place, but a bit of a dichotomy exists with the

frenzy of a large city and the attitudes of a small town. On the
one hand, within a two-mile ra-
dius you will find monasteries
constructed in the styles of
Thailand, Burma, Sri Lanka,

> *"I was amazed to see how much the values of my life overlapped with the Buddhist way."*

Japan, China, Bhutan, and Tibet to accommodate all of the pilgrims that flow into town, especially in the cooler weather (it can
get *very* hot in the earlier months of the program). There is also the
Mahabodhi Temple, the site where the Buddha attained enlightenment, with a descendant of the original Bodhi tree. So there is a
fair amount of activity and events in the town. For example, a group
of Tibetans come round every November to set up restaurant tents
for the pilgrims and tourists.

On the other hand, the students said that the town definitely had
a community feel to it. Getting to know the locals was commonplace—they know the Antioch program—and some even feel like
the students are their "adopted children," inviting everyone to
meals and festivals. Everyone also gets to know the peanut butter/
toilet paper Walla (vendor) very well.

Walking around town, students felt awkward and strange because of the Indian custom of staring at things they think are curious. And, trust us, you will always be a curiosity in India. One
student said, "I learned a thousand things from walking around
every day, but I felt like a big bumbling American fool a lot of the
time . . . people are completely shameless about treating you like
an outsider. They don't stare to be rude, it's just their way."

Advice from the students: "Stare back, it's fine."

Being a woman in India is something that you'll constantly be
aware of. The women we talked to said that the men had an easier
time interacting with people. Also, if alone, a woman will be frequently hit on. As one said, "Being a woman in India is tough, but
it doesn't hamper the experience."

Advice from the students: "Having a little cheap wedding band
and a picture of a little kid and a guy usually does the trick."

Housing

"It forces you to take an intense look at yourself and what your life means."

THE VIHAR

Your nine weeks in Bodh Gaya is spent in the Burmese Vihar, a monastery that was constructed across the street from the Phalgu River and within a ten-minute walk of both the central bazaar and the Mahabodhi Temple.

The rooms at the Vihar surprised most everyone as being better than expected, and soon these became places to get away from the hustle and bustle of everyday life. The rooms have beds with mosquito netting, desks, chairs, and candles for the usual electricity failures. There are single and double rooms. Those who desire singles must draw lots for them, then switch halfway through the term to doubles.

Here at the Vihar, you are expected to follow the five basic Buddhist precepts:

1. To abstain from taking life
2. To abstain from theft
3. To abstain from sexual misconduct
4. To abstain from lying
5. To abstain from intoxicants

These precepts were followed to a varying degree by the students—of course some went out for a drink or two every now and then, and a few relationships did form. As one person said, "When you're meditating, and there are a thousand mosquitoes flying around you, it's really hard to show the proper restraint and not swat at them." But these "slips" were not blatantly declared, and the program retained its air of total dedication to experiencing Buddhism.

"Once, we heard that a man from town was killed by a cobra . . . the strange part was that the people of the town thought that he hadn't encountered a poisonous snake, but that he had disturbed a pair of Naga (roughly translated as spirits) who had been mating, and they in turn killed him."

The Vihar requires that you participate in the upkeep of the facilities during your stay. While the work is not heavy, you should realize that it often includes dirty jobs: maintaining the toilet facilities (porcelain toilet seats over holes, actually quite good for most of India), sweeping, general cleaning, etc. Students said this made them appreciate the sense of community that began to form soon after they arrived.

Food

"It wasn't in me long enough to fully appreciate it."

Indian food "goes in hot, and comes out hot," and so, during the first few weeks, the Vihar provides meals (vegetarian, of course) that are easier on the stomach. This gives you time to develop a better tolerance for "real Indian food." Then you are given a stipend to get dinner on your own, and are forced to go out and explore the town. Since the town is a destination for tourists and pilgrims, there is a wide range of restaurants. To the great delight of the students, there is even an Italian restaurant owned by a man named Roberto from Florence.

Hygienically speaking, Antioch makes an effort to keep out the biological nasties that lurk in Indian water—your drinking water at the Vihar is boiled, then filtered. However, once you step out the doors, you're on your own.

Academics

"We studied all of the turns of the wheel."

The academic structure is by far the most unique aspect of the Antioch program. Rather than just being straight textbook learning in an appropriate setting, this program also focuses on the experiential education of Buddhism. To be precise, this is the study of Buddhism by becoming, if only for a short time, a practicing Buddhist. However, the goal of the program is not to convert students to Buddhism—they are encouraged to critically examine their experiences and discuss them with advisors.

> *"They treated you like a student . . . it was like 'ask me a question, and I will give you an answer.' What's more, if you acted like an adult, you were treated like an adult."*

Generally, the courses offered were less challenging than

courses in the United States, but students stressed that they learned so much more from them. And while you have plenty of free time to relax and explore on your own (which most students insist is the best way to actually learn about a culture), you certainly do not have a slack schedule. Here is a typical day:

5:30 A.M.	Meditation	12:00 P.M.	Language practice
6:30 A.M.	Breakfast	1:00 P.M.	Lunch
7:30 A.M.	Language course	4:00 P.M.	Tea
8:30 A.M.	Core course	5:00 P.M.	Meditation
10:00 A.M.	Tea	6:30 P.M.	Dinner
10:30 A.M.	Core course		

While in Bodh Gaya, students follow an academic curriculum divided into three parts: meditation traditions, language study (Tibetan or Hindi), and one core course (history, culture, or religion).

MEDITATION

The *Meditation Traditions* class is mandatory, and covers three separate types of meditation: Vipassana, Zazen, and Dzogchen. Besides meditating twice a day, the course examines the history, characteristics, and approaches of three very distinct Buddhist traditions. You're required to write three short handwritten papers (three to five pages) relating your experiences and thoughts about the different practices, and also to meet with an academic advisor to discuss what you're learning.

"I haven't come back and joined a Zen monastery or anything, but I can't get the program off my mind . . . which shows you how the program gets inside you."

This course, while difficult for nearly everyone, was also praised by all as being a great part of the program, and essential to understanding Buddhism. Many said that it provided insights to understanding themselves as well. Some people start out a little suspicious of the whole idea, but "soon everyone is very sincere about it, dropping any sarcasm and just doing it."

THE LANGUAGE COURSES

The languages offered are either *Beginning Hindi* or *Beginning Tibetan*, and they get mixed reviews. While they're extremely well run by terrific teachers and very challenging, some students felt that it was taking away from their other interests or courses. These classes meet five times a week, with language class in the morning, and practice for conversational skills in the afternoon. As for needing a language to get around, the students assure us that you can always

find someone who speaks English. However, people are a lot friend-
lier to you if you make an attempt to speak in *their* language as
well. You *can* get around Tibet with the Tibetan you learn, insists
one student. He does, however, add that he once mistakenly asked
his Tibetan friends, "what time that night they were going to eat
the neighbors?"

THE CORE COURSES

These classes meet three times a week, and were well liked by the
students. We heard nothing but praise about the *Contemporary
Buddhist Culture* course. People loved the idea of learning about
something and then going out into town and seeing it (which you
did as part of the course). It is also a discussion-based class, and
the students thought that is a plus. *The Buddhist Philosophy* course
is more lecture-oriented, with a lot of reading and a lot of information thrown at you. You are expected to digest a ton of information,
and students would have liked a little more discussion. Lastly, the
History of South Asian Buddhism course was described as excellent,
and was recommended in order to learn a little bit more about the
country you are living in. Students said the lectures were interesting and insightful.

THE INDEPENDENT FIELD RESEARCH

This, for a majority of the people that we talked to, is the most
rewarding part of the program. During your time at the Vihar, you
decide on a particular aspect of Buddhist culture that you wish to
research. With the help of the faculty, you choose your topic, develop the questions that you need to have answered, and determine
the procedures needed to complete your study. You have access to
the wide array of contact people that are linked to the program,
ranging all over India, Nepal, and Thailand. This research topic is
eventually turned into a twenty-page paper (average length). Each
project that we heard about was unique and fascinating.

For example, one student visited a group of Buddhist nuns in
Nepal and studied the role of women in Buddhism. During her stay,
she helped them build their nunnery in the highlands. Another
studied the neo-Buddhist movement among the Untouchable caste
in Bombay. Still other topics include Tibetan medicinal techniques,
Japanese calligraphy, Buddhist concepts of Hell, and the role of
Buddhism in the education of Tibetan children.

To accomplish these independent projects, Antioch provides
their students with a stipend to pay for expenses such as travel,
lodging, food, and particulars to their project's individual needs.
(This stipend is part of the original cost of the program.) From time
to time, someone connected with Antioch will check up on you. But

other than that, your time and efforts are entirely your own for nearly a month. Students felt that the structure of the program prepared them to do their own research. Some wished this section of the program was longer.

FACULTY

The professors participating in this program are all extremely impressive in their respective fields. The students had nothing but high praise for the efforts that their teachers made in relating their knowledge, which spans decades of doctorate dissertation, field research, and years of working on the program. In addition, the meditation teachers are all masters in their traditions, each from the major centers of Theravada, Zen, and Tibetan disciplines. Coordinating the program are the current directors, Robert Pryor and Tara Doyle, who have been with the program since its beginning in 1979. These two get rave reviews from the students, a few eve going so far as to say that they "made the program for them."

By the nature of the program, the professors are always available; they're living in the

> *"It was the feel-good program of the year."*

monastery with you. For most, you'll be on a first-name basis, and socializing with them is not uncommon. Anyway you look at it, there will always be someone around who has an answer to your questions, or just someone to talk to.

FACILITIES

Don't expect to study at an American university with all of the frills. You study at a monastery, with rooms set aside for classrooms. But remember, the classroom is also the monastery itself, and Bodh Gaya and all of its inhabitants. You can do your work in your room or in the common areas, and the library is someone's old living quarters stacked with books. However, the students said that it's an excellent library for what they needed to study, in a comfortable setting.

COURSES (1995)

Beginning Hindi
Beginning Tibetan
Contemporary Buddhist Culture
Buddhist Philosophy
History of South Asian Buddhism
Independent Field Research

There are no computers, which students thought might have been nice to type up individual research projects, but besides that they really aren't necessary. Also, due to sporadic electricity, it's hard to study after dark (at one time, they didn't have any electricity for five days because someone had stolen a kilometer of wire). All in all, the facilities are basic, but they serve their function and no one felt that anything more was necessary.

THE LAST WEEK

After the independent research project, students return to Bodh Gaya for one week to write up their papers, say goodbye to friends, tie up loose ends, etc. Everyone felt that it was a whirlwind of a pace compared to the rest of the program, and that they wished it would be extended at least a few more days. A few said that they were so busy writing their papers, they didn't have time to say goodbye to some of the people they met in town.

DOWNTIME

Away from the academics, away from the work—what are you doing? The students said that walking around town is a favorite activity. One student loved "just sitting in the sun with the abbot (of the monastery) as he was receiving people from the town." Others found that journeying out to the countryside was not only a way of relaxing and having a good time, but also a way to get different viewpoints on life in India.

Off the Track

As we've said, you have plenty of time to do things outside the program—regular weekends, two long weekends, and your independent project time. So here are some examples of what's happened to students of the Antioch program on their own time in the past:

One student got "kidnapped" in New Delhi. He and some friends were trying to get to a particular store and they got into a motorized rickshaw. . . . Soon, not only had they passed the store, but they had taken so many alleyways and shortcuts that they were completely dependent on the driver to get them to an area they recognized. They yelled at him, but the driver kept saying, "I'll take you somewhere better! My brother's store!" They got to the store and could not leave until they had bought something. The student still considers this a great experience for him.

In Varanasi a student met the owner of a shop she went into. . . . He took her to see parts of the town that she would not have ordinarily seen, as well as all of the temples that she wanted to see. Finally, he brought her home to meet his mother. She felt that just talking to him was enlightening. When she came back to visit him several weeks later, it turned out to be his birthday, which she celebrated with him and his entire family.

A student's birthday landed on the day before the program ended. They all took their meditation pillows to the Mahabodhi Temple, went to the porch (which is closed to most visitors), and sat underneath the branches of the Bodhi tree. No birthday since has compared to that experience.

On one of the long weekends, a student went to Varanasi, the holiest of holy cities for Hindus, located on the banks of the Ganges. He talked to an owner of a small store briefly during that visit. When he came back four weeks later, the owner remembered his name, declared that they were friends, gave him cold drinks, and bought him a few tapes of Indian music.

Nalanda, a tiny little crossroads of a town, was the destination for a few people's long weekend. It was here that an enormous Buddhist university was constructed around 400 A.D., which lasted until around 1200 A.D. The ruins of it are still there today. The students were awed by the fact that 1,000 years ago, people here had been studying the same subject that they themselves were.

A group of people went to a nature park that was nearby and got lost . . . they finally ended up spending the night in a tree for fear of being eaten by a leopard if they had stayed on the ground.

The Dalai Lama was speaking on a beach in Bombay while a student was in the area. When he approached the packed area, people who were in charge saw him and decided that since he was a westerner, he must be someone important, or from the press. So they took him by the hand and led them to the press table right in front, a few feet away from the Dalai Lama.

Advice and Warnings
from the Students

▶ "Read up on India before you go. Know something about the culture in which you're going to spend four months. Don't go in being ignorant of how 20 percent of the world's population lives."

▶ $700 to $800 is a good amount of money to bring for personal expenses. This is considered by all to be more than an adequate amount to let you do anything you want.

▶ "To the women: Don't be afraid to object outright to what someone is asking or saying!"

▶ "Know that you are going to get sick . . . and pack lightly."

▶ "Bring a little medicine chest of your own . . . and most importantly don't forget the Pepto-Bismol and the Imodium AD."

▶ "Don't underestimate how cheap things are over there, especially clothes."

The Best + The Worst

👎 Unanimously, everyone on the program thought that being sick was the worst. One student got so sick that all she could do was wear a dress and sit on a bucket; she would receive visitors that way. What most students said about this was summed up by one perfectly: "But that's India—so deal with it."

👍 The fact that Antioch "basically let you discover India for yourself, and yourself for yourself"

👍 Seeing the sunrise everyday

👍 The meditation time

👍 The free time

👍 Taking the bodhisattva vow. This was an option on the trip—you could take the bodhisattva vow underneath the Bodhi tree, dedicating yourself to helping others find enlightenment.

👍 Going to the cave where the Buddha practiced asceticism

HARLAXTON COLLEGE

LOCATION: Grantham, Great Britain

HOST SCHOOL: University of Evansville

DESCRIPTION: A semester or year-long stay in a nineteenth-century Victorian mansion, studying British culture along with other U.S. accredited courses

DURATION: Semester or year

COST: $8,760 (airfare and optional side trips to destinations in various European cities not included)

FINANCIAL AID: None. Federal loans and scholarships may be used.

PREREQUISITES: 2.5 minimum GPA, and dean and academic advisor approval

COURSE FULFILLMENT: Various, including British History

NO. OF STUDENTS: 350   M/F RATIO: 1/3

HOUSING: Dormitories in Harlaxton Manor or on its grounds

COMPUTERS: Provided. Personal computers allowed and recommended.

CONTACT INFORMATION
Suzy Lantz
Director of International Admissions
University of Evansville
1800 Lincoln Avenue
Evansville, IN 47722
Phone: (800) 856-2667
Fax: (812) 479-2320
E-mail: Not available
WWW: Not available

Overview

"It was like a dream."

Looking out on the grounds of the estate, contemplating the wood-work and murals inside, or simply staring at the 100-room, nine-teenth-century Victorian palace, students might fantasize hearing, "Another crumpet, my lord, or perhaps some more tea?"

A picture-perfect setting for examining British studies (as well as other topics), students of the University of Evansville's Harlaxton College actually reside and study in a lavish manor house built in 1837. The program offers solid academics, and it also organizes countless optional trips around the U.K. (with a few to mainland Europe as well). Additionally, students can "adopt" local families to get a closer look at the English culture through the "Meet a Family" program. If you are a little nervous about being in a completely foreign country, want to live in a palace, soak up the English cul-ture, and receive a solid academic semester to boot, then this pro-gram is for you.

While students are free to choose their classes from a variety of subjects, there is a mandatory British culture survey course. This class covers Great Britain from the start of its recorded history up until the present day, exam-ining British literature, art his-tory, and politics. Other courses offered range from *Medieval Art*

> *"Everything is great, from the grounds to the faculty."*

to *Principles of Macroeconomics*, and are taught by a mixture of British and American professors.

Throughout the entire semester, the administration is very ac-tive in getting the students out into other parts of the U.K. and Europe, to experience the history and cultures they are studying firsthand. There are scheduled optional trips every weekend, offer-ing students a hassle-free way to get to a variety of destinations, and the program supplies them with enormous freedom once there. For those who want to travel by themselves, the administration is more than happy to help with the arrangements. Travel is a big part of the program, and students usually have three-day weekends to take advantage of, since there are no classes on Fridays.

Environment

"It was like our own little world."

Of course, the first thing that everyone wants to know about is the palace, or castle, or manor house, or whatever one chooses to call it. There is something innately romantic about living in a nineteenth-century manor house, but it is also historic, and many said that it set the academic tone for the program. They were, after all, living in a piece of architecture that they could enjoy and study at the same time. Of course, it's also everybody's dream at some point to live in a castle. More than one person said they felt like Cinderella or King Arthur. (The manor is described in detail in the "Housing" section.)

The village of Harlaxton itself is not much to look at, but it does offer students a post office, the Gregory Arms pub, and is only a mile down the manor driveway. Grantham is a slightly larger town three miles away, and the college runs a regular shuttle to and from it. This is the more frequented town, as it holds all the basics that students overseas need—including a McDonald's, a Woolworth's, a Marks and Spencer, a market, a small mall, a bank, post office, and numerous pubs from which to choose.

Most people mentioned the pubs in Grantham—as pubs are basically the social setting all across the U.K. There are many different demeanors of pubs in Grantham, ranging from the more typical American bar for the younger crowd, to the quiet pub for those seeking conversation rather than a pickup game of snooker. The beer is very British, of course, and usually lukewarm. It is also very good, and can be quite strong. A big difference between pubs and bars is the fact that the pubs announce last call at around eleven o'clock, sometimes earlier.

> *"The Gregory Arms pub had a weekly trivia night—we lost every time, but we met a lot of people."*

Of course, the city of London is a mere hour away by train. Many students opted to use their weekends to go there to sightsee, take in a play or an opera, visit one of the museums, or just be in one of the world's great cities. London is not only a cultural center, but also a gateway to the rest of Europe—with daily flights from Heathrow, a quick jaunt to Switzerland on a three-day weekend is a very real possibility.

Housing

"It was like living in a museum, except nothing was off-limits."

You approach the manor house via a mile-long driveway, pass through the gates guarded by the Harlaxton lions, and enter the courtyard and circular driveway. In front of you is something out of a fairy tale. It has everything a castle should, including secret passageways, grounds with walled gardens, a great hall, and more. There are three sections, really, to the Harlaxton manor—the main manor, the Cottage Block, and the gym.

> *"Oh my God, I'm living in a castle."*

To start with, it is *very* large. So large, in fact, that many students claimed they were lost for the first few weeks, and that there were times when they suddenly realized they hadn't been outside of the manor for days. There are over 100 rooms for students to explore, as well as 110 acres of grounds and gardens.

ROOMS/COTTAGE BLOCK

Students live either in the old servants' quarters in the manor or in the old stables (you can make of that what you will). Surprisingly, the old stables, called the Cottage Block, is the preferred lodging. The rooms there are preferred simply because they're away from the manor and force students to get outside that building.

Most rooms are doubles, but there are some singles available. Rooms range from large and beautiful to small and a bit shabby. All come with sinks, beds, desks, chairs, and a small amount of closet space. Not all rooms have windows, but those that don't are supplied with skylights. Room selection is done by lottery, so it is only luck that puts someone in a great room. The Cottage Block has its own laundry, as well as study lounges.

THE MANOR

The classrooms are by far the most talked about rooms in the manor. These are decorated in a manner one would think that most of the rooms would have been decorated back in 1837. Angels stare down from the ceilings, numerous mirrors hang from the walls, and gold trim adorns the doorways, which themselves are elegantly carved out of rosewood. They are, typical of the style, gaudy and beautiful at the same time. As one student said, "Even in the last weeks of classes, I was still noticing new details about the rooms."

Other inspiring rooms include the Great Hall, a mammoth room made of stone and wood, complete with an enormous fireplace taller than a person. Weekly meetings are held here, as well as all of the dances and the Super Bowl party during spring semester. The Conservatory is also a wonderful room for studying or socializing in, with a ceiling composed entirely of glass, climbing vines scaling the stone walls inside, and even a goldfish pond.

The Bistro, housed in the basement, is the center for student activities at the manor. Besides drinking, there is something going on there almost every night, ranging from movies to pajama parties. It's also the meeting place for the societies that are organized, with past societies even including a Star Trek society and a Cricket society. There are also weekly functions, including a fancy dress ball, a formal, a beach party, as well as the infamous "Drain the Bistro" night at the end of the semester.

The dining room is apparently unremarkable in its capacity, being simply a large room with tables. The food is done cafeteria style and is reportedly of average quality. On Sundays there is a formal meal, which is generally lamb or roast beef. Students from the year we interviewed asked for, and received, a vegetarian option for each meal. There is also a gift shop that has small items such as candy and drinks for sale.

THE GYM

The gym is separate from the main building, and contains step machines, stationary bikes, and free weights. There is a decent indoor basketball court, and outdoor tennis courts are located behind the manor. Sports play a vital role among the activities of Harlaxton students. School teams, including football (that's soccer to Americans), rugby, and even basketball vie against the local English college teams. Students can also take horsemanship through the college at a nearby stable, or borrow mountain bikes to bike into town or explore the countryside.

THE GROUNDS

The grounds of the manor are just being "rediscovered." Yorkshire Television's expert gardener explored the 110 acres of wilderness and overgrown gardens around Harlaxton, and he decided that they could be turned into one of the best gardens in England. He and his crew, along with student volunteers each semester, have been working on the grounds since the summer of 1993. They have already discovered a forgotten lake, an ornamental canal, numerous pathways and avenues, as well as stone seats and steps with beautiful views of the Vale.

However, it needs to be mentioned that it isn't all a fairy tale, as the manor can become a little too oppressive. Students eat there, sleep there, study there, take classes there, and do just about every-thing there. There is nothing else around, really, except the Gregory Arms pub down the road. Luckily there is the shuttle into Grant-ham, and the three-day weekends to travel in.

Another complaint about the manor is that the students, as well as most of the administration, are all American, which stifles the amount of cultural immersion possible. "There is the danger," warns one student, "of the school becoming its own island of cul-ture—American, regrettably." The school used to accept students from all around the world a few years ago, and past participants would have liked for this aspect to still be in effect.

MEET-A-FAMILY

One of the many attractive aspects of the Harlaxton semester is their "Meet-A-Family" program. Designed to get students in touch with their neighbors, this endeavor matches up participants with families and other people from town. This program got consistently good reviews from students, and most found new friends in their "adopted moms and dads." The families are always a great way to get away from the manor, or just to get a home-cooked meal. Some students in past years even went on weekend trips with their adopted families—to London, their summer cottages, or even the coast.

Academics

"It's not just a building or a school, it's an entire experience."

The academics occasionally take a backseat to the traveling, but they are still the main focus of this program. The simple fact that students are in the English countryside, living in an architectural wonder provides the inspiration for academic discipline. After all, to be studying Henry V and then go see a production of it at Strat-ford is a wonderful opportunity few people would pass up. Of course, the main studying is done from Sunday night until Friday at noon, because of the traveling.

The only required course is the British Studies course, which meets twice a week. Other classes either meet three times a week or twice a week, Monday through Thursday.

COURSES

The British Studies course, or what the students call simply "ID," is the main course of the semester. It covers the aspects of British history from the beginnings of recorded history to the present. Topics include the British Empire's influences on philosophy, literature, and theology, plus the developments within those disciplines. ID is the only mandatory course in the Harlaxton curriculum and, unfortunately for non-morning people, is held bright and early at 8:30 A.M. twice a week.

ID is primarily taught by British professors, and the majority of class time is spent in lectures. This course can be taken on the 200-level, or, for those who require a higher level course, at the 300-level as well. Requirements for this course include essay exams and an extensive reading list.

> *"The classes weren't easy, and they were always enlightening."*

The rest of the courses offered are anything from politics to economics. Typically, there are twenty-five to thirty courses offered each semester. All classes are comparable to classes in the U.S., with the same intensity and workload. Students generally found their courses to be interesting and informative, especially the ones that had a British or European theme to them. Past British courses include *Shakespeare, British Culture, English Literature, British Politics,* and *British Social Problems.* Requirements for classes typically include a large reading list, a few papers, and a few exams.

The attendance policy was repeatedly stated as one of the worst things about the program. The policy is this: If a class meets three times a week, you are allowed to miss that class three times. If it meets twice a week, you are allowed to miss it two times. Students felt the policy was unfair, as it made it practically impossible to plan long weekends. Harlaxton has no plans to change the policy (and we don't find it particularly harsh, anyway).

FACULTY

The faculty is a mix of American and British professors, which was a small sore point for some of the students. They would have preferred it either one way or the other, as each nationality seems to have very different teaching styles and expectations. British professors tend to lecture more, and their tests are centered around essays instead of multiple choice or true/false tests. Students reported that they tend to grade a little tougher as well. Perhaps demonstrating what is wrong with American education today, one student said, "The British professors really expected you to think for yourself."

Some of the professors live at the manor itself, and most are readily available and very approachable for whatever questions students may have, even if it is to simply have some tea and discuss

British culture. Although the American professors were perhaps a bit more personable, students were on a first-name basis with nearly all of their professors.

FIELD TRIPS

Both mandatory and optional field trips are common in most classes. As mentioned above, trips to Stratford to see Shakespeare performed in the Bard's hometown are offered, as well as trips to Lincoln, York, Bath, Stonehenge, Oxford, the Lake District, and Cambridge.

Additionally, there are trips offered every weekend that are not class-related (although certainly educational). Several very popular trips mentioned were to

> *"Do everything while you're there, or you'll come back with regrets."*

Scotland and Ireland. The trips are extremely well run and, from the students' accounts, reasonably priced as well. They are certainly a value—the school takes care of all travel and hotel arrangements, and some meals. Once at the destination, they give students a sheet of recommended things to do and see, and then allow them to go off on their own (lectures are also held beforehand to supply historical background).

There are also two week-long trips offered at the end of the semester. Typically, they go to either Rome, Florence, and Venice, or Prague, Vienna, and Munich. They are organized and run in the same way the weekend trips are, allowing students freedom while taking care of all the "busy-work." All organized trips are highly recommended, although most students suggested eventually traveling on your own as much as possible. One said, "This program gave me the confidence that I can travel anywhere, by myself."

FACILITIES

Facilities are more than adequate for what is required of the students. The library is open to students twenty-four hours a day, and is well suited to fulfill the needs of the curriculum of the program. Those needing additional materials can go to the library at Nottingham University, part of the British Library system. The computers are mainly IBM compatibles, and in "crunch time" it's hard to get time on them.

COURSES (1995)

A large and varied curriculum is offered.

Off the Track

With a three-day weekend nearly every week, as well as two four-day weekend breaks, students have plenty of time for their own explorations. Here are a few of the things that happened to students of Harlaxton College:

Hiking in the Swiss Alps was a highlight for one student. He managed to get himself to a remote little town, and took one of the small, winding trails up the mountain. After hiking alone for two hours, he was startled when a hang glider sailed into sight—a mere thirty feet above his head. The ridge he had just gotten to is evidently notorious for its favorable winds and gorgeous views.

One student decided to walk the three miles into Grantham rather than take the shuttle. On her way she got lost and asked directions from a woman working in her yard. The woman said that she could give her directions into town, but insisted that she come in for tea first. The two became close friends, and the student had an open invitation to come for dinner anytime she wanted.

Tradition is important in England, and it is no less so at Harlaxton. The mile-long drive was used daily as the perfect jogging ground for students, either to get to town or for exercise. However, tradition decrees that those who do so must participate at the end of the semester in the "Naked Mile" (you have to find out about this yourself!).

One student's adopted family was her most memorable experience while in England. Arranged through Harlaxton's "Meet-A-Family" program, she started out simply having dinner once a week with them for a home-cooked meal. But they all soon became very close, and the family would take her to the local sightseeing stops, and even took a weekend with her up to Edinburgh.

A few students "accidentally" wound up in a nude bar. They claim complete innocence, even though the women they were talking to at their table were dressed only in their underwear. The surprise came at the end of the night, however, when they were charged 250 pounds for the conversation.

Switzerland was the favorite country for one student. He and a friend went to Zermatt to go skiing and encountered one of the winter's biggest snowfalls, with drifts up to five feet. On that trip he discovered that one could ski from the town of Zermatt across the Swiss/Italian border—so you have to ski with your passport.

Advice and Warnings from the Students

▶ "Don't be the loud, obnoxious American!"

▶ "Take sweaters and jeans and turtlenecks—it gets cold and rainy!"

▶ "Understand that Britain is an entirely different culture, and try to learn as much as you can about it."

▶ $3,000 to $3,500 is a good amount of money to bring for personal expenses, including travel.

▶ "Make sure you get out of the manor as much as you can!"

▶ "Bring film because it is expensive in Europe!"

▶ "Try to find the secret passageway in the manor that you open by 'moving the shield.'"

The Best + The Worst

For your general enjoyment and information, here are a few of the best and worst things that happened to former students of the University of Evansville's Harlaxton College program:

👍 The traveling

👎 English food

👍 The manor house

👎 Too many Americans

👍 The "Meet-A-Family" program

👎 The attendance policy

👍 Seeing Shakespeare in England

👎 The pubs close early

👍 ID class

👎 The fact that there were no good science-related classes

👍 The Bistro nights

SEMESTER AT SEA

Courtesy Semester at Sea

LOCATION: Global

HOST SCHOOL: University of Pittsburgh/ISE

DESCRIPTION: A four-month academic voyage around the world, focusing on global comparative studies

DURATION: Semester

COST: $12,580 (airfare to and from the embarkation/disembarkation ports and costs of port activities not included)

FINANCIAL AID: Work study, scholarships, nontraditional aid (for those who don't normally qualify) is available. Federal aid through home institution may be used.

PREREQUISITES: One full semester of an accredited college program with a 2.75 GPA

COURSE FULFILLMENT: Various

NO. OF STUDENTS 400–500   M/F RATIO: 1/2

HOUSING: Rooms aboard the S.S. *Universe.*

COMPUTERS: Provided. Personal computers allowed and recommended.

CONTACT INFORMATION
Director of Admissions
Semester at Sea / Institute of Shipboard Education
2E Forbes Quadrangle
Pittsburgh, PA 15260
Phone: (800) 854-0195
Fax: (412) 648-2298
E-mail: shipboard@sas.ise.pitt.edu
WWW: http://www.pitt.edu/~julesh/
   SemSeahome.html

Overview

> *"Around the world in 100 days in an old cruise ship, visiting nine countries . . . not a day has gone by that I haven't thought about Semester at Sea."*

Twice each year, Semester at Sea travels the globe aboard the S.S. *Universe** (see footnote, p. 41). The program mixes academic concentration on comparative global studies with actual visits to the countries involved. The itinerary, though varying from year to year, consists of 100 days of travel, an average forty-five of which are spent in eight to ten countries. Emphasis is placed on visiting the nonwestern nations of the world. Recent itineraries included visits to Brazil, China, Egypt, Hong Kong, India, Japan, Kenya, Malaysia, Morocco, Turkey, Russia, South Africa, Spain, Taiwan, Venezuela, and Vietnam.

Semester at Sea begins preparing students for the voyage months before they even get on the ship. Inoculations and international visas compose the bulk of the predeparture requirements. Students also receive constant updates on their itinerary, U.S. State Department information regarding specific countries, and registration materials for courses.

Once at sea, students are in full "university mode." There are classes nearly every day, tests, and papers due. There are also "interport lecturers" who give orientation talks and discussions: they are either experts on the next country of visit, or people from the countries themselves.

> *"Semester at Sea was definitely the best choice I've ever made."*

The staff occasionally plan special events that are a lot of fun, and there's plenty of time to "get to know everyone." In essence, the *Universe* becomes exactly what the program literature states: a floating campus.

While in port, however, the students are required to complete field practica for specific classes. These field trips provide the opportunity to go out and see the very things that they've been learning about on board ship. Other than this requirement, however, they are free to explore each country on their own to their hearts' content, provided that they are back on board when the ship departs.

Environment

"I can't imagine any other way of getting such an experience in one semester."

Because of the nature of the program, the main environment for the semester is the S.S. *Universe*. Since students experience a new culture on nearly a weekly basis, the ship soon becomes a comforting, familiar home. A few students affectionately called it "their big white security blanket on the sea."

The *Universe* is well equipped to be a floating campus. Constructed originally for use as a light cargo freighter in 1951, its hull was later modified to serve as a passenger liner. The ship is now fully air-conditioned and stabilized and has six classrooms, a library, weight room, darkrooms, a 200-seat theater, hospital, swimming pool, sports

> *"Are you kidding me? It's 500 college students on the* **Love Boat** *going around the world!"*

and sundecks, student union/pub, campus store, cafeteria-style dining room, and a snack bar. A pickup linen service is also provided, and cabin attendants clean the bathrooms.

Life aboard a ship can be rewarding and fun, but also confining and frustrating. It's *hard*. Imagine taking 500 students and putting them all in a space perhaps as big as a large university library. Float that on the water so no one can leave and you're getting a pretty good picture. Now add a few students from international schools, around forty to fifty professors and their families, staff members, and administrators. There are also the 125 Asian crew, cooks, cabin stewards, and bursars to consider.

Which obviously makes the time spent on the water hell, right? Evidently, the answer is "wrong." So many of our interviewees *loved* being on the water for all that time; it's an incredibly romantic way to travel. As one student said, "I never missed a sunrise or a sunset, and I saw as many of the moonrises that I could. Three hundred and sixty degrees of water and sky all of the time is hard to beat."

As for the small space, a community feeling develops almost as soon as you step on board. You not only have to be considerate toward everyone, but these are all people with whom you have an extraordinary thing in common: the experience of traveling around the world on a ship.

WHAT DO YOU DO?

Life on the ship isn't limited to studying. Volleyball, table tennis, jogging, basketball, and aerobics are some of the activities that students can participate in. There's also the option of using the darkroom, the weight room, the library, and the field study office, which are all open at selected hours of the day. On warm days, others simply take advantage of the sun and seek the perfect tan out on the lounge

> *"Life on the ship was really laid back because 1) there were a lot of people from California, and 2) what are you going to do? Just sit down and hang out."*

chairs by the pool. Past spring semester students warn to bring plenty of sunblock; the spring itinerary brings you close to the equator for a good portion of the journey.

Occasionally special events are held. Formal dances held to benefit charity organizations create a social focus as well as help to give the ship more of a college campus feel. Events like the "Sea Olympics" are just for fun, while other events include celebrating occasions such as crossing the equator. Religion also holds a place on the *Universe*, and services for many faiths are encouraged.

On selected nights of the week, the Student Union becomes a nightclub, where students can buy beer at a reasonable price and dance out on the dance floor. Movies are shown in the theater, and often the selections reflect the mood or appeal concerning the part of the world that the ship is about to visit (for example, *Gandhi* right before India).

ADULT PASSENGERS

Besides the students, there are also approximately forty adult passengers on board. These are people who have paid to go on Semester at Sea, but have no need for the academic credit. They always choose a clever name for themselves like "Globetrotters" or "Seasoned Salt," and students love having them aboard as they add to the community feeling. Many of them audit classes, and nearly all of them participate in the "Extended Family" program. This program links students to adult passengers, so that the student has a shipboard "parent" or "grandparent."

Housing

"It's overwhelming at first, but then it gets so much better!"

Looking at the rooms on the *Universe* certainly will wipe away any images of a luxury cruise around the world. The rooms are small. Very, very small. This can be tough, because there is certainly a lack of privacy in such tight quarters. However, the students added that it doesn't really affect the trip at all, since you're hardly ever there. Many also grew to love being "rocked to sleep" every night, claiming that they got the most restful sleep they'd ever had aboard the ship. The rooms all have bunk beds, lockers (like a gym locker), one desk, one chair, and a private bathroom. You can live in inside or outside doubles or triples. "Inside" means that there is no porthole.

Advice from the students: "Get an inside room, and you'll save around $1,000!"

FOOD

As with everything else, the food is not cruise line quality. The food is plain fare, with a few occasional "treats" in the menu for variety. If you're a practicing vegetarian, you will find that your options are limited, and you will have to pick over the menus carefully. There are always fresh fruits available, bread and sandwich fixings, as well as the ever-present rice dishes. Overall, the food is pretty wholesome despite the fact that it does get routine after a while. Some students even went as far as saying that it was better food than their own home university. For those who miss a meal or two, there is a snack bar on one of the upper decks that serves items like ice cream and burgers every afternoon. Snacks are also served every night to the delight of most (one person called it the "ten o'clock feeding"), with tea, coffee, and sandwiches.

Advice from the students: "Bring a lot of food in a footlocker! As you eat it off, replace it with stuff from the countries!"

Academics

In the past, Semester at Sea has been called "Semester at C-minus," "Party at Sea," and "Semester at Sex"—all jokes referring to Semester at Sea's supposed lack of academic vigor. However, recent students have been *very* surprised at the amount of work they found themselves doing, and the difficulty of it. Although it's not a semester at Oxford, it's not a cruise line vacation either; students should expect to be doing a fair amount of studying while on board, although probably less than they are used to at home. One student warned, "Remember, you're constantly traveling and seeing the world, so it's a lot harder to focus."

The academic curriculum is based on global studies and structural changes occurring in the world today. Besides focusing on specific topics in selected areas of the world, all courses offered are taught within a global and comparative framework. In supplement to this, students are traveling around the world, visiting the places of study.

The days at sea are divided into "A," "B," and "Free" days. Free days occur perhaps once every few weeks, as class time is limited to days at sea. Classes meet either on A or B days, and last for seventy-five minutes.

COURSES

In keeping with its role as a floating campus, the courses on Semester at Sea, while not as numerous as those at an American college or university, are almost as varied. There are approximately sixty courses offered each semester, ranging from anthropology to fine arts to biological sciences to philosophy. Students are required to take twelve credits, but can take no more than fifteen. In general, the students thought the courses were all interesting and relevant to the larger theme of global studies, and their field experiences were well integrated with the curriculum aboard ship.

THE CORE COURSE

There is one required course: the *Core Course*, which meets every day while at sea for seventy-five minutes (with the entire 500 students in attendance), and focuses on the countries being studied. The course gives valuable information about specific cultures and history, and it provides a framework by which the entire semester can be examined. "Core" is also a bit unique in its format. Rather than just straight lectures, there are also debates, panel discussions, student presentations, videos, and role-playing. The Core Course coordinator, a faculty member from a previous semester, does some of the teaching, but not all of it. Guest lectures are frequent, given by either interport lecturers or another member of the faculty.

While hailed as the most important course of the semester, Core gets mixed reviews. For some, it proved to be just what the program literature promises: interesting, useful, and informative. Others felt that Core tried to bite off more than it could chew. Covering the issues and cultures of nine countries in one course and keeping the attention of 500 students is a difficult job, perhaps a little too difficult. Also, if the Core coordinator specialized in something like economics, the entire course tended to have an economic slant to it, which would be fascinating to some but tedious to others. "Despite its faults, Core can be a great course for an intensive overview of what the semester entails, as long as the irrelevant topics and discussions are avoided."

COMMUNITY COLLEGE

Each evening at sea, students and faculty informally gather to engage in group discussions and activities. These events, referred to as "Community College," touch on a wide variety of subjects ranging from the serious to the whimsical. One night the subject might be the role of women in the indigenous tribes of the Amazon, whereas the next night the interport lecturer could be teaching the group the latest dances from Brazil. Community College is also the setting for "preport" briefings, where students and faculty get the latest information on the next port of call. After departure, students relate their adventures and observations to one another at the "postport" talks.

FACULTY

Living on the same ship with your professors can be a mixed blessing. The faculty for the most part is always available. You eat in the dining room with them, chat with them on the promenade deck, or down a few beers with them in the Student Union. In fact, once you get a glance of, say, your Econ professor trying to samba, or your Lit professor in her muumuu and straw hat out by the pool, they all seem a bit more human. Remember, the faculty is just as excited to be traveling around the world as you are. Having the faculty so close at hand also makes the learning more personal, and it's natural to be on a first-name basis with them.

The program takes care to ensure that the ship has an experienced and credible faculty on board. Virtually all are Ph.D.s from top-name schools, backed with years of experience in their individual fields. Rounding out the group are experts from other areas of international study, such as U.S. politicians, and members of private research groups. Selections of faculty are made on the basis of their track record in teaching and experience in one or more of the countries or regions on the itinerary.

FACILITIES

All things considered, the ship has quite a lot in the way of facilities. However, for a full complement of students, the resources occasionally get stretched thin. The ship's classroom environment is Spartan, equipped with the usual desks and chalkboards. The library, which one student compared to her high school library, provides the bare essentials in research materials. Those looking for more specific works or materials probably will not find them on board. This is not really a problem, as most professors stock the library with references their classes will need before the ship sails.

There are a few lounges on board dedicated solely to "quiet study," or the Student Union is available, provided it's not during Community College or pub night. As for computers, students could be disappointed. With 500 people writing up to three papers each, even a dozen computers networked to laser printers can seem to be inadequate.

THE INTERNATIONAL FIELD EXPERIENCE

With nearly fifty days in port, students have plenty of free time to go out and explore by themselves or take an organized Semester at Sea trip. These trips are in two categories: field practica that may be required for specific classes, or trips that allow students to see places and do things that would be extremely difficult

> *"This is the adventure of your life, so don't let a moment of it slip away!"*

to do on their own. They range anywhere from a half day to a week in length.

On the field practica, students are investigating a specific theme. For example, students in a world religion or music class may observe a Sufi Dervish

> *"This is something you can't really put a price tag on."*

meeting in Istanbul. Art students may visit an Indian temple compound, and anthropology students may take a boat trip through a Hong Kong fishing village.

The other trips offered by Semester at Sea are incredibly far-reaching in scope. There are the "big trips"—like package tours to Beijing from Hong Kong, safaris in Kenya, or journeys through the Brazilian Amazon. In every port there are city orientation trips and "Welcome Student" gatherings, which are basically small parties held with students from local universities. These are particularly recommended, as students are able to meet people their own age all around the globe.

Almost everyone stressed

> COURSES (1995)
>
> *A large and varied curriculum is offered.*

taking organized trips only at the beginning of the semester, when people are still learning how to travel by themselves in other countries. It's more rewarding, and cheaper, to do it on your own. The exception to this are trips that you'd love to do, but feel you can't on your own, like getting to Beijing and back.

Off the Track

The time in the ports is the real reason for going on Semester at Sea. Students are on the voyage to go around the world, and visit nine cultures completely different from their own. Here, then, are some of the experiences that students had while in port:

A few students organized their own safari in Kenya. They spent four days camping out on the savanna with a guide and two Maasai warriors to guard them, as hyenas were frequent visitors to their campsite. Not only did they "avoid all the touristy places," but it was cheaper as well.

A night out on the town in Malaysia was certainly an experience for one student and his friends. They roamed the town until they found a great local bar. At the end of the night, the guys got a check for the beer, and the girls got a check for "competing with the locals for men."

One of the planned trips in Venezuela included a plane flight to see Angel Falls and the surrounding jungle. The waterfalls themselves were incredible, but the plane trip was also a surprise. To the amazement of some and to the horror of the rest, the pilot took the DC-3 to treetop level. He then dove down into what is know as "Devil's Canyon," leaving a mere twelve feet between the wingtips and the faces of the cliffs.

While trekking through a small mountain town in India, a few students were startled to hear an old Indian man say, "You are from America? My son is going to America, come inside." They did, climbed upstairs and met the son, who ended up reading all of their palms as well as showing them how to properly meditate to achieve peace of mind.

Most students stressed that the best thing they did in the ports was simply walk around the cities, look, learn, and explore. The people of each country, in particular the children, remain very vividly in all of their memories.

Climbing Mt. Fuji was the goal of one student in Japan. It soon became a real feat as the national park was closed for the season.

Despite this, he hitched his way to Fuji and befriended a few of the local park rangers. Together, they climbed up to the snowpack.

The Taj Mahal was targeted by a lot of students as a "must see" in India. However, all of the organized trips had been canceled, due to civil unrest in northern India. Some ignored the advisories and warnings of Semester at Sea, and went anyway. Five students ended up being on a plane that got hijacked, an experience that was doubly frightening because they couldn't understand what the hijackers were saying. Everyone came out of it okay.

For one young woman, the highlight of the trip was bumping into Nelson Mandela in Nairobi. The famous leader of the ANC was visiting while the *Universe* was in port, and she and her friends found him surrounded by a crowd of supporters, on a corner of the Kenyan capital.

Advice and Warnings from the Students

► "Try to learn about the culture and hang with the locals, don't just hang out at the bars."

► "Bring a lot of film! It can be expensive overseas!"

► $2,500 to $3,000 is a good amount of money to bring for personal expenses.

► "While you're in a port, stay away from other Semester at Sea students!"

► "Bring 'hanging shelves' to put in your locker so you have more room to store your clothes."

► "Before you leave the States, change $25 into the local currency of each port! This way, you don't have to change money as soon as you step off the ship."

► "Bring a tape recorder for audio letters back and forth to the States."

► "Bring something nice to wear for the formal events."

► "Flip-flops or Teva sandals are great for wearing around the ship—the deck surface gets hot and they don't let you go barefoot into the dining room."

The Best + The Worst

👍 Meeting all of the people, both on and off the ship

👎 The "bad" element on the ship—those who just wanted to party and go to bars in the ports

👍 Learning how to travel on your own

👎 "The laundry facilities on board are terrible!"

👍 The opportunity to learn things that aren't from a textbook

👎 The time change as the ship crossed time zones

👍 Being on the ship for fifty days

👎 Being on the ship for fifty days

👍 "Traveling around the world on a ship, and getting college credit for it"

👎 "Fish and rice, fish and rice, fish and rice"

👍 The sense of adventure, freedom, and the responsibility of making your own choices

---

*At the time of publication, Semester at Sea was using a new ship for the first time—the SS *Universe Explorer.* By all accounts so far, this ship is simply a larger, slightly better-equipped version of the *Universe.* The University of Pittsburgh assures us that it has comparable features in every way. As no students were available yet for interviews, we have no other information at this time.

LONDON AND FLORENCE: ARTS IN CONTEXT

LOCATION: Great Britain, Italy

HOST SCHOOL: Associated Colleges of the Midwest (ACM)

DESCRIPTION: A 17-week program studying the history, literature, arts, and architecture of two historical European cities. Students also receive Italian language study.

DURATION: Semester

COST: $1,800 (Program fee only. Students from ACM colleges will pay one-half their yearly tuition. Non-ACM students should contact ACM for information. Meals in London not included.)

FINANCIAL AID: Students from ACM affiliates can use their regular financial aid.

PREREQUISITES: None (though juniors, seniors, and advanced sophomores are eligible to apply)

COURSE FULFILLMENT: Theater Production, Theater History, Art History

NO. OF STUDENTS: 50   M/F RATIO: 1/1

HOUSING: Homestays (Florence) and apartments provided by the program (London)

COMPUTERS: Not provided. Personal computers not needed.

CONTACT INFORMATION
Admissions
Associated Colleges of the Midwest
205 West Wacker Drive
Suite 1300
Chicago, IL 60603
Phone: (312) 263-5000
Fax: (312) 263-5879
E-mail: acm@midwest.netwave.net
WWW: http://midwest.netwave.net/acm

Overview

"I usually describe this program in one word: 'Amazing.' "

Perhaps two of the most fascinating and exciting cities in Europe, London and Florence herald visions of Michelangelo's David, Shakespeare's Romeo, and architecture, ranging from London Bridge to the Cathedral of Santa Maria del Fiore with its great dome. Art lovers are in paradise in these cities, as both are filled with incredible galleries, museums, churches, and palaces containing virtual treasure troves of sculpture, paintings, and architecture.

Once each year, the Associated Colleges of the Midwest's London and Florence: Arts in Context program takes nearly fifty students to these cities for more than four months. Students affectionately call the program "A Tale of Two Cities in Europe," as they have the opportunity to live in two of the world's great cities for eight weeks a piece, as well as intensely study their rich history and culture.

The Associated Colleges of the Midwest (ACM) was created out of an alliance with a dozen or so American colleges. ACM draws part of its faculty from its members, and allows the curriculum of its programs to vary from year to year. Students of ACM programs typically come from ACM college affiliates, but students of any college or university may participate.

Stressing the experiential as well as the scholastic, the program offers a homestay, Italian language study, and tickets and tours to an impressive amount of plays, museums, churches, cathedrals, and other sites of interest. Indeed, the cities *are* the classrooms, more so than in any other program we've encountered. In short, the students are studying the cities themselves. The program is divided so that for the first eight weeks half the students are in Florence, and the other half are in London. There is then a ten-day break, after which the two groups switch cities.

"I was always interested in art, but wasn't an artist—this was perfect."

In Italy, the Florentine culture soon envelops the students as they live in Florentine homes, study the Italian language, and examine Italian literature, art, and architecture. Short field trips are constantly scheduled, as students visit sites in and around Florence on an almost daily basis. Day and overnight trips may include visits to Pompeii, Rome, Siena, and Pisa.

In England, the students examine London's theater, art, and architecture. The theater aspect is a highlight of the trip for most students, as the program offers nearly four plays a week, ranging from Shakespeare to Stoppard. The students have the opportunity to see performances that will eventually be hits on Broadway, as well as meet some of the playwrights, directors, and actors of the productions they see. As for the art and architecture class, students are studying in much the same style as they are in Florence—daily field trips in and around the city are the norm. Other field trips may include visits to Bath, Stonehenge, and Stratford.

This program is best for those who have an intense interest in the arts of Europe. Previous work in studio art, art history, theater, and literature is encouraged, although not required. In fact, most students stressed that the course work is aimed at those who are not art history majors. However, as one student said, "It's amazing to actually visit the places you've been seeing for years on slides in dark rooms."

Environment

> "It's Old World, romantic, and you can walk from one side of it to the other."

As the focus of the program is the two cities themselves, the immediate environments are London and Florence. This is not such a bad deal, as both are interesting, cultural, and modern, yet with a strong respect for their past history. We'll briefly touch upon both, just to give an idea of what's in store:

Florence is a city where students can still experience a bit of the Old World, as it hasn't *completely* succumbed to the American standards of McDonald's, CNN, and Levi's. It is world famous for its Gothic and Renaissance buildings, primarily because Florence was arguably the capital of the Renaissance, and the city's inhabitants have preserved their history with a passion. Within the city borders are masterpieces of architecture from the thirteenth, fourteenth, and fifteenth centuries, and work from artists such as Benvenuto Cellini, Giovanni

> "I want to live in Italy the rest of my life."

da Bologna, Raphael, Titian, Tintoretto, Il Perugino, Michelangelo, and Brunnelleschi, just to name a few. The Biblioteca Nazionale Centrale in Florence is one of the finest libraries in Italy.

Located at the foot of the Apennines on the Arno River, Florence is a romantic city, and by all student accounts an imminently walkable one as well. Small streets wind through the city dotted with cafes, bars, and shops. Many students take walks along the banks of the Arno, where there are horse tracks, walking paths, and soccer fields. Florentines are also extremely friendly, provided, students warn, that you try and learn the language and the culture. The pace of life in Florence can be glimpsed in the fact that most everything, including the buses, shuts down at midnight.

The city, however, is also a modern one, with all of the problems inherent therein (pop. about 500,000). Pollution in the city is bad, and many students complained of sinus problems until they were able to adjust to it. Public transportation is reliable, but can be quite an experience sometimes due to overcrowding and some interesting local characters. Italian men, women warn, will get on your nerves, especially if you are a blond American woman (who apparently have a reputation in Italy for being very promiscuous). One woman's worst moment came when a man strutted up to her and said, "Marry me and I will make you the mother of a football team."

Advice from the students: "If you're a blond woman, dye your hair!" (We're not sure if she was kidding or not.)

London is a precarious mix of characters and institutions, where bankers in three-piece suits can be seen on the same city block as skinheads with

> *"Every day you see something completely new."*

pierced noses and lips. The capstone of the now defunct British Empire, London is one of the world's most important centers of banking, theater, and architecture. Named loosely after the Roman settlement of Londinium, one can trace the history of the region back to the first century. In the 1,900 years that followed, London survived the fall of the Roman Empire, the conquest of Britain by its first King, William the Conqueror, and the extensive bombing by the Germans in World War II.

Today's London is a huge, sprawling city, to the point that students can feel overwhelmed at the prospect of learning about it. London is one of the most modern cities in the world, and hence is "unforgivably expensive," crowded (pop. 6.3 million), and fairly polluted. There is, however, a lot of culture to be experienced here. There are

> *"When I say we did Rome, I mean we did Rome—we saw everything."*

more museums, churches, castles, and libraries, perhaps, than any sane person can navigate in eight weeks (although a good portion of the students give it a try). The theater is also the best in the world, and the program takes in plays in the Fringe (London's "Off-Broadway"), as well as the West End ("Broadway"). The public transportation is excellent, and the double-decker buses, London's subway system (the Tube), and British Rail all get high marks from students.

The downside of England is, notoriously, the weather. Regardless of which half of the program you stay in the U.K. for, the weather is not going to be particularly fabulous. In fact, it may rain on you every single day that you are there. Fortunately, there is no real danger of you getting terribly homesick or culture-shocked, too. London has all of the fast-food chains, movies, video arcades, and TV shows that we have in the U.S.

Housing

"I learned more Italian around the dinner table than I did in class."

While both locations have more than adequate housing, Florence far surpasses London in the students' opinions. While in Florence, students are placed with homestay families. This not only gives students the opportunity to practice their Italian (or rather, forces them, as few of the families speak English), but also lets them in on Italian culture, and gives them two home-cooked meals a day!

Most students get very close with their Italian families, and some students even take vacations out to their family's summer cottage with them. Of course, everyone mentioned the home-cooked meals, and more than one person put on weight. As a few said, "You will never have a bad meal in Italy."

ACM does a credible job screening and monitoring the families, and all the families either live in the city, or are directly on bus routes. No one is more than twenty minutes away by bus. Be sure to take the word "families" with a grain of salt—students in the past have stayed with large families with five kids, and also with single, widowed women.

London's housing situation changes from year to year. ACM does, however, keep the accommodations simple and in the same general area, very near to the center of the city. In past years students have stayed in one large flat (apartment), where they all shared the same kitchen and bathrooms, and classes were held in the living room. Students have also stayed in individual efficiency apartments, sharing the flat with two or more people.

Regardless of the setup, the apartments are always small, and a bit dingy. Some years the apartments have even lacked proper kitchen supplies, which is quite a drawback when students are providing all three meals for themselves! However, the accommodations are always in an excellent location, near a tube stop, a good grocery store, and Hyde Park.

Academics

"You get to see what you're learning."

The academics on the London and Florence program are perhaps the most tiring we've encountered. You will walk *a lot*—down small city streets, through large museums, around botanical gardens of palaces. One student said, "You realize how amazing what you're doing is when you get back to your room and your feet are hurting from walking around the sites you're studying."

In both cities, there are two principal courses—a theater course in London and a litera-

> *"The courses were really tied into the experiences."*

ture course in Florence, which are taught by visiting professors from one of the ACM colleges, and an art and culture course in each city that is headed by the resident faculty. In addition to this, there is a language component covered at Linguaviva (an international language school) while the program is in Italy.

The shining star of the academics are clearly the art and culture courses, which effectively take students on well-guided walking tours of the architecture, museums, and galleries of London and Florence. Students told us that they were enormously impressed with the resident faculty's knowledge of both individual pieces of art and the city itself, and quite a few described them as "walking encyclopedias." One student claimed, "There was more information on those daily trips than I could have learned in two years at home."

The schedule in both cities is intense and, in a slight contradiction, relaxed as well. Classes are held four days a week, leaving students with three-day weekends for their own explorations when field trips are not

> *"I was so busy with the program for a few weeks I didn't have time to get a postage stamp."*

scheduled. However, those four days can be extremely busy. Typically, classes are held in the mornings, field trips around the city are held in the afternoons, and, while in London, the group attends a play at night. In Florence, language classes are held in the early evenings a few times a week, and the rest of the night is occupied by dinner (which some said could take up to two hours!), and then a few hours of homework.

FLORENCE

While in some ways the academics in Florence are the most rewarding, they can also be the most frustrating. Although there is language study and intensive examination of the arts, students can get caught up in trying to balance learning the culture and hunkering down with a book every night. There is so much to *do*—talking with your Italian family, going out with your new international friends, exploring the city and country, and trying to do all of the reading and work for the classes. Students put in different amounts of time on the pure scholastic side—some we talked to worked for a solid four hours every night on homework and "did every line on the syllabus," while others did far less. All we can say is what ACM offers is excellent—there is the opportunity to learn an incredible amount about the arts on this program.

The language study is taught by the staff of the Linguaviva, where the program holds all of its classes. The students are usually divided into two groups according to ability. Language study is centered on conversational rather than written Italian, and the staff also throw in tips on Italian culture and customs. The staff changes every year, and they received fair to excellent marks from past students. There are other international students taking instruction here, affording the opportunity to be exposed to more than one culture. The Linguaviva staff also arrange for the group to go on a few cultural trips, such as a visit to a Chianti vineyard, and organize events like a volleyball tournament for people attending the school.

For those that choose to go to Florence first, there is the option of arriving three weeks earlier than the program starts for intensive language study (for an additional charge). Most students recommend this, as the extra time is extremely helpful both for learning the language and for getting to know Florence. In addition, it is also the best time for the weather in both cities.

The literature course involves a different topic each year. Past topics have included *Mythological Sources in Renaissance Art*, *The Italian City in Twentieth-Century Literature and Film*, and *Expatriate View of Italy*. Most students felt that this was an important part of the Florence component, although many thought that the workload was a bit prohibitive and kept them studying too much.

> "It was a good balance of the academic and the experiential."

Students have a lot of reading, a few short papers, and comprehensive tests on the material (which may include a slide test for the art and culture class). There isn't much homework for Italian, but there are small quizzes every week. The facilities are very limited, and all papers are handwritten. There is no library other than what ACM has put together over the years, and all of the ones in the city are mainly in Italian. Field trips may include visits to Pisa, Rome, Venice, and Sienna.

LONDON

The London segment is much less complicated. There are only two courses—the art and culture course, and the theater course. Obviously, no language segment is needed (although some would disagree), and while the culture *is* different from America's, it's still very familiar.

The theater course is a highlight for most students. Seeing up to five plays a week is an amazing opportunity, especially with the great seats the program provides. However, when you add lectures by playwrights, actors, directors, and theater critics, backstage tours of some of the leading theaters, in-depth preparation for upcoming shows, as well as analytical discussions on what the group had just seen, this becomes a truly remarkable class. A field trip to Stratford-upon-Avon, the birthplace of Shakespeare, compliments this section well.

While the program leans toward seeing more plays in the Fringe (where the best theater is anyway, students tell us), a good amount are also seen in the West End. Nearly every type of play is covered, from classic to contemporary, with works by such writers as Shakespeare, Harold Pinter, and Tom Stoppard. All around, this course provides an excellent examination of British theater. During the semester, students are also given ten pounds in case they want to see a production or two on their own. (One student saw fifty-two plays in the span of eight weeks!)

The facilities are usually sparse, with classes being held pretty much wherever ACM can find a spot. Previous years have held classes in living rooms and in a basement of a hotel. Nevertheless, students had no real complaints about these setups. There is a small library that ACM has put together over the years of relevant material, which students said cover any topic the program touches upon. If more resources are needed, London

COURSES (1995)

Theater in Performance
London: The City as Visual Text
Italian Language and Culture
*Ancient Mythological Sources for
    the Art of the Renaissance*
*Medieval and Renaissance
    Florence*

does have some of the best libraries in the world, and they're all in English, too.

The workload is comparable to the Florence section, with a few short handwritten papers, and a test or two for the art and culture class. The theater course requires a journal of play reviews, as well as a presentation about a play of their choice. The main bulk of work is note-taking and reading. Field trips in the past have included Bath, Stonehenge, and Oxford.

Off the Track

With occasional three-day weekends and a ten-day break between cities, students have ample time for their own explorations. Here are a few of the things that happened to them:

Hiking on the Italian Riviera was one student's most memorable three-day weekend. She and a friend went to a place called Cinque Terre, which are a group of five small Mediterranean villages nestled in the cliffs of the region. There are winding trails that connect them all and pass by olive groves, vineyards, streams, and lemon trees. The students would spend the night in one village, hike the next day to another, have lunch there and watch the fisherman haul in their nets, and do a sunset hike to the next village where they would stay the night.

Late one Thursday night, one student was trying to convince his roommate to take a trip. He wanted to use his Eurailpass up with a long journey, and was rattling off a bunch of potential cities. His roommate suddenly said, "I'd go to Nice," which is a fifteen-hour train ride from Florence. They both were packed in five minutes, said good-bye to their disbelieving host family, and on the 1:00 A.M. train to Nice. They had a one-hour layover in Pisa, where they got to see the famous tower lit up at night. They woke up the next morning in France, had a day to enjoy Nice, and then boarded the train for the ride back.

Carnaval in Viarregio is a standard visit for students on the London and Florence program. The big celebration before Lent is really a combination parade/party in which the whole city takes part. There is usually a political theme, such as floats with the Pope spanking a scientific group doing genetic testing, or Italian politicians dressed up as clowns. Students report that there is also a lot of confetti and shaving cream thrown about.

Warmer climates lured a pair of students to the south of Italy. They decided on Capri, considered one of Italy's most popular tourist towns. The two made it to the island, which was thankfully free of tourists since it was the off-season. They explored the famous blue grotto set in the rock shoreline, dove off cliffs, stared at the turquoise waters, and wandered through the small, friendly villages. They spent their nights in their own private villa that the owner had built with his own hands.

Another student decided to travel to Oxford on one of his free weekends. He went to see what he could find out about his favorite author, J.R.R. Tolkien. He went on a tour group and began talking with the tour guide, realizing that there weren't many others on the tour that spoke English. The guide took him to various sites, such as the college that Tolkien taught at, the pub that the Inklings (the writing group that C.S. Lewis formed) had gathered at, and even went to go see J.R.R.'s grave site.

Advice and Warnings from the Students

▶ "Go to Italy first so you can get the three extra weeks of language study."

▶ "Get a guidebook for London—it can get very confusing."

▶ "Buy a *Let's Go Europe!* The opportunities for travel are endless!"

▶ "Put a cover on your *Let's Go,* so you don't look, and feel, like a complete tourist!"

▶ "Buy a 'Young Person's Rail Card' for Britain."

▶ $3,000 is a good amount of money for personal expenses.

▶ "You can get cheap, great bootleg CDs in Italy."

▶ "Get away from the group as often as you can!"

▶ "Save your money for England—London is much more expensive than Italy."

The Best + The Worst

👍 The plays in London

👎 The pollution in Florence

👍 The ten-day break and the three-day weekends

👎 Not getting to interact with students in London

👍 Studying two different cultures in sixteen weeks

👎 Italian men

👍 Going to all of the museums

👎 The hectic schedules

👍 The homestays

👎 Being with the group *all* of the time

👍 Italian meals

CHARLES UNIVERSITY, PRAGUE

LOCATION: Prague and Podebrady, Czech Republic

HOST SCHOOL: Council on International Educational Exchange (CIEE)

DESCRIPTION: A fourteen-week study of the culture, the language, and the history of Prague and the Czech Republic

DURATION: Semester or year

COST: $6,750 per semester (airfare not included)

FINANCIAL AID: None. Federal loans and scholarships may be used.

PREREQUISITES: 2.75 GPA

COURSE FULFILLMENT: Various

NO. OF STUDENTS: 40   M/F RATIO: 1/1

HOUSING: Dormitories

COMPUTERS: Provided. Personal computers allowed.

CONTACT INFORMATION
Ellen Bahr
Director
Council on International Educational Exchange
205 East 42nd Street
New York, NY 10017
Phone: (212) 661-1414
Fax: (212) 972-3231
E-mail: 6424659@mcimail.com
WWW: Not available

Overview

"It's the best program for Eastern Europe."

How would you like to see *Don Giovanni* in the opera house where Mozart first presented it? Or walk through the streets of an old-world city that emerged virtually unscathed from World War II? Or stroll across the Charles Bridge, built in the fourteenth century, while looking up at the dominating presence of Hradčany Castle, formerly the residence of the kings of Bohemia? The city for all of this, of course, is Prague, "a city that made you feel like you were in a different time." This is the setting for the Council on International Educational Exchange's (CIEE) Charles University Prague program.

Twice each year, CIEE sends thirty-five to fifty students to the Czech Republic to study its culture, language, and history, both by itself and in relation to the rest of Europe. Participants take classes at one of the oldest universities in existence (Charles University), are given intensive Czech language training, and are assigned a Czech suitemate. However, this is not a rigid and "hand-holding" program. Students have considerable freedom while there, both to travel and to just be a student in Prague.

The Council on International Educational Exchange (CIEE), although itself not an educational entity, has established over its fifty-year history a vast network of sponsorships and affiliations with foreign institutions and educators. CIEE maintains hundreds of programs covering the globe, and all their courses are accepted at the university-level nationally.

The first two weeks are spent in the spa town of Podebrady, an hour east of Prague. In this town, students are given an orientation into Czech culture and customs, as well as an intensive language class five hours a day, every day. From there, the program moves to "the magical city of Prague," where it stays for the remainder of the semester. Students reside and take their meals at the Komenskeho student hostel, which is more like a combination dorm and hotel than just a grubby place for backpackers.

A short walk away is Charles University, where students take four classes ranging from the Czech influence on the humanities and sciences, to art, history, and politics. The language course is also continued here, although not as intensely. At this point, CIEE fades into the background and allows the students to experience the academic life in Prague for themselves. Students are adamant, however, that CIEE was always there if they needed them, for whatever reason.

Students have the weekends free, and nearly everyone takes advantage of this by arranging their academic schedules so they have three-day (or even four-day) weekends for traveling. CIEE also hosts two weekend trips during the semester, to Moravia and Southern Bohemia.

Environment

"It was a wonderland."

When the wall finally fell, and the road to the former Eastern Bloc countries was reopened to the tourism of the West, the magnificence of Eastern Europe was once again realized. Prague, with its history dating back to the ninth century, is undoubtedly one of the more picturesque cities in Europe.

Built on seven hills and located on both sides of the Vltava River, the city is a mixture of old-world charm and modern industry. The eastern bank of the Vltava River is the site of the Old and New towns, as well as Charles University. In the Old town, crooked streets seem to cross the city in aimless fashion, and sudden turns reveal stunning architecture dating from the fourteenth century. Looming above the city is Hradçany Castle, which is now the seat of the government of the new Czech Republic. As one student said, "If you love to explore while walking, Prague is perfect." When you get too tired to walk, Prague also has an excellent public transportation system, consisting mainly of trams.

"Prague was an unbelievable city."

The New Town is primarily an industrial and commercial center, and home to most of the banks, museums, and other public buildings. Because of all the manufacturing, however, students warn that the city is very polluted. Those who have sinus problems should be prepared to bring medication, as the pollution will aggravate a sinus condition.

As for Charles University, it was founded in the mid-1300s by Holy Roman Emperor Charles IV. The university was relocated early in its history, and has since stood in the same square, the Carolinium, for over 600 years. The main buildings are a complex of Gothic structures that could themselves be the subject of an architecture class. The CIEE program is located at the Faculty of Philosophy, only a block away from the Vltava River, with good views of the castle.

Yet all of this history still doesn't give a good idea of what the city is actually *like*. For starters, the arts are very important in Prague. The students we interviewed went out to the opera or theater almost constantly—and for the equivalent of $6 a show! One student rattled off all of the operas she had seen until we lost track (*Don Giovanni, La Bohème, The Magic Flute*—we couldn't keep track of the rest). However, another student insisted that "the best shows in town were not the operas—they were the churches." She went to every church she could find and claimed that seeing the church services was the best way to get a feeling for the people of Prague. Museums were also hot spots for students to spend an afternoon in.

> *"You're never bored, there's always something to see."*

> *"I would go into the pubs just for a cheap beer and to speak Czech."*

Past students found they spent a lot of time in the pubs, not because CIEE recruits drunkards, mind you, but rather because pubs are the typical social settings for the Czech Republic. They are a great place to talk, to eat lunch, or to make new friends. Not unlike the pubs in Britain, where the atmosphere is more like a get-together than a rock concert, the pubs of Prague range from quiet, smoky bars to the kind you might expect in an American college town. There are also dance clubs that students said were almost as good as those in the hotter spots of Europe. Czech beer, reportedly, is supposed to be fantastic.

Most students also mentioned how safe they felt while in Prague. As a tourist spot, the city is still growing, and hasn't yet succumbed to the problems of crime and violence that appear with rampant tourism.

> *"It's a fantastic introduction to the Czech Republic, and the problems of all of Eastern Europe."*

Advice to female students: "One of the greatest reasons for a woman to go to Prague is because it was one of the safest places I have ever been."

Housing

> "My Czech roommate was the greatest person in the world."

Despite the fact that it has "hostel" in its name, the Komenskeho student hostel is actually a fairly nice place to live for fourteen months. Most students simply referred to it as "the dorm," although it does take patrons from all over, giving it that much more of an international flavor. The students unanimously praised their housing situation, as it is across the river from the university, and only a half-hour walk to the scenic parts of the city.

Students are placed in four-person suites with at least one other person from the program. Most participants we talked to also had Czech suitemates, although not everyone did. They blamed this on the bureaucracy of Charles University, as CIEE pushes as hard as it can to integrate the program. Having Czech suitemates is a definite advantage, as students can practice their Czech while their roomies (who already know the great places to go in Prague) practice their English.

Each room also has a fairly good kitchenette, as well as maid service to clean the floors, and linen service for the towels and sheets. The maids, students warn, will always wake you up *very* early in the morning.

Food

"Don't miss breakfast—it will ruin your whole day."

Most of the food at the hostel is lousy (see, we told you we'd tell you the truth). During one semester, the students actually refused to eat at the cafeteria in the hostel, and CIEE has since implemented full stipends for students to cover the cost of all meals. However, to be completely fair, not all students thought the food was *that* bad.

Indeed, breakfast at the hostel is a highlight of most students' days. As one student said, "The breakfasts were fabulous—I used to sit there for two or three hours and just eat." Besides the abundant good food, it is evidently an extremely social thing to do as well. The people who complained the most about the food, we found, usually also skipped breakfast. Besides the stipends, breakfast at the hostel is included in the program fee.

As for dining out, there *are* a bunch of options, but expect almost every meal to be centered around some sort of meat. It's hard being a vegetarian, but apparently there is a vegetarian food stand just around the corner from the hostel. Some students recommend buying your own groceries instead, and cooking in the suites.

Academics

"I took courses I wouldn't be able to take back home."

True of nearly all semester abroad programs, the axiom "you get what you put into it" applies to the Charles University program as well. Some students described the academics as comparable to their home campuses, while others thought they were a little lighter. We tend to see the workload as staying on the lighter side, with one test and/or paper at the end of the semester being the norm for each class.

The hardest part of the semester is at the very beginning, during the two-week stay in Podebrady. Besides orientation material, students are also attending Czech-intensive language classes, for at *least* five hours a day. While in Prague, students are taking four classes at the university, taught in English. They are also continuing the language classes, albeit at a slackened schedule of three times a week.

The schooling system conforms to the European standard, rather than the American, and some may find this a little hard to adjust to. There is reading, but information is mainly gained through the lectures during classes, which only meet once a week for three hours. It's grueling for those used to fifty-minute classes, but students remark that after that, it's over for the week. There isn't really much work until the last few weeks, but be prepared then to be tested on the entire semester!

There really are no typical class schedules, as some people had one class on each day of the week, while others had all four classes on two days (except the language class, which meets three times a week). As we mentioned before, most students arrange their schedule to have three- or four-day weekends for traveling.

COURSES

Classes are composed of one of four courses that students pick as their elective classes, and the mandatory Czech language course. There are ten course offerings, covering Arts and the Humanities, Economics, Political Science, and History. The elective classes meet once a week for three hours, totaling three credits each, while the language course meets three times a week for an hour, totaling four credits. The daily workload is light, with small reading assignments for the elective classes, as well as a lot of memorization and exercises for the language class.

Elective classes are extremely lecture-oriented, which some students found a little stifling since there are no discussions allowed. One student remembered a class in which the students began having a heated discussion during the lecture, until the professor haughtily said, "Well maybe I ought to turn the class over to the students now." Although the professors do tend to drone on a bit, most students stressed that if good notes are taken, the amount of information you receive is enormous. Remember that you will need all of that information for the tests at the end of the semester.

> *"Other programs didn't even know if they were going to have class that day—with CIEE it was no problem."*

All classes are taught in English, although those students who are fluent in another language from the region may opt to enroll in a course taught in that language. Students found that not only is this a way to keep up on their fluency, but also it is a great way to get integrated into the local student scene.

> *"CIEE cuts through the red tape for you—which is considerable."*

FACULTY

Most students found their professors to be treasure troves of information on their subject. One student mentioned that his professor had almost every fact needed at the tip of his tongue, and there was never a question that stumped him. Others were impressed with the fact that some of the faculty were involved in the early underground roots of the Czech Republic's democratic movement, and would supplement lectures with personal stories. They did find their professors, however, to be much less approachable than their U.S. counterparts. Contrary to American standards, professors have no office hours, and students who wish to discuss a point after class have to hustle to catch them before they go out the door.

COURSES (1995)

Judaism and Jewish-Christian Relations in the Central European Context
Music in Bohemia
History of East and Central Europe
Modern Czech Literature
Art and Architecture in Prague and Its Environs
Czech Film
Czech Theater
Czech and Slovak Politics
Globalism and Regionalism in European Politics
Recent Economic Developments in the Czech Republic and Slovakia

The only concrete link to CIEE is the resident director, who is more of an administrator than a professor. Their main job is the orientation in Podebrady, and then making sure everything goes smoothly once in Prague. They host one or two meetings with students a month, to see how everything is going and if the students have any complaints, suggestions, or needs. From students' past experiences, the resident directors are always available if there are any serious problems.

FACILITIES

There are computers available with E-mail access, which was helpful as mail can be slow. Students did say, however, that they didn't use the computers for writing papers as much as they did back in the States. All the textbooks used in the program are CIEE's, and they are generally "recycled" year after year, though the texts aren't out of date. There is a good English library in one of the buildings of the university, although it took some students a while to find it. Classrooms are usually large lecture halls.

FIELD TRIPS

Nearly everyone that we interviewed mentioned the whirlwind excursions that the program led on two weekends. "We seemed to stop everywhere," one student remarked. "The tour guide took us everywhere, no matter how trivial—vineyards, the largest fish farm in the republic, even a dance hall to hear oom-pah-pah music." The tour guide actually was one of the program's professors, whose knowledge of the republic was so vast that he would be constantly commentating on what they saw outside their bus window, as well as singing old folk and beer-drinking songs.

The program goes on two bus tours to the Bohemian and Moravian regions, and the students unanimously agreed that it was a great way to see some of the other parts of the country. Although the days are packed with things to see, students usually have the nights to do what they please.

Off the Track

With most students arranging a three- or four-day weekend, there are plenty of opportunities for adventures outside of the program. Here are a few things that happened to the students on the Charles University program:

An abandoned castle on the outskirts of Prague was one student's most memorable experience. A Czech friend took her out there—for an outdoor production of the opera *Othello,* under a full moon.

Since the program is located in Eastern Europe, the students are able to visit countries usually off the list for normal "Eurailpass" trips. Many past students visited Poland, Turkey, Hungary, or even Austria, besides the standard trips to Germany, Switzerland, and Italy.

Four men with accordions walked into one student's favorite bar. He had been talking to one of his Czech friends and was surprised when the men started playing Czech national songs right at the counter. He was even more surprised when everyone in the bar started singing along wholeheartedly. The student said that this was a perfect example of pub life in Prague.

One woman traveled to Krakow, in order to see the famed markets. She stopped briefly in Lithuania, and missed her bus because her watch was set to a different time zone. The bus station attendant informed her that they couldn't return her money, didn't accept credit cards, and hadn't ever heard of traveler's checks. She made her way to the embassy, where she ran into the father of someone she once knew, who lent her $50 out of his own pocket. She finally got to Krakow—where the market was closed for the holidays!

Advice and Warnings from the Students

▶ "If you go in the spring—bring your tux or ball gown for all of the balls that are held!"

▶ Make sure you ask in advance for a Czech roommate!"

▶ "Go to the opera, have a dark beer at a pub, live the life of Prague."

▶ $1,500 to $2,000 is a good amount of money to bring for personal expenses.

▶ "Don't change money on the street!"

▶ "Bring a lot of deodorant—you can't buy it over there!"

▶ "The pollution is bad, so bring a lot of Kleenex and medication for sinus problems!"

► "Don't miss breakfast!"

► "Bring a simple cookbook, because you can cook in your suite."

► "Speak as much Czech as possible—the people of Prague respond better."

The Best + The Worst

👍 The organized tours

👎 The food

👍 Breakfast

👎 The fact that Czechs get up with the sun

👍 The pubs

👎 The pollution

👍 The professors who knew everything

👎 Not enough integration scholastically with Czechs

👍 The city of Prague

👍 The intensive language class

BRAZILIAN ECOSYSTEMS

Joan Horn

LOCATION: Southern Brazil, South America

HOST SCHOOL: Antioch College

DESCRIPTION: A firsthand look at environmental issues at five separate sites in complex and diverse regions of southern Brazil. Students investigate ecological issues of the various climate zones of Brazil, as well as undertaking intense language study.

DURATION: Semester

COST: $9,200 (round-trip airfare to London is not included)

FINANCIAL AID: Federal aid through home institution. Scholarships from Antioch and Antioch New England are available.

PREREQUISITES: Two years of academic study at college level and recommendation of home campus advisors. Previous Portuguese or Spanish language study recommended.

COURSE FULFILLMENT: Ecology, Field Biology, Portuguese

NO. OF STUDENTS: 15   M/F RATIO: 1/7

HOUSING: Hotels and on-site dormitories

COMPUTERS: Not provided. Personal computers not suggested or needed.

CONTACT INFORMATION
Joanne Wallace
Brazilian Ecosystems
Antioch Education Abroad
Antioch College
Yellow Springs, OH 45387
Phone: (800) 874-7986
Fax: (513) 767-6469
E-mail: jraw@college.antioch.edu
WWW: http://192.161.123.121:125/academic.html

Overview

"I wouldn't trade this experience for anything."

You are waist deep in mud, looking at a bright green bird that has just flown into view, hearing its name whispered to you by your guide, Jorge. You don't mind the mud—you'll take a quick dip in the Amazon River to wash it off, and stare at the pink river dolphins playing as you set up your hammock for the night. You are, of course, on Antioch's Brazilian Ecosystems program.

> *"This is a very dirty program—you're tromping through mud constantly."*

Once a year, Antioch College takes approximately fifteen people through Brazil for three months, to study some of the hottest environmental issues facing the world today. Traveling to sites such as the Amazon, the world's largest wetlands, and subtropical forests, the Antioch program studies the complex and intricate diversity of the ecosystems in Brazil, as well as methods of how to balance its development with its preservation. This is not just a "Save the Rain Forest" campaign dressed up in academic clothing—Antioch does its usual good job of showing students both sides of every issue.

> *"It's an amazing experience and an incredible opportunity."*

Traveling from the depths of the rain forest to the Atlantic coast, students have the opportunity to see an incredible range of ecosystems, many of which are threatened to disappear forever. Lectures, both in the classroom and in the field, are by some of the top scientists on the subjects in the world, all of whom are down there doing the research that can be read about in *Time* and *Newsweek*.

Not only do students receive a firsthand look at some of the leading environmental issues and controversies, but they have intensive Portuguese language training, a month in which to conduct their own Individual Research Project, and even participate in a short urban homestay. Although the accommodations throughout are generally excellent, this program relies heavily on field work, and those students squeamish about being wet, dirty, itchy, and generally sodden should think twice before applying.

Environment

"We were there in mosquito and snake season—and I loved it."

The entire goal of the program seems to be to expose the students to as many different environments as possible, as it travels throughout the Amazonas and the southern regions of Brazil. Students trek through jungles, forests, coastal rain forests, cities, and towns, while staying on a riverboat, in dormitories, homes, and motels.

As for the host country, Brazil can be considered very different from its South American neighbors. Speaking Portuguese rather than Spanish, in the south its citizens are a European mix in most of the coastal areas, and it is not uncommon to see European names on hotels or menus in German. In the north, its citizens are African/native, with a small part European. The pace of the country is slow and relaxed, even in the larger cities, and this can be both a relief and a frustration to Norte-Americanos. However, many students were amazed at how similar the cites are to those in the U.S., as long as you ignore the language and things like avocado popsicles.

The program passes through some incredible natural environments, although it doesn't stay in any of them too long. Although the program visits seven locations, Antioch actually has nine sites from which to chose. Listed below are brief descriptions of the sites visited during our interviewing process. The order and length of stay vary from year to year, depending on guest lecturer schedules and availability of accommodations.

Many students found the **Manaus** segment to be one of the most incredible experiences, even though it's at the very beginning of the trip. After a brief stay in the city of Manaus ("not worth mentioning," as most students said), the program moves up the Rio Negro River, a northern branch of the Amazon, on a South American version of a houseboat. During the day, it docks at several landings along the shore, where local guides meet the program for long lecture hikes. Each day students said they saw every type of insect, mammal, fish, or plant

"The Amazon, of course, was incredible."

imaginable, including piranhas, jaguars, boa constrictors, toucans, dolphins, and, most notoriously, mosquitoes. Here the program is really in the depths of the jungle, where there are no roads except the one the boat floats on.

Foz do Iguaçu is one of the largest and best protected areas in South America. The weather and the vegetation here are much drier than the Amazon, and there is the looming effect of technology and development—Itaipú Hydroelectric Dam, the largest hydroelectric works in the world, is nearby. "You could walk or drive to over 170 waterfalls, each one better than Niagara Falls could ever be." Here you are surrounded by the jungle, endless flocks of birds, and the resounding cry of the jaguar.

The city of **Londrina** ("little London") is another small, friendly city, by all reports—small enough that the students can hike from town right into the hills. Here, students talked about going on early evening hikes while swarms of bats flew overhead.

Curitiba, the capital of the Brazilian state of Paraná, was one of the longer stays for the students we interviewed. This is considered by many to be the ecological capital of Brazil, with generous amounts of open, green space for its million-plus residents. The city is also the site of a few of Brazil's larger university and environmental groups. Students are matched up with Brazilian families here, for their urban homestay.

Apparently, the most breathtaking place of all is the coastal town of **Ponta Do Sul.** A marine research station, it is located practically on the beach, looking out over the bay. Dunes and mangroves dot the coast, while close by is Ilha do Mel (Honey Island), which boasts pristine white beaches, clear water, and even good surfing waves. Students can walk from the research station to the town of Ponta Do Sul for a beer, or a stop at the post office. Across the bay is the city of Paranguá, one of the busiest ports of southern Brazil.

Volta Velha Reserve is the final stop before students go off on their Independent Research Projects. The region surrounding Volta Velha is what is known

> *"I would walk out of the forest with tears, it was so beautiful."*

as Atlantic Plain Rain Forest, and is some of the last remaining areas of its type. Volta Velha is an ecotourist center, and within its borders are rain forests, a mountain range, and wide fields that run from the forests to the sea. One student claimed that the area is so filled with species of different birds, researchers have barely scratched the surface of categorizing them.

Other Antioch sites include the **Pantanal,** which is the world's largest wetland, **General Carneiro,** an Araucária forest, and **Guaraqueçaba,** where the group studies coastal wetlands. These areas were not visited by our interviewees.

Perhaps the most stable environment, though, is the group itself, which has both advantages and disadvantages. Traveling in a small group can be difficult, as the hours on the road can get very long, cramped inside the two vans which Antioch uses for transportation. "Long days mean short tempers," as one student put it. However, good group dynamics can make some of the experiences that much richer, as well as provide students with lifelong friends.

Although the traveling is diverse, there *are* certain images that can stick in your mind—hiking through knee-deep mud in the Amazon, staring out at night at the bioluminescence in the protected bay on which Ponta do Sul is stationed, watching a flight of bats in the moonlight.

Housing

"I would wake up to a chorus of birds, and go to sleep to thundershowers."

The students unanimously voted the first housing stop as the worst. The motel in Manaus was described in many ways, but one student summed it up perfectly as "a dump." However, it's only for a few days, and the group soon moves onto the riverboat while exploring the Amazon. The boat was considered to be quite nice, albeit simple. Students hung hammocks from the second floor of the boat when they wanted to sleep, and there was room to hold occasional classes as well as have a meal. For showers, students would "jump in the soft waters of the Amazon and play with the dolphins."

In Foz do Iguaçu, the group is housed in what was described to us as "a large Victorian house in the middle of the jungle." Called the "House of Hospitalities" (visiting researchers stay here while doing field work), the house is enormous. It has beds for over two dozen, a kitchen, dining room, and a large living room filled with overstuffed furniture.

The hotels that the group use during their stay in Maringá aren't particularly extravagant, but the students said that they are comfortable (nearly all had air-conditioning), safe, and clean. Some were disappointed by the fact that although they are in the same towns as some of the major Brazilian universities, they have little opportunity to interact with the local students more.

Students are placed with host families in Curitiba and Londrina, offering them the chance to get exposed to a little more Brazilian culture. Students that we interviewed loved their homestay families in general, in particular for the chance to practice Portuguese. "My host mother," one student remembered, "was great. She knew I was struggling with the language, and so she would talk to me really *loud* and *slow*." Any students we talked to who had problems with their families were quickly relocated by the program.

When the program moves to Ponta do Sul, the group stays in the dormitories at the research station. "The rooms are great and clean, but they feel a little like barracks" was how one student put it. Needless to say, these barracks are right on the beach—so much so that people usually went for a swim before going to class.

Finally, the group reaches Volta Velha and stays at the ecotourist ranch. The amenities are basic, but clean and comfortable. There is an outdoor kitchen to cook in, and one of the women on the ranch bakes fresh bread every day. There is no electricity here, although the people we interviewed mentioned that they were so tired from hikes, they were asleep right after sunset anyway. Larger groups end up staying at the new Vila da Gloria ecotourism hotel, which is much more modern, houses two to three students to a bungalow, and even had a great pool to cool off in.

FOOD

As for food, the diet is heavily centered on meat. Vegetarians will have slim pickings, but students claimed they could always rely on fruits, vegetables, and pasta. The influence of the Amazon is evident in the cuisine in the north, as food is typically cooked in some manner in Dende oil (palm oil) and can be heavily spiced. While on the hammock boat, students should expect to eat *a lot* of fish.

Academics

"You are learning twenty-four hours a day."

Striving more for an overview of the problems and issues facing the ecosystems of Brazil than for in-depth examination, Antioch touches upon regional problems while actually visiting the regions themselves. Antioch gives its students a broad perspective of what a diverse country Brazil actually *is*—from its incredible resources to its formidable problems.

Listed below are the sites visited with their academic content, in the order they were visited:

Manaus—Students get a quick orientation to the culture and customs of Brazil in the city of Manaus, as well as a rundown of their itinerary and safety tips. Then it is immediately off to the Amazon for ten days, where students may participate in jungle hikes, research trips on a hammock boat, visits to research sites and indigenous organizations, as well as meet with faculty researchers from the Federal University of Amazonas. The Amazon, being perhaps the richest place in the world in terms of genetic diversity, is one of the more memorable places for most students.

Foz do Iguaçu—"Foz," as the students call it, is a subtropical forest, one of the largest and best protected areas in South America. Activities here may include intensive language study in Portuguese (although the location for language study varies year to year), and studying Itaipú Hydroelectric Dam and the environmental management problems it presents.

Londrina—The next destination for a few days, where students study the ecology of birds and bats at the state university. Some of Brazil's top scientists do research here, many of whom lecture to the group.

Curitiba—A high point for most students, the program stays here with host families. Students resume their intensive language training, as well as receive lectures and combined field trips studying agriculture and soil erosion, soils and vegetation, and city planning and waste management.

Ponta do Sul—Generally staying here for a week, the program comes out of the trees and studies the coast. At the Federal University Marine Studies Center, students examine mangrove ecology and dune vegetation, while also enjoying the water and surrounding islands.

Volta Velha Reserve—Here the program tackles an ecosystem just as diverse and important as the Amazon—the Atlantic coastal rainforest. Staying inside the reserve so as to be completely immersed in their surroundings, students study topics such as soils, bats, botany, animal tracking and mammals, gap and forest ecology, and tidal pools. While visiting the new luxury hotel nearby, the program looks at ecotourism, casual research, and their impact on fragile ecosystems.

The final month is devoted to the students' individual research projects, which are conducted in any of Antioch's program sites. The final three days are spent back in Curitiba, where students present their IRPs and the program has its final meetings.

COURSES

There are only three courses for the Brazilian Ecosystems program—*Brazilian Ecosystems: The Protection and Management of Diversity* for eight semester credits, *Portuguese Language* for four semester credits, and *Brazilian Ecosystems: Field Research* for four semester credits.

The *Protection and Management* course is simply what Antioch decided to call all of the lectures that the students receive. The diversity, quality, and quantity of the lectures are tremendous, whether they are in the classroom or in the field. Past lectures include numerous jungle hikes/lectures, visits to fisheries, birdwatches, examining soil composition, tracking a jaguar that has been fitted with a radio collar, or simply explaining the effects of Itaipú Hydroelectric Dam on the indigenous tribes. Students unanimously were amazed at the quality of the lectures. As one of them said, "It was like being in an outdoor class for eight hours a day!"

While it may seem impossible for students to retain all of the information that is thrown at them, nearly all of the past participants were surprised by how much they *did* remember once back in the States. Of course, students also warn that you will never take more notes in your life.

The *Portuguese Language* course formally has class for only two weeks (and two separate weeks at that—one at the beginning, one at the end), a time frame that may seem incredibly skimpy for learning a language. Indeed, most students wished this component was longer. However, they also concede that they can hold a conversation in Portuguese fairly easily now, which is the goal of the course.

The class is very intensive both weeks, and the language is taught in inventive ways. There are "no English" times scheduled, even during such difficult times as cooking dinner. (How do you ask if the water is boiling in Portuguese?) Signs are placed all over the house in which they are staying—words for "television," "floor," etc. Although the formal sessions end after two weeks, students are being guided and taught by local scientists who usually do not speak English, which practically forces them to use and expand their skills.

The *Field Research* class is simply the Independent Research Project (IRP). During the first two months, students work

> *"The shining star of the program is the internships."*

with their field directors and local scientists on constructing a project, or an internship. Students may contribute to ongoing research at one of the sites, or do their own research. Past projects include studying the behavioral pattern of pumas, growth patterns of bromeliads in the Atlantic rain forest, the urbanization and morphodynamics of coastal processes, and an internship with the mayor's office in Curitiba to study an ecotourism presentation, to name a few.

WORKLOAD

The workload is considerably lighter than what students may be used to. There are only two papers to write—an ecology paper on a topic of the student's choice, and a paper describing their Independent Research Project. The ecology paper is about ten to fifteen pages, while the Independent Research paper averages out to about twenty pages (even though some student we talked to wrote as much as fifty!). Both papers are due at the end of the semester. However, extensions are easily attained, and some students were still writing their papers months after the program was over! There are small assignments and a final oral exam for the language course.

> *"It is so much more than writing papers and reading books."*

There are also two journals to keep—a scientific and a cultural. In the scientific journal, students keep class notes, observations from the field, descriptions, pictures, etc. The cultural journal is less stressed, and even turned into many people's "personal" journal.

Students aren't graded; rather, they are evaluated in all three courses by their professors and advisors to find if they have achieved a proper level of proficiency.

FACULTY

As we've mentioned, the faculty and lecturers on this program are the top people in their field of study. They are all approachable, as many of them simply lead the group for hikes through the forest and explain about the environmental phenomena or problems they are looking at. A lot of the lecturers, however, do not speak English, and translators are used until everyone in the group attains a proficient level of Portuguese.

> COURSES (1995)
>
> *The Protection and Management of Diversity*
> *Portuguese Language*
> *Brazilian Ecosystems: Field Research*

As for the Antioch staff down there, nearly all of them get good marks from the students. There are four different people associated with Antioch who live in Brazil, located at different locales. One faculty member from Antioch College travels with the group the entire time.

We have generally found that the staff and administration from Antioch is also highly receptive to students concerns and requests, and makes changes accordingly.

FACILITIES

The only facilities that the group always has access to is its "traveling library," which is basically a crate filled with books from years past (supplemented by material gained from lectures at universities during the semester). Although it may sound extremely limited, students said that it was more than sufficient.

Since students are based in the research sites they visit during the program for their Individual Research Projects, they have access to all the equipment they may need. All of the research areas are adequately equipped, and one or two are even state of the art, with computers and laser printers.

Off the Track

Although there is hardly any time off (an afternoon off a week was standard, while a whole day was an exception), students still came away with incredible stories. Here are a few of the things that happened to the students on Antioch's Brazilian Ecosystems program:

Exploring a cave with some local spelunkers, one student noticed the water they were wading through was getting higher and higher. It finally stopped at waist level—just about the time she heard the sound of rushing water getting louder. The water eventually turned into a waterfall, which the group proceeded to climb down, emerging in the rain forest just as dusk was settling.

Seeing a jaguar was the main goal for one student during her IRP—but she never did. She did come very close, though. An avid runner, she was taking a jog right after it rained, her shoes sinking deep into the mud on the road. She began to get tired, and turned around. A quarter of a mile later, she looked down and saw the prints of one of the big cats interspersed with those her running shoes had made just minutes before.

Flora and fauna are a constant throughout the trip, but it's the fauna you have to look out for. Once, while going through the remains of an old building during a field lecture, a snake fell on one of the group. Only after she had flung it off and got her breath back did she realize it was a pit viper, one of the most poisonous snakes alive.

Hiking stories were repeated to us endlessly, all of them fascinating. One student recalled hiking up a waterfall under a full moon, while another loved going on long walks along the dunes near Ponta do Sul. During the IRPs, one student walked daily along a dirt road, looking for predator prints, while still another would take a daily walk to the magnificent waterfalls in Foz.

One student's homestay experience was so great that she stayed with her family again during her IRP. They taught her how to samba, took her on walking tours of the city, or just out to the movies. They even took her to a Paul McCartney concert when he came to town.

Advice and Warnings from the Students

▶ "Don't be afraid to speak Portuguese."

▶ "Get used to insects, they're everywhere."

▶ "Bring insect repellent!"

▶ "Don't bring a lot of traveler's checks, and don't change a lot of money at one time!"

▶ "Bring hiking boots and Tevas!"

▶ $500 is a good amount of money to bring for personal expenses.

▶ "Invest in good raingear! It pours in a lot of the places you go!"

▶ "Bring an English/Portuguese dictionary."

▶ "Make sure you bring both warm and cold clothing."

The Best + The Worst

👍 Being in the Amazon!

👎 The insects

👍 Sleeping in hammocks on the boat

👎 The first hotel in Manaus

👍 The group dynamics

👎 The trips in the vans

👍 The Independent Projects

👎 *Constantly* talking about Antioch (a large proportion of students are from Antioch)

👍 The homestays

👎 Being a vegetarian on the program

👍 The lecturers

👍 Brazilians

SEA SEMESTER

Kathy Sharp Frisbee

LOCATION: Atlantic Ocean, Caribbean Sea and Woods Hole, Massachusetts

HOST SCHOOL: Sea Education Association

DESCRIPTION: A three-month program that combines nautical science, oceanography, and maritime studies, including a six-week sailing voyage

DURATION: Semester

COST: $11,250 (airfare to all locations and meals in Woods Hole not included)

FINANCIAL AID: SEA offers several scholarships and interest-free loans to those who qualify. Federal aid packages are also accepted.

PREREQUISITES: One college level lab science course

COURSE FULFILLMENT: Oceanography, Field Sciences

NO. OF STUDENTS: 49   M/F RATIO: 1/1

HOUSING: Program facilities at Woods Hole, and on SSV *Corwith Cramer* or SSV *Westward*

COMPUTERS: Provided. Personal computers allowed at student's own risk.

CONTACT INFORMATION
Admissions Director
Sea Education Association
P.O. Box 6
Woods Hole, MA 02543
Phone: (800) 552-3633
Fax: (508) 457-4673
E-mail: Not available
WWW: Not available

Overview

"I'll be sailing the rest of my life because of SEA."

SEA Semester is run by the Sea Education Association based out of Woods Hole, Massachusetts, and provides their participants with a learning environment unlike any other. SEA teaches both science and nautical techniques with powerful hands-on methods, and considers "learning by doing" to be their main philosophy in an atmosphere of comprehension and teamwork.

SEA Semester offers students the setting to immerse themselves in the marine sciences in a unique way—the last six weeks of the course are spent sailing the Atlantic Ocean or the Caribbean Sea on board a tall ship. This program gives students an excellent introduction into the marine sciences, the opportunity to do an Individual Research Project at sea, and, more importantly, the chance to "learn by doing." It is an academically, mentally, emotionally, and physically challenging semester.

The program does not start off by putting you on a schooner and wishing you good luck as you leave the dock. During the first six weeks, forty-nine stu-

> *"SEA Semester is something that you will never have the chance to do again."*

dents live and study at SEA's campus at Woods Hole, Massachusetts. They are, in effect, in training for the six weeks at sea. Here they study all aspects of oceanography, nautical science, and even the human fascination with the sea in a maritime studies course. The nautical science course is especially important, as here students learn all the theory and navigational skills necessary to sail a ship. Students also learn how to handle group living situations—an important ability to have while at sea.

The culmination of the shore component is the six weeks aboard one of SEA's ships. Students sail aboard either the SSV *Westward*, a 125-foot staysail schooner, or the SSV *Corwith Cramer*, a 134-foot steel brigantine. Both are fully equipped research vessels under sail. Regardless of which ship students take, the voyage is generally 2,500 miles long, ranging from sailing around the Caribbean to sailing in New England and Canadian waters.

While at sea, the oceanography course continues (on a more relaxed schedule), students conduct their own individual research projects, and, of course, they are sailing. Students are an intricate part of the sailing environment—they take turns as cooks, as assistant engineers, as deck crew, as scientists, as navigators, and even as watch officer for a day. The time at sea is especially hard—students are either participating in sailing their ship, cleaning the ship, attending class, or doing research. Besides that, they sleep.

There is precious little free time, but students do have the weekends in Woods Hole to themselves, and the brief port stops.

Environment

"I love the fact that it was November and I was still able to wear shorts."

As was mentioned in the beginning, SEA Semester has two segments, the shore component and the sea component. The shore component takes place in Woods Hole, Massachusetts, which is the home of several world-renowned marine and research institutions. The Woods Hole Oceanographic Institution (WHOI), the Marine Biological Laboratory, and branches of the United States Geological Survey and the National Marine Fisheries Service all make their homes here. The presence of such distinguished groups sets a very scientific tone to the program.

Woods Hole is a small village in the southwestern corner of Cape Cod, about ninety minutes outside of Boston. It's a tourist town in the summers, but during the off-season it sinks comfortably back into the role of a small town with a few extra conveniences thrown in. There are some good restaurants, and a couple of small and interesting bars that students can go to for "study sessions."

Mainly, however, students spend their weekday free time on and around campus. The campus is about three miles outside of Woods Hole, so it is isolated with nothing to disturb it but the birds and the deer. Many students either run or mountain bike on the trails around the

"Everyone really focuses on the sea component, but the shore component was just as great."

campus, as getting into physical shape for the six weeks at sea is second only to getting into shape mentally. A sports center with tennis courts, aerobics classes, and a weight room is nearby.

Also within walking distance are beaches, marshes, and rocky shores, available for field trips or for simple recreation. For longer weekend trips, Martha's Vineyard is just a short ferry ride away, and Boston can easily be reached by car or bus. In the winter months, some students even go north to ski in Vermont and New

Hampshire. As for the social scene, the different student houses throw parties in their basement or hold coffeehouses to showcase student talent.

Life at sea is a mix of inspiration and challenge. On the one hand, there is the water itself. Dolphins playing in the ship's bow wave is a common occurrence; whale sightings are rarer but certainly not unheard of. Sunsets, sunrises, moonsets, and moonrises over the water are "unbelievably beautiful." The relaxing feeling of sailing across the Caribbean Sea with a good breeze can calm nearly anyone's nerves, while battling a tropical storm is a thrill few people get to experience.

On the other hand, students are sharing the space of a 130-foot ship with 35 other people. There is little, very very *very* little personal space, and some

> *"You're on the ship for six weeks, and you really develop a relationship with her."*

students contended that there isn't any at all. One student mentioned that he would volunteer for any climbing jobs available, simply so he could have a bit of time by himself up in the rigging. There is a flip side to the confines of the ship, however, as a few students mentioned that it makes them very dependent on one another, thus becoming "closer to the people on board than to anyone else."

SEA does try to ease the strain as much as possible. Swim breaks are held when the weather's right—the ship is anchored and students are allowed to dive into the sea to cool off. Many students mentioned swimming with dolphins, and some swam within a short distance of minke whales. The ships also stop for a few days at two ports during the voyage, allowing not only a respite from the shipboard life, but a glance into Caribbean culture. Bonaire, Jamaica, Bermuda, and the

> *"Swimming is weird because you can't touch the bottom."*

Windward Islands are frequent choices for ports of call. Each semester usually organizes group activities for themselves as well. One fall semester group assigned "secret Santas" for the December holidays—every person had to give a shipmate a handmade gift.

Housing

"It's truly a floating classroom."

While at Woods Hole, students are housed in cottages that hold ten people each. The group of houses have affectionately been called

"The Smurf Village" and "Waco" in the past. Despite the names, they are excellent housing with ample room for everybody. Typically two to three people share a room, and the houses also have large living room/dining rooms and a kitchen. The students decide how the cooking and the grocery shopping is done—but most people we talked to opted for the communal system. Students organize who cooks, who cleans, who shops, etc. This is all an exercise and a preparation for the cramped group living situation that they will experience while aboard ship.

While at sea, "you learn to get over being bashful very quickly." Students are each assigned a bunk, and the bunks line the inside of the ship from bow to stern. The bunk has a small storage shelf in it and a curtain for privacy, although most students never closed them because it can get very hot below deck. Other than that, there is the galley, the main salon, and the engine room. Above deck there is the bridge, the lab, and the "doghouse" (where the charts are kept and the navigational equipment is housed). Each ship is equipped with two radars, several radio-telephones, a satellite navigation system, LORAN, and depth sounders, in addition to scientific and safety equipment aboard.

FOOD

The old saying goes, "An army travels on its stomach," and evidently so does the navy. Three square meals a day, plus three snacks, is apparently not a problem for SEA Semester, as there is a full-time steward aboard who creates fare loved by the entire crew. Students also take turns as assistant stewards, helping to prepare the sometimes extravagant meals for the three-dozen crew members. There is little that is left out of the menus—freshly baked bread, pizzas, and seafood right off the hook are regular fares. The only missed item was cold, fresh milk, but that's a little hard to keep fresh. Snacks are usually fresh fruit and cookies. Cooking on a stove constantly in motion takes students a while to get used to, and on rough days the entree occasionally ends up on the deck instead of the table.

Academics

"It's not all fun and games, but I guess that's what makes it a great program."

The academics are neatly divided up into two segments, as is everything else. While at Woods Hole, the work is centered around classroom learning—studying all aspects of oceanography, nautical science, and maritime studies. Once on board ship, however, the focus shifts to the task of learning how to actually run the ship—from the sails down to the engine. The oceanography course does continue, though, and students have the added task of conducting their own research. Throughout both the land and shore components, the quality remains excellent and the intensity moderate to hard.

The classes at Woods Hole are comparable to any university, and there is the added bonus of learning the same material with the same group of people, day in and day out—everyone you are living with is studying the exact same topics. That is an advantage and also a hindrance—with challenging academics, intense living conditions, and bright students, it can get a little competitive.

The class schedule is pretty full as well, and one student even remembered pulling all-nighters on a Saturday night. Classes are Monday through Friday, and meet every day in the morning for an hour each. The afternoons are reserved for labs, which vary from class to class. They may be actual lab work, such as practicing charting, or field trips, such as going to the maritime museum or a local salt marsh. Labs usually last three or four hours. A typical day would be:

8:00 A.M.	Oceanography	11:30 A.M.	Lunch
9:15 A.M.	Nautical science	1:30 P.M.	Lab
10:30 A.M.	Maritime studies		

The time at sea is an entirely different scenario. The oceanography and nautical science courses are still held, one meeting in the morning and one in the afternoon. Some felt that this is the worst part academically, as they are held outside and "people would put on their sunglasses and go to sleep." Classes last for an hour each, and are typically held four to five days out of the week.

The days at sea, however, are really centered around the "watches." These watches define life aboard ship as follows:

3–7 A.M.	Dawn watch	7–11 P.M.	Evening watch
7–1 P.M.	Morning watch	11–3 A.M.	Midwatch
1–7 P.M.	Afternoon watch		

The group itself is divided up into watch groups of eight or nine people. Each person is assigned a task to do for their watch. There is "Deck," to which three people are assigned. They are in charge of helping the captain and mates steer the ship, navigate, etc. One person is always on Bow watch, to look for obstructions or other ships in their path. There is "Engineering," in which one person is assigned to be the assistant engineer and help out. There is also "Lab," where the remainder of the people are conducting tests that the scientists aboard ship want done. One person from Dawn watch is assigned to be assistant steward, and has to help out the steward in preparing and cleaning up for all three meals, and snacks.

The watch schedule is on a rotating three-day schedule, where a group is on for one watch, and then off for two. So if a group starts at Dawn watch, it will take three days to again have that watch.

NAUTICAL SCIENCE

To be able to sail the program's vessels, the students must learn the proper methods of seamanship and the principles of navigation and simple marine engineering. This is covered in the Nautical Science class. Leading the class are the captains whom students will serve under during the sea component. In addition to skills such as rope work, chart work, and navigation, the students learn the principles of buoyancy and the physics involved in keeping ships afloat and on course. Students also learn the elements of electrical generation, the intricacies of diesel engines, and the mechanics of pulleys, levers, and the other "simple machines" that make up a sailing vessel's rigging.

"There are things that I learned that I won't realize for years to come."

The students use lab models to determine the forces that act on a ship's hull and sails, and even disassemble and reassemble a small diesel engine. Students also work with charts and sextants in order to completely understand the elements of navigation and determining position on the open sea. Finally, the students learn about the processes involved in predicting weather and how these forces are important in conjunction with sailing.

OCEANOGRAPHY

Oceanography is the course that runs the entire twelve weeks of the semester. The course covers the broad topic in four different categories—biological, chemical, geological, and physical oceanography. A fifth, environmental studies, is added during the sea component. There is a large amount of lab time involved in the Oceanography course, the majority of which is conducted while at sea.

On shore, this course helps the student understand the work that is completed while at sea, as the course requires students to design a research project and implement it while aboard ship. In addition to the research project, students also must do a minipresentation on a particular marine species, known as a "creature feature." There are occasional papers and exams, and a fair amount of reading.

MARITIME STUDIES

The one course mentioned repeatedly as outstanding was the Maritime Studies course. Covering the lore rather than the science of the sea, this course examines the aspect of nautical affairs and the maritime heritage in two distinct parts. The first part covers the history and legends of the early Americas—investigating topics such as the fishing trades of the colonial and precolonial eras. These historical lectures are enhanced with assigned readings of selected American and British authors who wrote of the sea, such as Melville, Hemmingway, and Conrad.

The second part of this course covers the more contemporary issues that are problems for today's mariner. Topics include the fishing industry and the ways that technology is affecting its production. It also looks at the future of the American merchant fleet and its role in the post–cold war era. This course gives students a more romantic view of what can be very demanding work. There is one short paper due each week for this course.

INDIVIDUAL PROJECTS

The main project aboard ship is the individual research project, officially titled *Practical Oceanography II*. This project is entirely of the student's own design, with heavy consultation with faculty members. However, it must be thought of and proposed while still at Woods Hole, and it is implemented under the direction of the chief scientist while at sea. It is considerably easier to conduct research either as a continuation of someone else's project, or to use someone's research as a stepping-stone instead of starting from scratch. Since SEA sails the same routes year after year, students have the advantage of collecting data on the same areas over an extended period of time. The research must be conducted either aboard ship or in port during the student's free time. Projects range from examining an underwater volcano, to measuring currents, to investigating plastic and tar deposits on islands and beaches. Project write-ups are typically ten to twenty pages long, and the sophistication of each usually reflects students' individual backgrounds.

JWO + JSWO

A special aspect of the watches occurs for the final two weeks of the voyage. Students each get a chance to be Junior Watch Officer (JWO), as well as Junior Science Watch Officer (JSWO). As JWO, they are in charge of the Deck watch, overseeing the running of the ship and reporting directly to the captain. More than one student mentioned being particularly nervous about this, but extremely elated whenever they did something right. As JSWO, students direct all of the scientific work that is done during watch in the labs.

FACULTY

The faculty are all specialists in their fields, all Ph.D.s., and many have been with the program for years. The students were highly impressed with the faculty, in particular the ones teaching the Maritime Studies course. For some, these were the best teachers they had ever had. One member of the faculty becomes the chief scientist while at sea, and there are three assistant scientists aboard as well.

The captains of the ships are all licensed professional mariners, and most have also been with the program for a while. They teach the Nautical Science

> *"Even when we were in port I was anxious to get back on the water."*

course on shore, and it is there that SEA sags a bit. All of the captains received A's for effort, but a few scored lower on the teaching ability scale. The students complained that they just do not have the background to clearly convey the complicated issues or topics at hand. However, at sea they are all more than competent. The captain's personality will extend itself to the entire ship, which is generally good, but can be a drag as well. Because of this, some ships are "dry ships," while others do allow a celebration or two when in port.

There are also three deck officers, an engineer, and a steward aboard. The stewards, in particular, received enormous praise for the quality of the food.

FACILITIES

The facilities available to SEA Semester students are probably some of the most prestigious in the U.S. In Woods Hole, many hours are spent in the Marine Biological Laboratory, where students have access to the world-famous library. Students also have access to any local scientist's lectures from the Oceanographic Institution, and there are the occasional trips to the labs there. The SEA campus also houses its own classroom, lecture hall, laboratory, as well as a computer lab and a student library. Most people we talked to felt that the facilities on campus were more

---

COURSES (1995)

Oceanography
Nautical Science
Maritime Studies
Practical Oceanography I
Practical Oceanography II

than adequate. The computer room was felt to be a little small, and students advised to plan ahead so you didn't need a computer during peak time.

Once at sea, there are smaller, yet quite adequate, facilities aboard the *Westward* and *Cramer*. Both vessels carry sounding instruments, such as a mechanical bathythermograph for determining temperatures at various depths, and more technical devices that help study characteristics of water masses. The lab on board has analytical aids to further the study of samples taken, as well as a main desktop computer for data storage and analysis. There is a small library on board as well, containing reference materials, scientific journals, and texts. The library also has four laptop computers, which are very handy to write up reports or papers.

Off the Track

While there is not a lot of free time, students do have the weekends in Woods Hole, the ports of call, and there is always an adventure at sea. Here are a few of the things that happened to students of SEA Semester:

On bow watch one night, a student noticed a few dolphins playing in the bow wave of the ship. There was a warm breeze, the stars were out, and the bioluminescent organisms in the water made the dolphins look like "comets doing synchronized swimming."

Most people mentioned the days they were Junior Watch Officers as the highlight of their experiences. To be in complete charge of the ship, to make every decision and have the crew follow those orders out, and, what's more, to make the *right* decision is a feeling of accomplishment that nearly all said never goes away.

Jogging early in the morning through the fresh snow was the daily routine for one student at Woods Hole. One day she was leading a few friends over her usual route when they all stopped suddenly—in front of them was a herd of very startled deer. The deer looked at them, snorted, and continued down the path, making the humans walk slowly behind them.

Weather is a major factor while at sea. One woman said that despite the dangers, rough weather was her favorite time during the voyage. Apparently they had five days of rough weather, and those on watch would go out in their foul-weather gear and clip in to the cables that ran the length of the deck and hang on for a wild ride. There are times, however, when the captain restricts all the students to below decks.

On New Year's Eve, one captain anchored the ship near a reef and broke out the ship's stores of rum for a mini-celebration among the crew. The ship remained at anchor there for the next day as the crew went snorkeling on their day off.

During one night watch, a sail needed changing out on the bowsprit. One student and the mate on duty clipped into the safety line and went out on the rigging. The sea was rough and they would sink up to their thighs in "green seas" as the ship nosed her way through a swell. As the ship came back up, they would get tossed up into the air only to be stopped by the safety cables attached to their waists.

Advice and Warnings from the Students

▶ "Bring clothes you don't like, they'll get ruined."

▶ "Make sure you're able to get along in a group."

▶ $150 is a good amount of money to bring for personal expenses.

▶ "Bring a lot of suntan lotion, and a lot of film."

▶ "Get on a boat before you do this program, to see how it feels."

▶ "Bring a small battery-powered fan—it gets hot below!"

▶ "A good pair of sunglasses is important!"

▶ "Bring a Crazy Creek chair (a small, folding, *very* comfortable chair) for the lectures on board ship."

▶ "Be prepared to work hard!"

▶ "Your foul-weather gear can be expensive! Plan for this!"

The Best + The Worst

 Learning to sail

 Sailing on a small boat with thirty-five other people

👍 Dawn Watch

👎 Cleaning the ship

👍 Being JWO

👎 Leaving half of the group after the shore component

👍 Deck watch

👎 Getting seasick

👍 Swim Calls

👍 The Maritime Studies course

EDINBURGH PROGRAM

Courtesy of British Tourist Authority

LOCATION: Edinburgh, Scotland

HOST SCHOOL: Beaver College

DESCRIPTION: Students are placed directly in Edinburgh University, which offers a full range of courses at the university level.

DURATION: Semester or Year

COST: $6,350 (Cost per term. One-way airfare from New York included. Full year cost: $16,000; two spring terms: $10,850. Optional excursions through Beaver College not included.)

FINANCIAL AID: None. Federal loans and scholarships may be used. Beaver College offers a limited number of scholarships.

PREREQUISITES: 3.0 GPA

COURSE FULFILLMENT: Various

NO. OF STUDENTS: Not available   M/F RATIO: 1/1

HOUSING: Dormitories houses or arranged apartments, and a one-week homestay

COMPUTERS: Provided. Personal computers allowed and recommended.

CONTACT INFORMATION
Center for Education Abroad
Director of Admissions
Beaver College
450 South Easton Road
Glenside, PA 19038
Phone: (800) 755-5607
Fax: (215) 572-2174
E-mail: cea@beaver.edu
WWW: http://www.beaver.edu

Overview

"I can't pick what was the best about this program—that's too hard."

If you want a program that will immerse you in Scottish culture, station you in a top-notch international university, take care of all of your housing and busywork, offer you side trips all around the U.K., while still leaving you plenty of freedom to lead your own life, Beaver College at the University of Edinburgh is perfect. This is a program for people who don't want to have to deal with another language (just a difficult accent), and who will enjoy the simple pleasure of going to school in an international setting.

Students are enrolled by Beaver directly into the Edinburgh matriculation process. They take classes alongside the other students at the university, which most students feel is an important aspect. Academic topics at the university are diverse, ranging from Artificial Intelligence to Classical Literature, and the university is also the home of the School of Scottish Studies.

As for Edinburgh itself, it's a wonderful city. From the quaint streets to the bustling marketplaces to Queen Elizabeth's official palace in Scotland, it was the city itself that students raved about. "If you're going abroad just for a city," one student remarked, "go to Edinburgh." There is ample time to explore and participate in all the city has to offer, as most students arrange their schedules to have four-day weekends.

This isn't to say, however, that the Beaver program does nothing for you. In fact, we heard nothing but praise for the entire job that the people from Beaver did. The first week in the U.K., Beaver places students in a homestay. This is a good way of exposing them to how Scottish people actually live, while allowing time

> *"I remember everyone walking around going, 'I love Beaver College.'"*

for an orientation to prepare for the months ahead. After that, it's off to Edinburgh where Beaver's role quietly fades into the background as students are allowed to immerse themselves in the community of Edinburgh.

For those in need of a bit of structure, Beaver organizes day trips to the surrounding areas, and events like a Thanksgiving retreat to the Highlands. In addition, if students encounter problems of any sort, the program director is always there to assist them. "If you had a problem, Beaver was always there for you."

Environment

"It was more like I was a student of Edinburgh."

Edinburgh has repeatedly been called one of the loveliest cities in Europe. Only four and half hours away from London by train, the capital of Scotland mixes the past and the present with ease and grace. Edinburgh castle, dating from the sixth century, looms above the city even

> *"It was fun going out and getting lost in Edinburgh."*

while the world-renowned International Festival and Fringe Festival fills the streets and venues with theater, music, and dance.

The city is wonderful for walking—with historic buildings, galleries, and museums throughout housing art, armor, and the legends of Scottish royalty. Small, winding side streets contrast with avenues filled with stylish boutiques and stores. Old stone houses ten stories high compete with office buildings.

Edinburgh is also the site of the infamous Rose Street—reportedly home to more bars per yard than any other street in the world. There is also something called "Fresher's Week" at the beginning of the school year. This evidently is a week of "partying, pub crawls, and going out and getting rowdy." For one student, the highlight of this was when a techno band played in the school's wood-paneled debating hall.

With miles of coastline for boating, several beaches, numerous golf courses, public football fields, cricket pitches, and tennis courts, the city offers plenty of recreational facilities. Finally, students report that while the weather is just as horrible in Edinburgh as it is in London, the food is a little tastier.

As for the university itself, it is centered in two main sites—one at the King's Buildings Science Campus, and the other two miles north adjacent to the Old Town. Student residences are located in between the two cam-

> *"It was a lot more than I expected."*

puses, both being a ten- to twenty-minute walk away. The most important aspect of the university is that it is truly an *international* school. People come not only from Europe, but from all over the world to study here, giving students a glimpse of more cultures than one would normally get in a semester or year.

Students also talked about the people of Edinburgh, and how there was a terrific community feel about the entire city. As one student said, "The people are friendly, they're really into the arts, and the pubs stay open later than in England."

Housing

"The homestays are great—they're such an important part of the program."

When students first arrive in Britain, they are placed in local homes for a week-long homestay. This offers them the opportunity to get acclimated with the locals and, as one student said, "really get to see how Scottish people live." This part of the program is also designed to give students a small orientation into what they will experience in the next few months, as well as afford them the opportunity to make a few friends outside of a university setting.

After the first week, students move on to Edinburgh and have three choices for housing: student dorms, student houses, or student apartments. All choices mix Scottish students with international students. The dorms house large numbers of students and have shared rooms, shared bath, and a full board plan. There is also a linen and maid service. Dormitories are the least favorite option, as they were described as "kind of depressing." One astute student pointed out, "Don't live in the dorms. Most of the dorm people are freshmen, and you're not going to be a freshman."

The student apartments got fair reviews. Four to six people live in the apartment, with shared rooms and bath. Students are expected to provide their own linen and food. This option was more desirable than the dorms, as it allows you a bit more freedom and has more of a sense of "home."

"The Beaver College program was nice because it took care of all the paperwork."

The most popular housing option by far was the student houses. These typically hold twenty-five to thirty students, with shared room, bath, and kitchen facilities. There is a greater feeling of community at these, and while they allow you to meet a lot of different people, they are not as overwhelming as the dorms. The houses also have maid service for "light cleaning." Occasionally the houses had a theme to them—for instance, one person we talked to lived in the Mountaineering House, and on the weekends she would go climbing with her housemates.

FOOD

The food is, of course, Scottish. Although Scottish fare doesn't end up being as bland, rubbery, and gray as English food, dining can be an interesting experience. Remember, this is the place where they came up with haggis (boiled sheep stomach—the national dish) and porridge (like oatmeal, but more dense). Then again, the Scottish did invent the single malt whiskey. Favorites for sandwiches include Marmite and Vegemite, two yeast extracts that take Americans a while to develop a taste for.

Advice from the students: "Never, ever let your family make you a sandwich."

Academics

> *"It was great to have the flexibility of a different curriculum."*

As with all programs overseas that reside at a foreign university, the academic rigor will vary from student to student. The Edinburgh program illustrates this perfectly, as student descriptions of the academics ranged from "I worked harder there than I ever did in my life" to "They weren't really that important."

This emphasizes the fact that it's up to students how seriously they want to take their classes and homework. The schooling system is run a little differently in Scotland, and students were quick to point out that there wasn't any serious work until the end of the semester, when finals and term papers seem to leap out at you. For self-disciplined students, keeping up with the class lectures and readings should be no problem. For those (the majority, we found) who want to get out and experience Edinburgh and Scotland, the onrush of work at the end is a bit of a surprise.

Compared to class schedules in the States, most students had light workloads. As was mentioned before, almost everyone we talked to organized their schedules so they had four-day weekends. There really were no typical days for our interviewees, but most had three classes that met twice a week for an hour and a half.

COURSES

As with most large universities, Edinburgh's curriculum is extremely diverse. The fields of study range from Art to Engineering to the Social Sciences, with numerous course titles in each department. Students may find themselves a bit lost at first, as the teaching methods of the professors reflect that of most British colleges.

(Don't use the term "school" when referring to Edinburgh—in the Queen's English, that's elementary school.) Courses emphasize class lectures rather than required reading or daily assignments. However, students should remember that there is work to be done—it's just not due until the end of the semester.

The lectures are held in large group settings, but tutorial and upper-level courses generally have only six to ten students. Students are required to take three courses per term, providing them with twelve to fifteen semester credits accreditable to their home university.

Advice from the students: "Make sure your credits will transfer before you go! My university is still deciding how to count the courses I took!"

FACULTY

For the American student, the faculty is probably the weak link of the academics at Edinburgh. Some students said that although the professors are well-versed, the curriculum was poorly formulated. "There were times when I was under the impression that they really didn't know what they wanted." In contrast, others felt that the professors were some of the best that they had encountered in college, perhaps the tops in their areas of study. A few students mentioned that they didn't think the Edinburgh professors knew how to deal with foreign students, as well as the confusion students may have dealing with a different style of teaching. Almost everyone mentioned that the Scottish accent, especially in technical-oriented science classes, took a while to get used to.

FACILITIES

To put it quite simply, the University of Edinburgh is the leading university of Scotland, so there is hardly anything that students will feel a lack of. There are excellent computer facilities, a large library, lecture halls, well-equipped classrooms—the works. However, one student was amazed that a card catalog system was still in use at the library (as opposed to microfiche), while another remarked that it seemed to be mainly Americans who used the computers since "we're so used to them."

As for sports facilities, there is a sports center and playing fields that students can use for a small fee. Students did take advantage of these, mainly by joining "Societies." There seems to be every sort of society there to join, from a Rowing Society (where the canal is only large enough for one boat and they go to the pub before practice) to an Ultimate Frisbee Society to a Rugby Society. There are also nonathletic choices, from the Jewish Society to the Whiskey Drinking Society. A favorite was the Dirty Weekenders, a society where the members travel every weekend to clean up the environment in some way. In all, there are around 130 clubs or associations for students to join.

FIELD TRIPS

Throughout the school year, Beaver offers field trips to various points of historic and cultural interest. This can mean a day trip to places like Bath, York, or Cambridge, or it can simply mean an evening watching *Romeo and Juliet* in Edinburgh. Occasionally, Beaver organizes bigger trips—the

> COURSES
>
> *A wide range of university-level courses are always available.*

Thanksgiving weekend excursion up to the Highlands got rave reviews from the students. Once there, the students could hike, kayak, bike, ski, or just explore on their own. All the trips were described as well-organized and fun, and they get you somewhere interesting while still allowing you a generous amount of freedom. The trips are available for an additional fee.

Off the Track

With a four-day weekend every week, as well as a week-long break during the semester, there is plenty of time for the student's own explorations. Here are a few things that happened to students on the Edinburgh program:

Nearly everyone mentioned Arthur's Seat, the rock outcropping on the outskirts of Edinburgh. Rising behind Holyrood Palace, in the midst of King's Park, the trip to the top is an amazing day hike with great views of the spires of Edinburgh. As one student put it, "I looked back and sighed. These were the best days of my life."

A production of *The Blithe Spirit* in Edinburgh was how one student spent her free time. She played, not surprisingly, the American. It was an interesting experience for her, as the theater scene is much more lighthearted there, and she had never gone to a pub quite that often before.

The "typical student-around-Europe thing" is how many people spent their week-long breaks. Just a short hop away from Scotland, students roamed all over mainland Europe, from Amsterdam to Madrid to Rome.

One group of students traveled to the Orkney Islands, an island group on the northern coast of Scotland. Here in the isolated corner of the British Isles, they rented bicycles and toured the coast for a week and a half.

The best thing one student did was get a job. By taking on a job as a bartender in one of the local pubs, he not only met a good number of people and made some friends, but he was also able to pay off most of his expenses (U.S. students must secure a work visa to work in the U.K.).

A visit to the isle of Iona off the west coast of Scotland was a highlight for one student. They walked along the white sand beaches, gazed out at the turquoise waters, and "hung out with the sheep."

Advice and Warnings from the Students

▶ "Travel beforehand if you can. Once you start the program you'll feel so much more prepared, and it's a perfect time to do it."

▶ "Live in a student house!"

▶ $2,300 is a good amount of money to bring for personal expenses, including travel.

▶ "Don't go flying off to different places every weekend—get to know Edinburgh! That is, after all, why you're there."

▶ "Know your money limit!"

▶ "Bring a warm coat and a good pair of walking shoes."

▶ "Get involved in a Society!"

▶ "It gets cold there, so buy a good comforter!"

▶ "If you go, go for a whole year—it's such an experience."

The Best + The Worst

👍 The Beaver College administrator in Edinburgh

👎 The food

👍 The four-day weekends

👎 Leaving

👍 Living with people that weren't American

👎 Being homesick the first two weeks

👍 The freedom of being on your own in a different country

👎 The weather

👍 Edinburgh

👎 Not meeting as many Scottish people as possible

👍 The trips that Beaver organized

👍 The hostel system in Scotland

EAST/WEST MARINE BIOLOGY PROGRAM

J. Zarous Photo

LOCATION: Washington, Jamaica, Massachusetts

HOST SCHOOL: Northeastern University

DESCRIPTION: A year-long intensive study of marine biology, situated in three locations around North America

DURATION: Year

COST: $19,120 (Airfare to all locations and meals in Massachusetts not included. Scuba equipment not provided.)

FINANCIAL AID: None. Federal scholarships and loans may be used. Some universities allow their aid to transfer.

PREREQUISITES: 1–2 years of college-level introductory biology

COURSE FULFILLMENT: Marine Biology, Oceanography, Marine and Coastal Zoology, Botany, Field Research

NO. OF STUDENTS: 20   M/F RATIO: 1/1

HOUSING: On-site dormitories and private apartments (included in cost)

COMPUTERS: Provided. Personal computers allowed and recommended.

CONTACT INFORMATION
Sarah Jordan
Coordinator
Marine Science Center, Northeastern University
East Point
Nahant, MA 01908
Phone: (617) 595-5597
Fax: (617) 581-6076
E-mail: Not available
WWW: Not available

Overview

"Spend a year on three seas" is what the brochure for Northeastern's East/West Marine Biology program promises, and that is exactly what they deliver—from the extremes of the near pristine coastline of the Northwest to the clear blue water of the Caribbean Sea. Put this in a package with great facilities, extremely strong academics, and faculty who are renowned in their fields, and you have a program that students interested in marine biology dream of. Wipe away most of the starry-eyed visions of playing with dolphins and hugging whales, however. This program is designed for the serious student with a real interest in marine biology as a science.

Don't be scared away from this program if you aren't majoring in marine biology. Although it's recommended that you have a good working knowledge of the subject prior to attending, there *have* been people in recent years who had only briefly studied biology (one was an art major).

The East/West program is not a typical study abroad experience; there is little here in the way of cultural immersion and you are by no means far afield. The program is based in three separate areas around North America: the Pacific Northwest, the Caribbean, and the Atlantic Northeast. This is not an easy year, nor is it overly glamorous. But the amount of practical experience that students come away with will silence most critics.

The East/West program gives roughly twenty students an intensive overview of marine biology each year. It allows them the opportunity to experience a broad scope of the field before deciding on what element they wish to focus on for future study. For this, the program does a first-rate job. Students spend a year living and working in the same environments that they are studying: Friday Harbor on the Washington coast in the fall, Discovery Bay in Jamaica for the winter, and Nahant, Massachusetts, during the spring. Between each location is a break of three to four weeks.

The program begins in Friday Harbor, on the northern coast of Washington State. Here, students are eased into the intensity of the program with introductory courses to prepare them for the comparative

> *"People on other programs don't seem as happy."*

courses in tropical and East Coast marine biology that follow. Students are introduced to diving research methods with a course that includes mainly hands-on field research. This prepares them for better diving conditions and opportunities in the following semester.

Second semester avoids the North American winter and moves down to Discovery Bay, on the north coast of the island of Jamaica. Here, students study tropical biology within walking or swimming distances to sandy bays and coral reefs. Besides the weather and the usual impressive academics and faculty, a bonus of Jamaica is the opportunity to experience a different culture.

Last semester is spent thirty-five minutes north of Boston in Nahant, Massachusetts. Here, students take on the final aspects of the program's curriculum. Working out of Northeastern University's Marine Science Center, they tackle the most specialized courses in the program, with full access to the facility's extensive equipment.

Environment

"The greatest part was living in these areas for almost a season. You live there long enough to miss it."

WASHINGTON

Washington is the students' favorite location because it's an environment that's both beautiful and, in terms of labs and housing, well-equipped. The labs are located on San Juan Island, part of an archipelago that's between Washington State and Vancouver Island, Canada. San Juan is a tourist town in the summers, rather like Martha's Vineyard, in one student's opinion. In the fall, the tourists are all gone, leaving behind a quaint little island with a "small town feel to it" and locals who are relaxed about life. The town is no thriving metropolis, but it does offer, among other things, a movie theater, a few bars, and some interesting stores. It is also beautiful there, with Mt. Baker visible in the distance.

The weather, nearly everyone assured us, is not as bad as you think. "The rain stays in Seattle" is how one person put it. Apparently, it snowed only once between September and December, and half of their days were sunny. However, a few students from years past said that it *can* get very rainy, and they recommended heavy raingear and wool. Our advice is to bring what the program advises, and if you get nice weather, enjoy it.

Advice from students: "If possible, bring your car even if they tell you that you can't—you should know that you can. It's great to have to get around!"

JAMAICA

To most students, Discovery Bay did not feel like a lush, tropical setting—at least it didn't seem so then, despite being a hundred yards from the beach with daily temperatures normally between 70° and 80°. Once you get into the warm Caribbean water, however, it's a *very* quick reminder.

Discovery Bay is not near a resort town; the local income is derived from fishing and a Ca-

> *"Jamaica was insane."*

nadian-owned bauxite mine. Don't expect to find the Gap and Esprit here. The town is a ten-minute walk away and has a few things like a convenience store, a gas station, and a public beach, but little else. However, it's precisely because of this that students get treated better than the average tourist. Hanging out with the locals is commonplace, as are pickup games of soccer with them (for men only, the women tell us). You will, however, have to deal with attracting attention while studying in Jamaica. This applies especially to women, as the Jamaican men are *very* interested in you. Some found this to be flattering at times, while others thought it was just plain annoying. But, as one student said, "Whatever your view, you just have to deal."

MASSACHUSETTS

The last semester is spent on the island of Nahant, approximately ten miles north of Boston. Nahant can best be described as a small, New England island community. Everyone knows one another, and the police might pull you over if they don't recognize your car. It's one of the safest areas that we've heard about from students—people literally do not lock their doors. Since you arrive in spring, the weather starts out a bit cold, but soon turns beautiful, and residents walk almost everywhere. This isn't really surprising, seeing as the buses on the island run very infrequently. Again, advice from the students is, if it's possible, to bring your car. Although it's only a ten-minute walk to the labs, it would be useful to have for weekends.

Housing

WASHINGTON

Housing here was rated highly by the students. The dorms, in one person's opinion, were "the best that I have ever stayed in." There are two people to a room, with the usual modern dorm features—beds, desks built into the walls, and chairs. The bathrooms are shared, but separated by sex. A highlight for many people was the ability to live at the marine lab, and dive practically right off the deck.

The food situation astounded us. How does Belgian waffles with whipped cream sound for breakfast? As one person said, "They fed you like kings." Another claimed that she gained fifteen pounds here. She did, however, lose that right away in Jamaica. . . .

JAMAICA

The atmosphere in Jamaica feels crowded. Not only are you forced to see *everyone* nearly twenty-four hours a day, but the rooms hold four people. A saving grace for the rooms are the balconies with ocean views; after a long day of classes and diving, it makes for a good place to relax. Each room has two bunk beds and a private bathroom, but no hot water. Downstairs from the living quarters is the dining hall/meeting hall/classroom. Separate from the main building are the labs, offices, library and computer room. Other buildings hold faculty rooms and the dive shop.

Advice from the female students: "Women, get waxed! Shaving in cold water is not fun!"

Food-wise you might find the selections, well, unpalatable in some cases, especially if you're a vegetarian. As one student said, "Either you like goat or you don't." Yes, goat. The "tropical fish" that are served are generally grilled and offered whole—fins, tail, head, and all. However, some students did mention that the Jamaican cuisine was a great way to lose weight. Others went as far as enduring a forty-minute bus ride to get to Burger King, where they could get something that didn't come with its head still attached. However, Northeastern reports that they have hired a new cook, and the situation has drastically improved.

MASSACHUSETTS

For the groups of students that we talked to, housing in Nahant turned out to be a source of tension between the group. Although it changes from year to year, most recently students were split into two groups—nine of them were in an old Victorian mansion, and the other four

> *"The downside is, it's pretty expensive."*

were in an apartment. A few students arranged for their own housing. The ones in the apartment definitely lucked out—after living with the same twenty people for nearly eight months, you want as few of them around as possible. However, both arrangements turned out to be more than adequate.

It's entirely up to you to cook and fend for yourself in Nahant.

You'll have to set aside extra money for a semester's worth of groceries.

Group Dynamics

"You have to realize that anytime you're spending a year with the same twenty people, it's going to be a sociology experiment." It can and will be hell at times, especially in the isolated and close quarters of Jamaica. However, most consider the people they met on the program as some of their closest friends.

Here's how one student sketched the situation: "Everyone is friendly in Friday Harbor, but after a while the group breaks apart and cliques develop. In Discovery Bay, you have to deal with everyone twenty-four hours a day, and that's the catalyst. In Nahant, you really get into groups because you're in different housing."

But the basic point is this: Because it's such a small group, the times when you would normally walk away from somebody you can't, because you will always see them tomorrow.

Academics

"Molecular up to ecology; if you're not sure about what kind of biology you want to do, this program is for you."

GENERAL

Quality + Structure

Northeastern's program retains a high quality of academics over a wide range of areas associated with marine biology. Whether that means studying marine birds and mammals or tropical terrestrial ecology, students thought the academic content and the faculty throughout the program were outstanding.

Past year participants had complained that everyone was at a different level of experience,

> *"For my career, it was the best thing I could do."*

so students are now required to have one to two years of introductory biology. Students in the past who *were* majoring in biology or marine biology mentioned having no trouble applying Northeastern credit to their degree.

There's a lot of reading required for the courses, and taking copious notes in class is a must. Students also periodically collect data during the day while either scuba diving or on a field trip. Computers, provided by the program, are used constantly, as students do a lot of analysis throughout the entire program. Papers are required occasionally, and one student remarked that she worked harder and longer on them than any at her home college.

Of course, the best part of the program is the experiential side of it—the opportunity to live and work in the same environments that you are reading up on and learning about in lectures. Field practica may observe natural phenomenon (tides, full moon, nocturnal behavior, etc.), and you may even be dragged out of bed to go investigate them! As one student said, "You can't beat just getting out there and doing science."

FACULTY

The faculty are all highly respected in their fields, from organizations such as Cornell University, the University of West Indies, and the Smithsonian Institute. As for their teaching methods, one student remarked, "They were great. They really pushed you to succeed and to question everything that you were exposed to." The close quarters inherent to the working and living environment make for a casual atmosphere. It's common practice to call professors by their first names, although having a few beers with them takes a bit of getting used to.

> "Sometimes it's really hard to live with your teachers, but otherwise it was pretty cool."

FACILITIES

The quality of the facilities is generally excellent, which is fortunate for you'll be using them on a *daily* basis. Since many of the labs take place in the water, underwater, or on the shoreline, the information gained from those outings is brought back to the labs, classified, and written up on computer. In all of the locations, underwater photography equipment is also provided—both cameras and video recorders.

In Friday Harbor, the lab facilities include a research building and library, eight teaching and research labs, a dark room, cold room, microtechnique room, shop, analytical equipment and a forty-two-foot research vessel. Students felt they were "*very* well set up on the island."

The diving is reportedly wonderful, until it gets too cold to go into the water. Students dive during the research methods class, and people also dove with the dive master for his own research, as well as other resident researchers at the labs. The students said they averaged around twelve to fifteen dives in Washington, although the program is trying to schedule more diving for this part of the program.

The facilities in Nahant are excellent. "The Marine Center was incredible. Whatever I needed, they could provide." Among other things, the lab has a stockroom, darkroom, a great library, cold and culture rooms, electron microscope, image processing, histology and neurobiology labs, and an interactive microcomputer system that students were particularly impressed with. The building also has a flow-through seawater system, allowing long-term observations in a shirtsleeve environment. Small boats are available for near shore work, and a fifty-foot research vessel is at hand for more extensive observations.

Very few of the people we talked to did a lot of diving here; an average was maybe one to two dives the entire term. The work is concentrated more on

> *"Compared to the East Coast, the diversity and color of the animals was incredible."*

exploring the shoreline, individual projects, and the time in the labs.

In Discovery Bay, the labs are the worst of the program, but they are good enough to do the job. There are computers, and wet labs with water tables. The library was described as "yucky." If an individual project requires equipment that Discovery Bay lacks, the program will ship you what you need—provided that you ask while you're in Washington and the equipment is not outrageously expensive.

Diving, naturally, is the main means of research here. All of the courses make complete use of the reef that's close at hand, as well as other sites that are an easy fifteen minutes away by boat. One student loved the fact that she could just grab her diving buddy, hop in a boat, and fifteen minutes later arrive at a

> *"For an undergrad, it's a real taste of what research can be!"*

spectacular dive site. Of course, the easiest way is to dive right off of the dock and swim 1,000 yards. As one student said, "It's great to be able to swim out, grab a sample, and bring it back."

Don't get the wrong idea, however—this is no dive vacation. An estimated two-thirds of your day is in the lab or in the classroom. But rest assured, students insist that there is enough "playtime."

Advice from students: If you have one, bring your own computer. During "crunch" time, with twenty people all trying to write papers, it will save you a lot of hassle.

Friday Harbor Laboratories, owned by the University of Washington, is a near-perfect setting for marine research. The surrounding area is a biological preserve, and a tidal range of twelve feet allows students to explore and study the exposed intertidal shores of rock, sand, and mud. The local waters range from quiet bays to swift passages. "They're amazing. They're teeming with life and the diversity and size of the organisms will astound you. Even the barnacles are huge."

Here, the more basic theories of marine biology are presented to let students slide into the program, as well as prepare them for the topics of the following semesters. There are also a few required field trips, and destinations in the past have included Botany Bay, Seattle, and trips to neighboring islands or different parts of the coast. The students thought these trips were fantastic, but grumbled a little at what hours they occurred at, which sometimes was after midnight (which is necessary to study certain tidal phenomena).

COURSES

While in Friday Harbor, the choice of classes include: *Invertebrate Zoology* (five credits), *Marine Botany, Marine Birds and Mammals*, and *Ocean and Coastal Processes I* (four credits each), *Diving Research Methods* (two credits), and *Marine Biology Seminar* (one credit). These credits, it should be noted, are quarter credits by Northeastern's standard (most universities transfer four quarter credits as three semester credits). The schedule for Washington normally has classes in the mornings, labs in the afternoons, and weekends free.

The classes are excellent. Nearly all of them have field trips to a variety of local habitats, which students felt was an important aspect of the curriculum. The *Diving Research Methods* class is especially recommended because it forms the base of the work done in Jamaica, and students also get in some good div-

> *"Once you find something you like, there's always somebody who specializes in it."*

ing led by a great dive master. Students wish this course could be longer, but the northern climate does not lend itself to diving after October. People also loved the coastal processes course (OCP I); which gives a good overview of the surrounding area. This topic, joined with OCP II and III, runs the length of the program. The *Marine Biology Seminar*, which invites speakers to lecture on their latest marine research, received good reviews from students, as the lectures were all thought to be interesting.

Advice from the students: "Realize that you don't have to take *all* of the classes, and you'll have more free time."

JAMAICA

When compared to the other two sites of the program, Discovery Bay Marine Laboratory never falls in the middle range for anything. It has the best weather, the worst food, the best diving, the worst lab equipment, the most amount of stress, the least amount of privacy, and the most cultural immersion. It's located on a protected bay, with a coral reef 1,000 yards from the dock. The water is beautiful, warm, clear, and blue, but the reef that you have access to is a bit overfished. However, the students still claimed the diving was terrific and that "you lived, literally, in the water."

The academic focus is more specialized here compared to Washington, as you concentrate on a particular type of environment, rather than general marine biology. The academic schedule has courses in the mornings, labs in the day, and an additional class on Saturday. Also, people have the choice of doing an individual research project on a tropical marine biological topic that interests them.

COURSES

Here at Discovery Bay, you can take *Tropical Terrestrial Ecology (two credits), Ocean and Coastal Processes II, Biology of Fishes* (4 credits each), *Biology of Corals and Coral Reefs* (five credits), and *Directed Study In Biology* (two credits), which is the individual research project.

> *"I didn't appreciate it until it was over."*

Again, the students loved all of the courses. They described them as "even better than Washington" because of the strong links between the academic study and the field research. Discovery Bay has the advantage of being an around-the-clock "second classroom"— the water is warm enough for diving at any time. So every course offers an opportunity for daily field work, in addition to the usual field trips.

Since students are in an isolated area living, working, diving, and relaxing with their professors, the classes are not only more intimate, but the learning is on a more personal level. The reef fish ecology class was high up on people's lists, because most of the labs were all observatory ones. The independent projects were also top-notch, as students loved the ability to do their own research and make their own schedule.

However, one course in particular receives high praise—the terrestrial ecology course. The students declare that not only is the professor wonderful, but also the class is a nice change of pace, as it focuses on the *land*-based ecosystem. The high point of this course is climbing up into the Blue Mountains, a nice way to "get out of the water."

MASSACHUSETTS

"And then we went to Nahant." That's how most of the students described their final site—Northeastern University's Marine Science Center. It took enormous effort to get most of them to talk about the town, their housing, the labs, and what they were doing there. We attribute this to the fact that Nahant, in many people's eyes, is great, but not really exotic enough to stand out.

However, it's an excellent location to finish up the program. Students can investigate a variety of intertidal and subtidal communities as a result of the undisturbed shoreline with a 9.5-foot tidal amplitude. There is also access to the multimillion-dollar equipment gathered together at the Marine Center.

COURSES (1995)
Invertebrate Zoology
Marine Botany
Marine Birds and Mammals
Ocean & Coastal Processes I
Diving Research Methods
Marine Biology Seminar
Tropical Terrestrial Ecology
Ocean and Coastal Processes II
Biology of Fishes
Biology of Corals and Coral Reefs
Directed Study in Biology
Advanced Invertebrate Zoology: Research Techniques
Neuroethology
Molecular Marine Botany
Ocean and Coastal Processes III

But don't think that with the increase of technology there's less work. The course work is the most specialized of all three locations. Again, there is the opportunity of doing an independent research project. As for diving, though, the water is usually too cold for even the bravest of souls.

The structure of the academic week is similar to Washington, with classes in the mornings, labs in the afternoons, and weekends free.

COURSES

The selection of courses is: *Advanced Invertebrate Zoology: Research Techniques, Neuroethology, Molecular Marine Botany, Ocean and Coastal Processes III,* and *Benthic Marine Ecology* (4 credits each). The *Marine Biology Seminar* is offered again for one credit, and *Directed Study in Biology* for two credits.

As for the quality of the courses, they are all up to the usual standards, only tougher. The students had nothing outstanding to say about any one in particular, nor did they have anything terrible to add. While there's not much diving, the fieldwork takes you as far north as the Bay of Fundy, and as far south as Cape Cod. This work is mainly done in areas with sizable tidal changes, a common enough phenomenon among the numerous bays and inlets that dot the coastline.

The one major drawback of Nahant is that the social structure changes. Participants no longer live right next to the faculty, and socializing with them is not as frequent, nor as easy to do. It's still no problem to call them up with a question, but the semester lacks the previous feeling of camaraderie and the benefits of working with the professors in close quarters.

Off the Track

While there aren't a tremendous amount of opportunities to go and see exotic places, you *do* have free time. Here are some of the activities that people on the E/W program did:

Biking and hiking is evidently the thing to do in Washington. If someone didn't have a biking story to tell us, they had a hiking one. Or the two combined. It was easy just to take your bike, hop the ferry to another island, bike into the hilly country, and camp out.

In Jamaica, the Round Bar was a favorite watering hole of the students and professors. It's an outdoor bar where they occasionally set up huge speakers and have open parties. Walking there and back is a little frightening, though—there are no lights or sidewalks on the road that you have to take.

Sailing around the islands in Washington was a favorite pasttime of one student. The people there are so friendly, he said he would simply go to the local bar or marina, and soon someone would be dying to show off their "pride and joy"—and away they'd go.

Boston was the destination of choice for filling free time in Nahant. Either to see the sights, visit the clubs, or see friends they knew from home, there would always be at least one student from the E/W program in the city every weekend.

The Bob Marley Birthday Bash was a high point in Jamaica for a few students. They loved the music, the people, and the atmosphere. It was a terrific way to shrug off the academics and simply enjoy the fact of being in Jamaica.

In Washington, a few students had a favorite bar that they went to occasionally. It could be reached on foot, but jumping into a rowboat and rowing across the bay was much quicker. The row back, they assured us, was always very interesting.

Advice and Warnings from the Students

▶ "Bring lots of music in Jamaica! Don't take the treasured "four tapes" as a last-minute thought. Fill your bag!"

▶ "Mosquito repellent is a must."

▶ A good amount of money to bring for personal expenses is $550 for Washington, $400 for Jamaica, and $500 for Massachusetts, but remember that you have to buy your own groceries in MA as well.

▶ Scuba gear is an added cost that should be factored in as well. Scuba is not required, although most students highly recommended it. Tanks and weights may be rented at each site, and the program provides free air.

▶ "Bring you camping gear and your bike to Washington—you'll use it."

▶ "Make sure you like to be isolated. It can be tough on the social butterfly, especially in Jamaica."

▶ "Don't make enemies in Washington! You're living with these people for the next nine months."

▶ "Make sure you are a certified scuba diver before you go! Snorkeling is always an option, but you'll miss out!"

The Best + The Worst

👍 Being with all of the people all the time

👎 Being with all of the people all the time

👍 The Jamaican weather

👎 The Jamaican vultures that sun themselves and run around on the tin roof at 7 A.M.

👍 Getting "twisted" with the professors

👎 "Can I name names?" (They did, but we're not printing them.)

👍 Sneaking into the little cabins at Friday Harbor

👎 The housing in Boston

👍 The classes, the practical experience you get, and working with some of the top people in marine biology (the contacts you make!)

WOMEN'S STUDIES

I. Burmester

LOCATION: Poland, Germany, The Netherlands, Great Britain

HOST SCHOOL: Antioch College

DESCRIPTION: A three-month study of women's issues as they relate to four European nations. Students are exposed to not only the traditions and roles of women, but also to a variety of leaders and authorities on women's issues.

DURATION: Semester

COST: $9,400 (airfare not included)

FINANCIAL AID: None. Federal loans and scholarships may be used.

PREREQUISITES: Two years of academic study at college level and recommendation of home campus advisors

COURSE FULFILLMENT: Politics, Women's Studies

NO. OF STUDENTS: 25   M/F RATIO: 0/25

HOUSING: Hotels throughout Europe, with a month-long homestay in London

COMPUTERS: Not provided. Personal computers not suggested or needed.

CONTACT INFORMATION
Idella Burmester
Women's Studies
Antioch Education Abroad
Antioch College
Yellow Springs, OH 45387
Phone: (800) 874-7986
Fax: (513) 767-6469
E-mail: aea@college.antioch.edu
WWW: http://192.161.123.121:125/academic.html

Overview

"This program made me aware of what it was like to be a woman."

When asked why Antioch's Women's Studies in Europe program should be included in a "Best Of" book, nearly all past participants answered, "What other program does something like this?" In a world becoming increasingly aware of women's issues and problems, Antioch steps up to the challenge and provides a program that is academic, demanding, innovative, and flexible.

In three months, the program studies in four countries, traveling through Germany, Poland, The Netherlands, and England. In every location, the group is presented a series of lectures and speakers unique to each. Speakers include politicians, writers, health care workers, academics, lesbian rights groups, grassroots organizers, and journalists—giving participants a grasp on women's problems, challenges, advances, and the European women's movement.

While there are quite a few "standard" lectures, the program is extremely flexible and schedules discussions and events according to group interests. Additionally, each location exposes students to different aspects of women's issues in field trips that visit feminist organizations, women's centers, conferences, festivals, and performances.

> *"It's amazing getting to a point that you can fend for yourself in a completely foreign city."*

Another unique aspect of the program is the *Practicum in Feminist Group Process*. This class is there to help examine the stages of group structure. In plainer language, the "community meetings" help ease the strain of living and traveling in very close quarters with roughly twenty-five other people, by generating a forum in which problems, experiences, and topics may be brought up and discussed among the group.

While Antioch does provide a structured learning environment, they are adamant in their view that the bulk of the learning abroad rests on the individual. The hardest, yet favorite, part of the program is the Individual Research Project (IRP). Throughout the length of the trip, students conduct their own research on a related topic of their choice. Taking their questions to the streets of Europe, many find their projects an empowering challenge.

The final four weeks are spent in London with homestay families. The lectures and community meetings continue, but this month is really meant for finishing up the individual projects, and providing a bit of downtime from the constant traveling of the previous two months.

Environment

"The best part was learning from my peers."

"There were *a lot* of discussions about roommates," said one student, talking about typical community meetings. What's interesting to note about the Antioch program is that very few of the people we interviewed talked about the cities when asked about their environment. Instead, they talked about the group they were with, their problems, and how they dealt with them.

Since students are on the move for a fair amount of two months, it is hardly surprising that this is the only real stable environment people can talk about. They stressed that living and traveling with twenty-five people is *very* difficult, but also very rewarding. Privacy is merely wishful thinking, and everyone has a different tolerance level for any number of things—from rooming with other people to putting up with lost train reservations.

However, this is where Antioch capitalizes on an issue that practically every study abroad program has, but does little about. Instead of hoping for the best in group dynamics and leaving it at that, Antioch makes the group interactions an essential part of the program. The community meetings are designed to deal with this aspect, with the teaching assistant acting as the group facilitator to guide them through problems.

"The only way I could interview prostitutes in Amsterdam was if I paid."

As a result of this, people soon come to feel like they are very much a part of a group—accepted and an active participant. While every person's experience was profoundly different, it was *a group* traveling through these countries, experiencing and sharing as a whole.

A discouraging but perhaps inevitable part of this was that the women on the program felt that if a man had been on the trip the group dynamics would have been significantly changed (the semesters we looked into were comprised entirely of women). Essentially, the experience is height-

"It's an unbelievable experience to be in an all-female program."

ened because the group becomes its own women's community traveling through Europe, studying issues that they all have in common or can relate to. Men may feel ostracized in certain situations, out of touch and out of the loop simply because they aren't women, and cannot relate to many of the issues discussed or experienced. It needs to be noted, however, that Antioch does not discriminate because of gender.

But as with the majority of all study abroad programs, the cities themselves act as classroom environments. The program visits several cities ranging from the metropolitan centers of Berlin and London to the small outlying towns around Warsaw. This offers a substantial cross section of roles played by women in Europe, but it also allows the participants the chance to play tourist and cover a fair amount of territory in a few short months.

Most found Poland to be staggeringly behind the times, as if "in another decade." In stark contrast, most of our interviewees said that their favorite city was Amsterdam, and they assured us that it wasn't because drugs are legal. "The people there were so much more friendly than the ones we had left in Berlin," one student told us. "People seem to be happier there."

As the last leg of the trip, students spend a month in London. While everyone agreed that it was nice to stop moving around and stay in a place where people spoke English, a few would have preferred staying in Amsterdam. However, the city delighted and surprised most people. As one student said, "I thought London would be dark and dreary, but I loved it!"

Housing

"We were spoiled brats."

In general, the program puts students up in comfortable hotels or in upper-scale hostels. We never heard a single complaint about the lodging. The closest we heard was that the rooms in Europe tend to be smaller than in the States, but the quality everywhere was adequate to excellent.

While in London, students are participating in homestays. These got mixed reviews. One student said, "My family was terrific!", while another remarked, "It was just a place to live." But nearly everyone felt that the houses were too far apart from one another—up to an hour and a half away! After traveling in close quarters with the group for two months, it is hard to be with only one other person in a house. But generally the homestays are re-

warding and a welcome relief from the hectic pace of the previous
two months.

Food

Naturally, Europe has a wide variety of cuisines available, but the
differences in the standards of living in each country make the selections slim in some cases. In London, where the comparative
value of the pound is high, people had to rely on lower-cost food to
keep within their budget. Grimly, one student remarked, "There's
only so much falafel you can eat." In contrast, Polish fare was extraordinarily cheap, but not to the taste of many. "Polish food is
generally starchy. Everything usually has potatoes and some kind
of 'mystery meat.' "

Antioch gives students a daily stipend to cover the cost of buying
food. The amount given out reflects the economy in each country—
more is given in London, less in Poland. Still, many students felt
London to be extraordinarily expensive—so be prepared.

Academics

"You can't not learn something."

Wipe away images of classes that meet in classrooms three times
a week with a set syllabus and homework every other night. The
academic structure atually begins before the program starts,
changes radically while in Europe, and then finishes up back in the
States.

The summer before the program, readings and papers are assigned to give a solid background in the issues that students will
come face to face with. While in Europe, though, the academics are
focused much more on experiential learning.

The lectures are on issues that students can observe on field
trips or their own explorations, while the community meetings
focus attention on the group it-
self—a self-involved examination of a women's community.
Throughout all of this, students
research their independent proj-

> *"Knowledge just sits there if you don't discuss it."*

ects. There is also a "wrap-up" paper due at the end of the semester,
and a final paper that students complete while back in the States.

While there *is* free time to relax, typically the lecture class meets twice a day every day except weekends, and the community meetings are held twice a week. Students estimated that perhaps one out of every three weekends had field trips. Field trips are also occasionally in the afternoons. Add this up with trying to do an independent project, and there *is* a fair amount of work to be done. However, there is no hand-holding on this program. If you don't show up to the lecture class one day, students report that no one is really going to yell at you—but the issue will be addressed in class if you miss it repeatedly.

POLITICAL AND SOCIAL SYSTEMS IN WOMEN'S LIVES

This class is almost entirely lecture-oriented, with women coming to speak on a broad array of topics. Some former lectures have ranged from prostitution unions to the situation of Turkish women in Germany to a discussion with a lesbian rabbi. It's a very interesting idea for a class, exploring the social construction of gender, class, race, and sexual identity, all within a European context. It is also a fairly flexible class, with lectures being scheduled in accordance to the interests of the group, and an effort is made to have them reflect students' research topics.

> *"You get to live in four countries, and talk to people from all over Europe who have the same interests as you."*

Most people felt that the lectures were interesting to amazing. They are also useful for providing the students with strong contacts for their independent projects. However, they complained that there really wasn't enough discussion afterward about lectures they had heard either just for kicking around an idea, or for relating it to their own experiences.

PRACTICUM IN FEMINIST GROUP PROCESS

As already mentioned, this is a rather unique part of the program. Meeting perhaps twice a week, the group gathers to talk about any problems that may have arisen, whether they are personal or not, and in general makes sure the group functions smoothly. By far, this seemed to be the most cohesive bunch of students we talked to, and it was evident that they all had been part of a strong community. As one student said, "This course made me extremely confident in group situations, but also taught me how to be aware and sensitive to others." However, a few felt that the meetings perhaps were too much sometimes. Old problems were continually brought up, and some felt that the problems discussed were petty. As one said, "I couldn't believe how much we could beat the same dead horse." All, though, felt that in the end this was a very worthwhile class.

INDEPENDENT RESEARCH PROJECT

In addition to lectures and the creation of the thesis papers, students are required to choose an aspect of women's roles in society for their independent research project. Topics are chosen before students leave their home university, under the counsel of their academic advisor. However, as one student said, "It was no problem to change your project once in Europe." On the other hand, Antioch highly discourages changing topics unless it's absolutely necessary.

The topic must have a universal theme to the areas on the itinerary, as they will be expected to do research on their topic throughout the program. Although there are reportedly "typical" projects that are done each year, there are those who take on more unconventional topics. Past projects, typical and

> *"The only way I could interview prostitutes in Amsterdam was if I paid."*

unconventional, include *The Role of Women in European Rock Music, Lesbian Filmmakers, The Social Status of Women in Europe, Women in Grassroots Politics*, and a *Study of Prostitutes' Lives*.

Unlike the more structured components of the program, students are on their own for this part. Armed with a short orientation on methods of gathering research information, they decide how they are to conduct their research and to what lengths they will go to collect their information. It seemed from our conversations with students that this was the part of the program that gave them the best insight into why they were actually in Europe. By introducing themselves to this environment, people felt that they were learning by immersion in the countries just as much as they were from the material presented in the daily lectures. "You don't realize going in that you can do these things and get an education at the same time . . . it's different, but it's cool."

INDEPENDENT INITIATIVE

While this is needed in all study abroad programs, we were particularly impressed with the students of the Women's Studies program. Some felt that they were not getting enough discussion on the lectures, and so they formed a "lunch group." They would meet for lunch and talk about the lectures, their experiences, and journal articles they had found themselves. One person organized an eating disorder group, while another organized a body image group. This is another indication of how a tight-knit, separate community soon begins to form on this program.

WORKLOAD

Seemingly the most tangible result of the three months spent on the program lies in the Comparison Analysis papers. This project, which develops as a written thesis, is compiled in stages during the months before the term, and throughout the program duration. Before leaving the U.S., the program requires students to write on women's issues of the four countries visited, using the materials provided. Although it may seem a bit strange to write about each country even before you get there, by the time the program ends students understand why this was important to the curriculum. "When you read what you wrote back in the States, you realize how far off the mark you actually were."

The theme of the papers focuses on women's lives and the comparison and contrast of that topic among each European nation. As students travel through each country and gain experience from people and the lecturers, these four essays are rewritten and expanded.

Upon finishing the program, participants have roughly a month to think about their time in Europe. The information in the previous papers is then consolidated into a single twenty-five- to forty-page thesis. Students didn't seem to mind the fact that even after the program was over, they still had to produce a final analysis. "There weren't adequate facilities for us to really get into the writing of a major paper. Besides, when we came back to the U.S. it was a good way to reflect on what we had done and learned."

FIELD TRIPS

Although most of the semester can be viewed as an extended field trip, there are certain designated excursions that are supposedly outside of the curriculum. These include "doing the tourist thing" trips to places such as Stonehenge and the Lake District, as well as trips that pack a bigger emotional punch to sites such as the Auschwitz concentration camp. The years we surveyed also took a four-day break at a mountain retreat—to give the participants time to soak in all they had learned so far, and to unwind a bit.

FACULTY

There are two faculty who accompany the students for the entire program—the program director and the teaching assistant. These two are extremely important to the group, as their actions and attitudes can either make or break a program. They wear a myriad of hats throughout—from organizing all of the hotel reservations, to making sure the lecturers turn up, to giving lectures themselves, to acting as the group facilitator for the community meetings. As they generally change from year to year, no examination of any particular two would be fair. We have, however, heard only fair to glowing reviews and feel comfortable that Antioch does an admirable job in screening for the positions.

FACILITIES

The available facilities are, by any definition, Spartan. While traveling, the program meets in a variety of locales—from university classrooms to conference rooms at resource centers. The group occasionally meets in its hotel's lecture or convention room. If these areas turn out to be threadbare or, as happened in certain cases, nonexistent, classes are held in their own rooms. As far as printed materials are concerned, Antioch provides little beyond the reading materials. The rough drafts of preparatory papers and research journals must be handwritten as there are no available computers or even typewriters (there is one of each, actually, in London—but it's almost too much of a pain to use them). Final papers are completed after the program and must be typed.

> **COURSES (1995)**
>
> *Political and Social Systems in Women's Lives*
>
> *Practicum in Feminist Group Process*
>
> *Individual Research Project*

Off the Track

While the schedule is fairly full for weekdays, students have the nights and most weekends for their own adventures. Here are some of the things that happened to past participants of the Women's Studies program:

Women in Raves around Europe was one person's independent project. Doing her research meant actually participating in the all-night parties. She thinks that there was a stretch of two weeks that she lived on caffeine and never saw the light of day.

One student's favorite pastime was exploring each city they were in by herself. She would get on whatever the local mode of transportation was (bus, trolley, subway, etc.), get off at a stop that "felt like it knew its place in the universe" and see what there was to see.

Visiting the concentration camp in Auschwitz had a profound effect on most of the students. The fact that they were in a group helped to have people to share it with, but a few found traveling back to Germany afterward very difficult.

Walking around Krakow after dinner, a few students saw some street musicians playing and started to dance to their music. The musicians loved this, and the two groups soon began swapping folk songs on the guitar and laughing until the early morning.

One woman was studying the lives of prostitutes for her independent project. While in Berlin, she was beckoned inside by a pair of the local brothel's "employees." Because she had shaved her head, they assumed that she was a man. Of course, because they wore skirts and nylons she assumed that they were women. They all laughed when the truth on both sides was revealed.

The language was always a challenge for those who weren't as fluent as they would have liked. One student tried to mime out "pesto" in a Hamburg restaurant. Despite her efforts, she ended up with a plate of something that resembled lawn clippings.

Advice and Warnings from the Students

▶ "Speakers for your Walkman (if you're bringing one) are terrific to have while traveling."

▶ "Bring reversible clothing so you don't get bored of what you're wearing."

▶ "Make it your own experience, do the research, and try to immerse yourself in as much of the culture that you can!"

▶ $1,500 to $2,000 is a comfortable amount of money to bring for personal expenses.

▶ "Bring a Visa card for emergencies: it's generally accepted everywhere in Europe."

▶ "Make sure you're a motivated person and can work with a group."

▶ "Remember, it's not going to be perfect, and it's not going to be like going to school in the States *at all*."

▶ "Bring a good pair of walking shoes!"

▶ "Take a self-defense class before you go, although it's good to know anytime!"

▶ "Bring a winter coat! London can get cold!"

The Best + The Worst

👍 The freedom of doing your own research on a topic of your choice

👎 Trying to live with twenty-six other students

👍 Interviewing women from four different countries in Europe

👎 Not knowing the language in four different countries in Europe

👍 The community meetings

👎 The community meetings

👍 Learning how to work in a group

👎 A lack of a "home" for two months

👍 The friends made on the trip

👎 There wasn't a set way of matching up roommates.

👍 Getting stoned in a McDonald's in Amsterdam

SEMESTER IN SEVILLE

LOCATION: Seville, Spain

HOST SCHOOL: University of Wisconsin–Platteville

DESCRIPTION: A semester or year-long cultural immersion program in Seville, Spain

DURATION: Semester or Year

COST: $5,225 (Cost per semester for non-Wisconsin students; airfare not included) WI/MN resident cost, $4,975.

FINANCIAL AID: Students are enrolled in UW/Platteville, and are eligible for all financial aid and scholarships therein.

PREREQUISITES: 2.5 GPA (must be at least a sophomore).

COURSE FULFILLMENT: Various, including Spanish.

NO. OF STUDENTS: 250 per year   M/F RATIO: 1/2

HOUSING: Homestay

COMPUTERS: Provided. Personal computers allowed and recommended.

CONTACT INFORMATION
Dr. William Spofford
Program Director, Study Abroad Office
308 Warner Hall, University of Wisconsin–Platteville
1 University Plaza
Platteville, WI 53818
Phone: (800) 342-1725
Fax: (608) 342-1736
E-mail: spofford@ucs.uwplatt.edu
WWW: Not available

Overview

> *"It's one of the best study abroad programs because of the weather, the location, the low cost, the culture, and the history."*

"Viva Yo! Live for yourself and the hell with everyone else!"

While everybody doesn't have this exact view on life in Seville, it's practically written into the law books that people should relax, enjoy, and experience life while living in this city. It's a city that people fall in love with; winding narrow streets lead into small squares, cafés and bistros are as numerous as the nightclubs, cobblestone streets fight for space with modern pavement, and the weather's fabulous.

In the heart of all this is the University of Wisconsin–Platteville's Seville program. This is a program that allows approximately 250 students each year to *really* experience the culture of Spain, and of Seville in particular. It's not a program that will take you around the world, and it won't make you an expert on Spanish literature in a semester. What the wonderful people at the University of Wisconsin–Platteville do, however, is go out of their way to provide quality classes in Spanish and Spanish topics, while at the same time stressing that *experiencing* Seville is what students are really here for. The faculty of the Seville program consider the city to be, in effect, a classroom in itself.

The program is based at the Spanish-American Institute of International Education right in the middle of old Seville, occupying the top four floors of a five-story building. Small shops, cafés, and restaurants surround the building on all sides.

At the institute, students are exposed to quality education in both Spanish and English, and course topics range from business to liberal arts. The academic setting allows for the intensity to vary from student to student; each person gets back what they put into it. In addition to the U.S. contingent, there are also a few local Spaniards taking courses at the institute. Supplementing the course work, students are assigned an "intercambio": a young Spaniard with whom students meet once a week to practice Spanish, and to hang out with.

> *"My stay in Seville is one I will never forget."*

Students do not live at the institute, however. They participate in homestays, living in the home of local Spanish families. This proved to be one of the best aspects of the Seville program for students, and most of them are still in contact with their host families to this day.

Besides the homestays, the intercambio partnership, and regular classes, the Seville program also offers cultural visits during the week and field trips on the weekends. The cultural visits include sites of historical interest within Seville like the Cathedral and the Alcázar. The day trips go to places like Ronda or Cordoba, and overnight field trips include visits to Granada and Morocco. Three excursions are built into the cost of the trip, and the rest are optional.

While still in the States, the program bombards students with preparatory material so they know as much as they can about Spain. Once in Seville, the program starts off fairly structured, then gradually decreases as students gain confidence and become more independent in a new country. As one student said, "The program provides a base to work off and out of for your own personal experiences."

To make sure that no student problems go unnoticed, the administration sets up focus groups composed of small groups of students, the resident program director, the academic director, the director of student affairs, and the registrar. At these group meetings, students are able to voice their opinions on policy or discuss personal problems.

Environment

"Seville's a magical city."

Spain may frustrate Americans who are used to the fast pace of the U.S. Students found themselves getting angry when the bus was always late. They couldn't understand why they could never get the attention of their waiter and, when they did, why he looked so bothered. But they soon learned that that's Spain. Things

"I'm a lot more relaxed now."

go more slowly, and people are more relaxed. The bus will come eventually, and the waiter will some day be by to take your order. In the meantime, have a drink, talk with your friends, and enjoy the day.

As for Seville itself, students spoke about the charm of the people, the quaint sections of the narrow, winding streets, and the tiny squares scattered about the city. In the old part of the city, the houses have white limewashed fronts and usually a patio or courtyard. The town is full of history as well, with structures such as the Cathedral, one of the largest in the Christian world, and the Alcázar, a mudéjar palace rich with medieval legends.

Students unanimously loved the city. Seville is "small enough so you don't feel lost in a big city, and big enough so there are plenty of things to do." As one student said, "I traveled all around Europe, and Seville is still my favorite city."

Housing

"My Spanish mother," a student told us, "still bugs me about not eating enough—through letters."

While most students miss their families back in the States, they are soon just as much a part of a Spanish family in Seville. Since the Seville program lacks a real campus, it relies on local homes to provide room and board for the students. The homestays are an important part of the Seville program because they allow the student to learn about Spanish culture on a twenty-four-hour basis. It also helps students improve their Spanish: "You learn the little things that they would never teach in a classroom, such as how to say 'the remote control.' "

Two students are placed in each home, unless a student requests a single and has a good reason for the request. The Spanish family provides students with most meals. For an extra fee, around $40 a month, the señora will also do your laundry, including ironing. Among the

"I wish I had stayed the whole year."

people we talked to, the living conditions ranged from satisfactory to excellent, and most houses are within a ten-minute walk of downtown, although we did talk to a few people who were forty-five minutes away.

But besides providing a roof over their heads, the host family really does become a substitute family for the students. One student told us, "I was skeptical when I got there, but now I'm a homestay convert." Most students agree that the University of Wisconsin–Platteville has a good system of screening families and matching students to families. However, some students did have problems with their families, but they said that the director of student affairs moved quickly to correct any problems and even found them alternative housing.

Food

All the people who talked about the food that they were served in their homestays said that aside from the initial reluctance to try new cuisine, they loved Spanish food. In fact, one said that when she first got there she was a picky eater, but now she'll eat anything. Perhaps the term *"Viva Yo!"* extends to the way the Spanish eat, too.

Academics

> *"I learned more in one semester in Spain than I did in all of my other semesters combined."*

Classes generally are not as difficult as those offered in American universities. Nor, we feel, should they be. If you simply want great academics, stay home. This is a cultural experience, and the faculty and administrators of this program know this and treat it accordingly.

However, that doesn't mean that the academics are a joke. The classes surprised many of the students by being more difficult than they expected. Of course, almost all of the students told us that "you get out of the courses what you put into it them." If you want the academics to be challenging with a large workload, they will be. But if you want to skip all your classes and stay in the nightclubs . . . you can't really do that. Remember, you're trying to study Spanish in addition to other academic courses, while at the same time learning from simply walking down the street everyday. Because of this, the courses and the workload are never easy.

The classes meet Monday through Thursday, leaving a three-day weekend for students to go and explore. It's easy, some students said, to take a week off for travel if you clear it with all of your professors first. This can be done only with careful planning, however, as there is a strict attendance policy that allows only three unexcused absences.

> *"You learn so much from being there, on the streets or in a bar."*

The average days also do not seem extraordinarily easy to us. Here is a typical day:

8:00 A.M.	Breakfast with family	2:00 P.M.	Lunch and siesta until 5:00
9:00 A.M.	Class	5:30 P.M.	Class
11:00 A.M.	Class	7:30 P.M.	Class

Language classes meet four days a week for a forty-five-minute period. All other courses meet two days a week, for one and a half hours (compared to the fifty-minute classes typical in the U.S.). In retrospect, our interviewees felt that the structure of the academics kept them focused on what was going on around them and, more importantly, kept them *thinking* the whole time.

COURSES

There are some thirty courses to choose from, all with a Spanish concentration. From *Spanish Art* to *Twentieth-Century Spanish Literature* to *Economics, Business, and Commerce in Europe*, the Seville program has courses that will interest everyone. You can even take *Horsemanship* or *Flamenco Dancing* for physical education credits. The set cur-

> *"I wouldn't recommend it if you wanted to go over and study physics—this is a cultural experience."*

riculum requires you to take at least one course in either Spanish language or Spanish literature at your level of fluency.

In general terms, the students found all of their classes to be good, and even excellent at times. The workload for all of the classes was fairly easy, and one student said her work was composed of "maybe two or three quizzes and two tests for a class a semester, and maybe a few papers, but nothing you couldn't churn out in an hour." Some students, however, found their classes to be comparable to the ones back home, while a few others even went on to say that they were harder (especially ones taught in Spanish!).

A few students felt the business courses were too basic, attributing this to the fact that the Spanish professors underestimated the students' knowledge of the field. Everyone we talked to loved their Spanish classes, and especially their Spanish professors.

FACULTY

While not "big names" in their respected fields, the professors were well liked by the students. We never heard a bad comment about them. The faculty is always accessible to the students, partly because it's common practice to go to cafés, bars, and nightclubs with them. The stu-

> *"There's nothing bad I can say about the program."*

dents all thought this aspect was not only fun, but it also brought the teacher/student relationship to a much more personal level. The language professors in particular were praised for their enthusiasm, knowledge, and skill.

INTERCAMBIO PARTNERSHIP

While no one mentioned this as their favorite part, the intercambio partnership was always on people's "best parts" list. At the beginning of the semester, students are paired with young Spaniards, technically for help with their Spanish. But in nearly all of the cases the intercambios would do far more than tutor Spanish. They would take students out at night, introduce them to friends, and were, in general, great to know in a strange and new city. And, yes, they also helped students tremendously with the language.

FACILITIES

At first, students were disappointed with the Spanish-American Institute: they arrived with thoughts of their home campuses still on their minds to find a five-story building in the middle of a city. But soon they came to see it as their second home, a place to come to anytime, whether they had classes or not.

Occupying four floors of a five-story building, the Spanish-American Institute features

"It offers so much—you get so much for what you pay."

seven classrooms, four study lounges, and administrative offices. Televisions in the lounges allow students to watch CNN. Students raved about the rooftop patio where they could read, talk, or just hang out in the sun and relax. There is no smoking inside the building, so you will have to indulge outside or on the patio. Beverages aren't allowed into the classrooms either—the policy states that it's to keep them clean, but students find it a pain during their ninety-minute classes.

The University of Wisconsin–Platteville definitely listens to comments made by the students. Some said that they would have liked access to computers during the program. Recently, they dedicated the use of one of the lounges to serve as a computer room equipped with four IBM compatibles installed with WordPerfect. Class space was also a concern of past participants, and two floors of a nearby building now serve as an Advanced Language Center, dedicated to advance students' conversational fluency.

FIELD TRIPS AND CULTURAL VISITS

Normally, people are skeptical about "organized" trips. There is always the danger of being too "protective" of the student, or of having to visit mind-wrenchingly boring sites. The Seville program offers interesting and fun excursions that are designed to give both structure to the trip and enough freedom for the student.

The cost of three excursions is built into the program fee—people on the fall semester usually visit the Cathedral and the Alcázar, LaRabida and the beach at the Matalascanas, and Jerez with a visit to Bodega (a winery). The spring semester usually travels to the Cathedral and the Alcázar, Cadiz and Playa de la Victoria, and Italica (the original Roman outpost in Spain).

There are also the optional day trips and overnight trips for an additional fee. These are also recommended by the students, because they visit places that you wouldn't normally go to on your own. The day trips in the past have gone to Ronda (an ancient Roman city), a bull-breeding ranch, and Aracena (prehistoric caves). Overnight trips have gone to southern Portugal, Morocco, and Granada (with a chance to ski in the Sierra Nevadas).

The cultural visits are usually offered in the mornings, Monday through Thursday. They visit sites of historical interest and places that play an important role in modern-day Seville.

COURSES (1995)

History of Spain
Government and Politics of Spain
Spanish Art
Spanish Civilization
Cultural Anthropology
Flamenco Dance
Management of International Business
International Labor Relations
Comparative Economic Systems
International Finance
Economics, Business, and Commerce in Europe
International Marketing
Money and Banking
International Economics

Courses Taught in Spanish

Survey on Spanish Literature I & II
Nineteenth-Century Spanish Literature
Twentieth-Century Spanish Literature
Literature of the Golden Age
Cervantes
Art in Seville
Spanish Painting
Geography of Mediterranean Lands
Twentieth-Century History of Spain
Latin American History
Spanish Civilization I and II

Off the Track

With a three-day weekend every week, there is plenty of time for the students' own explorations. Here are some activities that students have done in the past:

The main diversion for most students in Seville was going out at night with their American or Spanish friends. The action doesn't usually get started there until around 10:30 P.M., and it usually doesn't wind down until 5:00 A.M. The night's activities entailed dancing, talking, eating, or just hanging out.

Two students skipped school for a week and took the train to Barcelona. Their main stop, however, was Switzerland. There, they toured all around Geneva, Zurich, Bern, and Lucerne, staying in hostels and seeing the sights. Another "skipping a week" destination for different students was Italy, where they visited Florence, Milan, and Rome.

A few students made friends with the owners of a prominent bull-breeding ranch. They often visited the ranch, and got to see the "up and coming" fighting bulls being tested for courage by the local toreadors.

The head administrator's brother owned a restaurant/bar that the students would go to. The faculty would go there as well, making the whole program, in one student's words, "very closely knit."

Traveling around Spain and Europe in general was what the students did on their long weekends. Taking the train and staying in hostels was the best way to do it. Destinations included Barcelona, Portugal, France, Italy, Switzerland, and even London!

Advice and Warnings
from the Students

▶ "Bring your dress clothes! Spanish people like to dress up when they go out at night." This was repeated to us on numerous occasions.

▶ "Go for a year! It 'makes the language yours.'"

▶ "Spend time getting to know your families."

▶ $2,500 is a good amount of money to bring for personal expenses.

▶ "Get immersed in the culture, stay away from Americans; learn the culture, learn the language, and go on as many trips as you can!"

▶ "Follow the suggestions of what to bring that UW–Platte offers."

▶ "See Europe! You're right there . . ."

The Best + The Worst

👍 The time when Spain played Denmark in the World Cup

👎 The frustration of learning another language

👍 The festivals in Spain, in particular "the Visitation" that runs for twenty-four hours on December 8th

👎 Hanging around with too many U.S. students

👍 Traveling around Spain

👎 Noise pollution like you wouldn't believe

👍 The variety of opportunities that the program offers you

👎 Small study areas, forced to study at the homestay a lot

👍 The people of Seville who are friendly and will always talk to you

👎 "My first homestay was a nightmare."

👍 Living with a Spanish family!

👍 Just being in Seville, learning the culture

School for International Training

General Description

"SIT was the opportunity to stop reading and to start experiencing things."

The School for International Training (SIT) programs received such high praise by their students and sounded so impressive to us that we decided to include six of their programs in our book. These programs expose you to out-of-the-way countries and cultures (as well as traditional destinations like Europe), teach you the language, provide leadership and support without inhibiting your own explorations, and give you the confidence and tools to do your own research in a foreign environment. For the past sixty years, the School for International Training (SIT), in conjunction with the Experiment in International Living and World Learning Inc., has provided students with international study at the very height of experiential learning. By introducing foreign cultures at a very personal and base level (SIT boasts that they practically invented the homestay as a tool for cultural education), SIT gives students a unique, academic, and highly involved look at individual peoples, countries, and the world.

Individual SIT programs may have specific components that pertain to either the focus of the program, such as Sustainable Development, or the area that it is based in, like the Amazon rain forest. SIT has programs all over the globe (nearly sixty in all), ranging from Greece to South Africa.

The skeletal framework of SIT programs is generally the same. To keep from repeating ourselves, this introduction will discuss the aspects that are shared by each of the programs we reviewed.

Orientation + Safety

All SIT programs have an orientation—usually a two- to seven-day preparatory stay in an urban setting that allows the group to get to know one another and get a feel for the country that they will be staying in for the next few months. During this time, the program addresses important issues such as health and safety concerns, cross-cultural barriers, and academic structure. Health and safety in particular are examined extensively, as SIT puts the well-being of its students above all else. Everything from AIDS awareness to street smarts is covered.

Coursework

> *"The four months on SIT was like four years at school."*

TOPICAL SEMINARS

Ranging from the Dalai Lama to belly dancers to the former vice president of Cameroon, the lecturers on SIT programs will give students an extremely diverse and intense academic look at the country and subject they are studying. The lectures, of course, depend on what the focus of the particular program is. However, there are generally lectures on the history, politics, arts, anthropology, economics, and ecology of the country. It is a fairly flexible class—student interest has a large effect on how the lectures are approached and organized, and they can be held anywhere from a large university to a small café. These lectures are supplemented by field trips of related interest.

The classes got good, solid reviews from every student, with some describing the lectures as "excellent and relevant," and others merely saying they were "all right." Of course, some lectures will bore one person while another is entranced. Lectures are a constant presence on the programs, making sure that students have something academic to do all the time. The lectures play an important role in the program—not only do they bombard the student with more information than they think they can absorb, but they provide strong contacts for their Independent Study Project (ISP)—many of the lectures are related to students' ISPs. If a lecturer can't help a student with their ISP, someone they know probably can.

METHODS AND TECHNIQUES OF FIELD STUDY SEMINAR

When we asked students about this particular class, more often than not they replied, "What was . . . ? Oh, yeah. I guess that *was* a class." This is a class specifically designed to prepare students for their month-long ISP. However, there aren't really any lectures for the skills you need for your ISP—how to interview someone, how to make contacts, etc. A few students remembered discussions over lunch or dinner, but no formal training.

Instead, students are thrust into interviewing and observing people in unexpected situations to try to give them experiential, rather than book-learned, preparation. (You can read a book on how to ride a bike, but will you know how to ride one?) For example, students are given the name of a town to get to and the name of something to find on a piece of paper (they don't know what it means in English). They have to get to the town on their own, find the object by asking the locals, and then meet at a prearranged place in the town. Other students spoke of "drop-offs," where they were dropped off in a distant part of a city, or another town, and had to find their way back. There are also less strenuous exercises, such as interviewing a homestay family to find out about their history.

A journal must also be kept for this seminar, and it is checked almost weekly. Students write down their observations, thoughts, joys, and frustrations about their exercises and experiences. This aspect of the program is really not structured like a traditional class, but as one student said, "It really taught you to learn, to observe, and to survive on your own in real-life situations. Would I have ever learned this at college?"

INTENSIVE LANGUAGE STUDY

Except for the programs that visit English-speaking countries, each SIT program implements a language course. These classes are taught by local university professors or qualified teachers in the area. The classes mainly focus on the conversational aspects of the language, as students will need these essential skills when they are interviewing someone or are simply out on their own. Most students felt confident, if not at holding a conversation with someone, of at least getting around using the skills they had acquired.

Classes typically are held daily and last anywhere from three to five hours per day. Some programs have the language classes throughout the first half of the program, while others limit the course to a particular period on the itinerary. Requirements for this class include papers, exams, and regularly scheduled assignments, as well as an assessment of the progress made by each student. This can arguably be called the most "classlike" of the classes, and students generally had nothing but high praise for it. In particular, students thought SIT did a terrific job at choosing their teachers, who were almost unanimously described as enthusiastic and easy to follow.

INDEPENDENT STUDY PROJECTS

For most, this is considered the culmination of months of preparation—the opportunity to challenge themselves and strike out on
their own in a foreign country. It is also considered by most to be
the highlight of the SIT experience.

Usually three to four weeks long, this part of the program enables students to research, independently, an aspect of the program
topic that interests them. Participants choose a broad subject in the
program's area of study early on in the semester under the supervi-
sion of the academic director. Throughout most of the semester,
students narrow their topic down by undertaking preliminary research and establishing contacts. The last month is devoted entirely
to the ISP, allowing students to visit other areas of the country to
conduct their research in. This work is turned into a research
paper, the average length being about thirty to forty pages long.

Students receive a stipend during their ISP to cover the costs of
food and lodging. Students reported that the stipend was usually
more than enough to cover these, as well as any other costs they
had need of (including, for example, money to pay for "infor-
mants").

Faculty

The only faculty that remain throughout the length of the SIT program are the academic directors. Two academic directors usually
lead the SIT program (it depends on group size), and their attitude
and actions can make or break a trip. They have a profound effect
on everything the group does—from deciding how serious the academics are going to be, to being there if a student simply wants to
talk, to finding interesting lecturers, to arranging the transportation.

Luckily, we've found that SIT does an excellent job at screening
for these positions. Generally, academic directors are people who
know the culture, language, and the particular countries extremely
well. Nearly all have advanced degrees and several years of in-country experience. The two directors tend to complement each other
as well—if one seems to be competent at handling the "business"
end of things, the other is usually more personable and in tune
with the group. The contacts the academic directors have in the
countries often end up being the lecturers for the group. Academic
directors change every few years or so.

AUSTRALIA NATURAL AND HUMAN ENVIRONMENT

LOCATION: Various locations in Queensland, Australia

HOST SCHOOL: School for International Training

DESCRIPTION: A 15-week program focusing on Rain Forest Ecology, Aboriginal Studies, and Marine Biology

DURATION: Semester

COST: $10,300 (travel expenses to and from departure point not included)

FINANCIAL AID: SIT offers scholarships on a need or merit basis, and accepts federal aid and loans.

PREREQUISITES: Previous course work in environmental studies, ecology, anthropology, or related field. A standard 2.5 GPA is required in all SIT courses.

COURSE FULFILLMENT: Natural and Human Environmental Studies, Field Research

NO. OF STUDENTS: 22   M/F RATIO: 1/2

HOUSING: Hotels, hostels, on-site dormitories, and a three-week homestay in Cairns

COMPUTERS: Not provided. Personal computers not suggested.

CONTACT INFORMATION
Admissions Office
College Semester Abroad
School for International Study
Kipling Road, Box DA1WA
Brattleboro, VT 05302
Phone: (800) 336-1616
Fax: (802) 258-3126
E-mail: 6424659@mcimail.com
WWW: Not available

Overview

"There were some days when I wanted to stay forever."

Australia is usually passed over by students for a study abroad program. After all, why not just go to Europe? But where else can you tromp through a rain forest, snorkel on the Great Barrier Reef, and listen to Aborigines sing? Australia hosts a wide spectrum of peoples, geography, and ecosystems, and SIT's Australia: Natural and Human Environment program delivers a solid introduction to many of these.

The program actually branches out into three areas of study: rain forest ecology, ethnic studies, and marine ecology, traveling all around Queensland, the northernmost state of Australia (the most tropical of the Australian states, and arguably the prettiest). This is a program for independent students with an interest in all three academic areas, who don't want to have to deal with a language barrier, and who are looking forward to four months of beautiful weather. But don't think that this is a pub crawl and tourist trip around the north. The work is taken very seriously, and the hours are long.

Beginning with a short orientation in Cairns, the program then starts the task of covering an enormous amount of diverse material—marine ecology, rain forest ecology, and ethnic studies. To accomplish this, students study in a variety of environments: a research laboratory on Orpheus Island on the Great

> *"It's a really fun program, but don't be fooled—it's not a party program."*

Barrier Reef, a hostel right in the middle of the Daintree rain forest, and an aboriginal community near the Atherton Tablelands. The group is split in half for one month, with one-half going to study the rain forest while the other goes off to the Great Barrier Reef. After two weeks, they switch.

In each location, the lectures are given by experts on the particular field of study, whether that means a rain forest specialist or an Aboriginal elder. Additionally, students have a two-week homestay near Cairns, and they also spend a few days in Brisbane and Townsville. For their ISP, students usually stay in North Queensland.

Students reported that SIT managed to relate the three topics fairly well to one another and present them all in clear, concise packages of information. Students remarked about the unique aspect of studying all three areas at once, in such an idyllic setting as the north of Australia.

Environment

"Every day I thought, 'Oh, it's so incredible that I'm here!' "

Despite what you may think, traveling around Australia *is* a cultural experience. They do speak English there, but have you ever heard of "auckers," "roo-bars," "bickies," or "whingeing"? There are things to experience and learn even in such a "similar" culture.

"The weather is beautiful all the time."

Life Down Under is distinctly Australian, not British, despite its colonial past. Perhaps this is because, with a size roughly comparable to the U.S., there are fewer people living in the entire continent of Australia than in New York State. Perhaps it's because, being so out of the way, it has remained more isolated from world affairs. Or maybe it's like California, and the weather has just made everyone a little more easygoing and laid back.

Whatever the reason, students unanimously described how friendly the people are, how vast and different the land is, how good the beer tastes, and how different and surprising the culture is. Not to paint a completely rosy picture, students also talked about being surprised by the amount of racism they saw, and at how women were still treated like "they were in America in the 1950s. *Maybe* the 1960s."

Housing

"I'll never forget my homestay experience."

The program uses a variety of accommodations. For two weeks at the beginning, participants are placed in homestays in Mossman, a town just outside of Cairns. This is a wonderful experience for many, as it gives students the chance to see how Australians live, and also to

"The program really focuses on getting immersed in Australian culture."

make some friends outside of the group. Some students on previous semesters returned to their homestay families later on during the ISP period.

During the Aboriginal studies, the group is basically camping and living out of the back of trucks while traveling around to different communities. For the marine ecology section, they stay at a marine research station on Orpheus Island, on the Great Barrier Reef. Finally, in the rain forest, students are placed at the Croccodylus Hostel, described by many travelers as the most beautiful hostel they'd encountered. Made entirely out of polished wood and tent fabric, the hostel is alone in the middle of the rain forest, with nothing around for miles.

Academics

"I can't think of a better way to get natural science credits."

SIT stresses experiential learning, and it does not shy away from that self-imposed responsibility on this program. How does hearing a marine ecology lecture in the morning and then snorkeling on the Great Barrier Reef in the afternoon sound? Or going on a night hike through the Daintree rain forest with a rain forest expert? Or listening to Aboriginal dreamtime stories round a campfire, told by an Aboriginal elder?

As was mentioned earlier, the program has a pretty full schedule. Students grumbled a bit about the lack of free time, but looking back they decided that they would rather have done the amazing things they did than have a bit more time to themselves. There are no typical days, but there are lectures nearly every day, usually coupled with some activity or assignment in the afternoon. Nights typically are free, and students do get an occasional day off.

WORKLOAD

In addition to the normal SIT course work, the Australian program includes an additional, smaller research project while on the homestay. This is to give students practice at focusing on a specific area, rather than just focusing on the broad topics that are covered in the lectures.

There are also specific activities that the students must do as a group. For example, as part of the rain forest section they must

"The depth and range of topics we studied was impressive."

map out a particular section of the rain forest. Other times, students meet with a local expert who lectures while leading them on a hike. "Lecture hikes" were common throughout, and students stress to be prepared to do *a lot* of hiking. While not a cut-and-dry example of "workload," it takes a while to be able to absorb information on the move.

There are exams for all three aspects of the program, as well as occasional short projects. For example, after their stay at Orpheus Island, students had to present a way in which to manage and preserve the reef. Students did feel that the academics were a little unstructured in terms of a goal, but felt that could be attributed to encompassing three areas of study at one time. As one said, "Keep yourself focused or else you'll be lost."

NATURAL AND HUMAN ENVIRONMENT SEMINAR

The main focus of the program is the Natural and Human Environment Seminar (the topical seminar), which consists of four sections. Three of the sections are on the areas that the program visits—Marine Ecology, Rain Forest Ecology, and Ethnic Studies. The fourth, Environmental Philosophy, runs the length of the seminar and acts as an underlying theme.

INDEPENDENT STUDY PROJECT

With roughly a month of time for their own research, students traveled all around Northern Queensland, with a few even venturing into New South Wales. Projects included: *The Use of Fire in Aboriginal Agriculture, Mines and Its Impact in the Outback, Declining Amphibian Population in the Rain Forest,*

> *"The independent study project was the best classroom I've ever had."*

Environmental Education, Watersheds in the Outback, Kangaroo Farming, Aboriginal Dreamtime and *Origins, Historical Significance and Future of the Great Barrier Reef.*

FACILITIES

There is not much in the way of facilities, as students are never really in the same place for most of the semester. Students carry around the books they need for readings, and supplemental articles are handed out periodically. However, both the research station in the Daintree and the one on Orpheus island are well-

> *"We did a lot of things that the average tourist wouldn't do."*

equipped for any work that needs to be done while there.

All papers and assignments are handwritten. There *is* the opportunity to type out ISPs once back in Cairns, as the local university students are usually on break and SIT has access to the computers.

FIELD TRIPS

When we asked students if they had field trips, one replied, "The entire *program* was a field trip." It certainly seems that way. White-water rafting, hiking, mountain biking—the group did all of these trips together, and yet they are not structured parts of the program. What can we say? The entire program is a field trip.

> COURSES (1995)
>
> *Natural and Human Environment*
>   *Seminar*
> *Methods and Techniques of Field*
>   *Study*
> *Independent Study Project*

Off the Track

There is not a tremendous amount of time off, but students still did have their own explorations and experiences. Here is what happened to some of the students of the SIT/Australia program:

One student went looking for frogs at midnight in the rain forest during her ISP, with a biologist she had met who was studying the nocturnal habits of amphibians. Of course, both of them had forgotten an important piece of equipment—their flashlights. So, with candles on top of their heads so as not to ruin their night vision, they slipped and stumbled barefooted down a riverbed into the late hours of the night.

Hitching a ride into the Outback to live in an Aboriginal community was part of one person's ISP. On the way there, he didn't see another car for ten hours. There were fewer than 1,000 people in the village where he was staying, and he was soon just another part of the community—fishing in the lagoons, hanging out with friends, etc.

Calling home for Thanksgiving was an odd experience for one student. He talked to his entire family, who were in Boston in the middle of a snowstorm. He, however, had just walked through the rain forest in 98° heat.

Visiting a pub early one morning, a student and some friends had apparently wandered into one of the rougher sections of town. For a warm welcome, one of the larger patrons bit into a glass and spat the bloody chunk onto the floor in front of them. Laughing, he then invited them over for a round of drinks, on him.

Tramping through the rain forest, looking for wild turkey nesting mounds, was one activity the group had to do. One student remembers being soaked to the bone, vines everywhere, cuts over her legs, lost, and looking for "big piles of dirt." She suddenly stopped and thought to herself, "When would I have ever had the chance to do this?" She remembers this as one of her best days.

Two students hunted sea turtles with a group of Aborigines. They chased after turtles all night long, either not finding them or just missing with the spears Aborigines use, until after midnight. Finally, long past being tired and cold, they managed to spear a turtle in the pitch dark. Aborigines are the only people allowed to hunt the turtles, and then only for ceremonial purposes.

Advice and Warnings from the Students

► "Keep your plane ticket open so you can travel afterward if you want to."

► "Bring a *light* sleeping bag and Teva sandals."

► $1,100 is a good amount of money to bring for personal expenses.

► "You'll gain so much on this program. Be careful not to lose it."

► "Pack light and appropriate—remember the weather is hot and beautiful!"

► "Drink Victoria Bitter—it's awesome!"

► "If you're bringing something electric, bring an adapter."

► "*Definitely* travel afterward—look where you're going to be!"

The Best + The Worst

👍 The homestay

👎 It was nearly a seven-day-a-week schedule.

👍 Exploring on your own

👎 Moving every week and a half or so

👍 The ethnic studies

👎 Living out of a backpack for four months

👍 How SIT pushes you to be independent

👎 Not being outgoing enough

👍 The ISP portion of the program

👎 The fact that the group split into two halves

👍 Climbing up to platforms thirty meters above the treeline in the rain forest

👎 Going back to Vermont winters after 100° weather

ECUADOR COMPARATIVE ECOLOGY

Nanci Leitch/School for International Training

LOCATION: Quito, Sangolquí, the Ecuadorian Amazon, and the Galapagos Islands

HOST SCHOOL: School for International Training

DESCRIPTION: A fifteen-week program investigating environmental sustainability and the ecological diversity of Ecuador. The semester also includes intensive language study.

DURATION: Semester

COST: $9,900 (travel expenses to and from departure point not included)

FINANCIAL AID: SIT offers scholarships on a need or merit basis, and accepts federal aid and loans.

PREREQUISITES: Previous course work in environmental studies, ecology, or related field at the college level. One year of college Spanish or equivalent, and ability to follow course work in Spanish, based on SIT testing.

COURSE FULFILLMENT: Comparative Ecology, History, Politics, Spanish, Field Research

NO. OF STUDENTS: 12   M/F RATIO: 2/3

HOUSING: Hotels, campsites, a chartered boat, and a homestay in Sangolquí

COMPUTERS: Not provided. Personal computers not suggested.

CONTACT INFORMATION
Admissions Office
College Semester Abroad
School for International Study
Kipling Road, Box DA1WA
Brattleboro, VT 05302
Phone: (800) 336-1616
Fax: (802) 258-3126
E-mail: 6424659@mcimail.com
WWW: Not available

Overview

"Ecuadorian culture is so different, and SIT puts you in the middle of it."

Ecuador has a fascinating and diverse array of ecosystems, from the Andes Mountains, to the Ecuadorian Amazon, to the famed Galapagos Islands—all in a space perhaps the size of Colorado. Within its borders are volcanoes, cloud forests, penguins, and piranhas. SIT's Ecuador Comparative Ecology program explores all of these in a semester, while giving students two homestays, intensive Spanish language classes, a trip through the Ecuadorian Amazon, visits to cloud forests, and even a week boat trip to the Galapagos Islands.

Starting off in Quito for a week-long orientation, the program then moves south to the towns around Sangolquí. This is not really a "rural" homestay, as most students described it more as suburbia, and some of the families are middle to upper class. Still, it is an exciting and well-chosen place to start off the program, as students are getting accustomed to the group and its schedule in a fairly safe, friendly, and comfortable environment. The stay here is three weeks long, during which time students are mainly concentrating on their Spanish classes and receive an occasional lecture for the Comparative Ecology (topical seminar) class.

"Few programs have this mix of travel and individual research."

After Sangolquí, the program then travels through the Ecuadorian Amazon rain forest for eight days. This is the students' first chance to be completely immersed in an environment they are studying, and it evidently is not a disappointment. Students travel in motorized canoes, exploring terra firma and flooded forests. They receive lectures and guided hikes from a biologist and indigenous guides, visit oil production sites, and participate in field study exercises.

The program then moves to the capital city of Quito. Quito is a large, bustling, European-influenced city that has everything to offer—from malls to nightclubs. The lecture series for the Comparative Ecology class really starts going here, as a large city offers many more resources than a suburban town. The intensive Spanish classes no longer are held. Students again are in a homestay for the duration of their time in Quito, which is three weeks.

The Galapagos Islands are the next stop, and the program spends a week exploring some of the islands that inspired Charles

Darwin to come up with his theory of evolution. Students live and study on a boat (the only way to get to, and actually see, the Galapagos), and they are guided and taught by an experienced naturalist who works for the national park. Although most people were a bit seasick for at least some of the time, everyone insisted that it was worth it.

The next four weeks are dedicated to the ISPs, and students went all over Ecuador to conduct their research. The last week is spent back in Quito and in a cloud forest, where students present their ISPs and are evaluated by SIT.

Environment

"The trees looked like something out of a Dr. Seuss book."

Roughly 9,000 feet above sea level, Quito is a wonderfully picturesque city. Nestled in a valley flanked by mountains, one can even spot a few snowcapped volcanoes visible in the distance on a clear day. The weather is springlike, due to the contrast of being so close to the equator and being situated so high up.

The program spends a total of four weeks here. Being the capital city of Ecuador, it has nearly everything a student could want. From the libraries and the university to the nightclubs and the malls, students are kept constantly busy for this portion of the program. In particular, dancing among South Americans is a favorite pastime, and Ecuadorians are no exception. Most nighttime activities include going out to a club and dancing until the early hours (students warn to bring something nice to wear as Ecuadorians dress up to go out). There are other things to do though, like going to a museum or seeing the Quito Symphony Orchestra.

The Sangolquí area towns, on the other hand, are much smaller and much less lively. Located about an hour outside of Quito, it is practically like a sub-

"I ate rabbits that my homestay raised on the roof."

urb. It's a fairly wealthy town, and several students said they were surprised at how well off their homestay families were. While it *is* a small-town area, it is not an entirely dead one. Students reported their homestay sisters and brothers taking them out to the local dance clubs and discos, and of family outings to the bullfights. Free time was spent exploring the town, perhaps a family picnic, and, of course, dancing. The first three weeks of the program are spent here.

The Amazon and the Galapagos Islands are by far the most beautifil and hands-on learning environments that students are exposed to. While camping in the Amazon, expect to be dirty and wet all of the time—it's a rain forest after all. Also expect to see caymans (like crocodiles), bird species too numerous to mention, snakes, beautiful plants and flowers—and to learn a fair bit about each in the process.

The Galapagos was a highlight for every student. It is one of the most pristine places left on the planet, although even that is being encroached upon by an endless stream of tourists and newly built resort hotels. Students get to observe the unique and often fearless wildlife firsthand for a week. From penguins to seal lions to blue-footed boobies, students study and observe the astounding array of nature there.

Housing

"My homestay family smothered me with love."

The program begins in Quito, where the group is housed in a local bed-and-breakfast. This is so that they can get to know one another, and to slowly get used to a different surrounding and a new culture.

The Sangolquí area is the first place where students spend more than a few days. They are placed in homestays. In the past, students complained that their homestays were located too close to Quito, and so weren't that big of a contrast to the homestays there. SIT has since moved the first homestay to smaller towns, to remedy this problem.

Moving on to the rain forest, the group basically camps out for the duration of their stay. The campsites range from actual camp-sites to covered porches at research facilities to lodges run by indigenous families. Plan to get wet for eight days.

When the group returns to Quito, the students enter their second homestay. The capital provides a vibrant setting for the students to experience Ecuadorian culture with their homestay families. Many students went to cultural events and to nightclubs with their adopted brothers and sisters. This second homestay was particularly mentioned as a great experience for the people we interviewed.

The week spent in the Galapagos is the most confining of all the housing. Students spend the time on a small boat and share double cabins with bathrooms. There is even less personal space here than during the rest of the semester. Add this to the fact that the group has already been together for two months, the ISP period is coming up, and people are a little seasick, and, as one student said, "Tempers need to be checked and rechecked."

Academics

"It's an incredible mix of science and culture."

Don't expect this to be an incredibly science-based program. While there is botany, biology, and mammology involved, they are not particularly intensive. Rather, the program is focusing on its title: Comparative ecology. This includes everything from an introduction into the different ecological zones of Ecuador to studying the environmental policies now in effect, and controversies surrounding them. It is, in short, a broad look at the entire topic of ecology in Ecuador—from what it is to the problems it needs to overcome.

s much as possible, SIT tries to incorporate Spanish into the learning process, so students should have a good background in Spanish to participate. The time in Sangolquí, then, is spent mainly trying to get everybody up to par in their Spanish skills. Students are in language class from eight in the morning until one in the afternoon, five days a week. Twice-a-week group meetings or ecology classes are scheduled in the afternoons as well. The language classes are primarily conversational, which is the skill that is most needed both for following lectures in Spanish and for conducting interviews during ISPs. Students felt these classes were excellent.

> *"You see animals that aren't anywhere else on earth!"*

The program then moves into the Ecuadorian Amazon, to concentrate more on the topic of the program. Here, students are receiving daily lectures from local experts of all kinds—from botany to environmental issues. There is no official classroom. Rather, students learn as they go along—perhaps having a shaman guide them on a hike and point out the various medicinal properties of plants. Or it may be having a lecture at the campsite about environmentalists vs. oil producers, and then traveling to one of the actual oil sites in the rain forest. This is one of the more memorable field trips, as students were shocked to see oil fields right on the edge of the rain forest, in some cases spewing oil and waste into the waters and surrounding lands.

While in Quito, there are more structured lectures in a class-room setting. Professors from various universities or visiting experts are common lecturers. The schedule is tough here—classes in the morning, and field assignments or homework in the afternoon.

> *"Seeing the oil fields right on the edge of the rain forest was shattering."*

In the Galapagos, however, it is back to the method of explaining about something and then going out and seeing it (or, if you like, seeing something and then asking a question about it). Lectures are by the directors and a naturalist guide from the national park service who stays on the boat with the group.

WORKLOAD

Keeping true to the SIT theme of experiential learning, there isn't a lot of work that would pass as assignments back in the States, although it is certainly not a joke semester. In addition to the normal SIT course work, there are two to three written assignments roughly each week (one to three pages handwritten), and assigned readings. In the

> *"It was pouring rain, but I was so psyched to be planting trees in the middle of a cloud forest."*

Amazon, students are expected to prepare a mini-presentation on some aspect of the environment they are in. Spanish classes in Sangolqui are conversational-based, so the only workload is memorization of vocabulary and grammar. Lastly, there is, of course, the ISP period and the accompanying paper (in either English or Spanish) and presentation due at the end of the semester.

COMPARATIVE ECOLOGY SEMINAR

This class is divided up into two sections. The first is a short introduction into the life, culture, history, politics, geography, and economics of Ecuador—examined, when appropriate, from an environmental perspective. The second section is the main theme of the program: *Comparative Ecology*. Among other topics, it looks at the ecological zones in Ecuador, the impact of tourism on the environment and human settlements, ecosystem diversity and management, environmental law and policy making, and ethnobotany and medicinal plant research.

INDEPENDENT STUDY PROJECTS

With four weeks dedicated to the ISPs, students range all over Ecuador—traveling even to the Galapagos to conduct their research.

Past projects include: *Oil Exploitation and the Environment in the Ecuadorian Amazon, Sustainable Development, Human Migrations in the Galapagos, Flora and Fauna of Cloud Forests, Mythology and Ceramics of an Indigenous Group, Ants in the Rain Forest,* and *Environmental Education on the Coast.*

FIELD TRIPS

The main field trips have already been discussed: The Ecuadorian Amazon and the Galapagos Islands. There are small field trips scattered throughout, visiting the places where many of the guest lecturers work, or simply taking a weekend to see places of historical or cultural interest. These are organized by academic directors, whose tastes can be a guiding force—from a rural visit to a trek in the high Andes. Many field trips include "mingas," or community/student work projects. There is also an organized weekend trip to a northern cloud forest—this is mainly for pleasure, but it is educational at the same time, as practically everything else is on an SIT program.

FACILITIES

Since the program moves around the country in the first half of the program, there is a limited array of facilities. The group carries around with them a small library of materials, consisting of scientific articles and research papers. Once in Quito, however, the group can take advantage of the resources of a big city, including universities and libraries. The program uses classroom space at Universidad Católica

> COURSES (1995)
>
> Comparative Ecology Seminar
> Intensive Spanish
> Methods and Techniques of Field
> Study
> Independent Study Project

for lectures and the students have limited access to its library. Fortunately, the lecturers that the program and the director bring in are more than adequate to convey information necessary to fulfill the curriculum. In Sangolquí, the Spanish classes are held in the local church. There are no computers or typewriters, so all work is handwritten.

Off the Track

With weekends occasionally off, and the ISP period, students had some (not a lot, but some) free time for their own explorations.

Here are a few of the things that happened to students of SIT's Ecuador Comparative Ecology program:

In the Galapagos, a few students were cooling off from a long hike with a bit of snorkeling. They ended up playing with two very curious and friendly baby sea lions. The babies would come right up to the noses of the students, then dart away before they could react. The students made a hasty retreat when the father sea lion looked like he was getting worried—adult sea lions can reach up to 2,400 pounds.

While the group was on a walking tour in the rain forest, their local guide, who was walking ahead of them, came running past them, apparently in a panic. The man had seen a bushmaster, considered one of the most poisonous snakes in South America, lying in the middle of the path. Later on, the guide told them that it was only the second time that he had ever encountered the deadly serpent.

During one student's ISP, she felt the need to work extra hard so that she could be done a week early and travel back to Quito. The special occasion was Quito's Fiestas, celebrating the founding of Quito. The week-long celebration is marked by parades and bull-fights and, of course, plenty of dancing all night long.

Playing Frisbee on one of the beaches in the Galapagos proved to be a larger game than a few students bargained for. The local sea lions would try to get the Frisbee by barking and making feints in its direction, and the seagulls would dive-bomb it whenever they had a chance.

Two students from the trip wanted to make peanut butter cookies for their host family. They discovered that the local brand lacked the preservatives that make the cookies stay together like American peanut butter does. The store manager, amid fits of laughter, politely showed them the aisle with the peanut butter and where the pharmacy section was. Of course they didn't realize that the word for preservative is the same in Spanish as condom!

The capital city of Quito has lots to offer those seeking a more cultured experience. One woman regularly took advantage of this, going to the Quito Symphony Orchestra every week. It was an even more rewarding experience for her, apart from most people in the audience, as her host "brother" was a member of the ensemble.

Advice and Warnings from the Students

▶ "This program is not for students who need to shower every day!"

▶ "Bring a good rain jacket, good hiking boots, and a lot of film!"

▶ "Don't bring *a lot* of nice clothes—but bring some."

▶ $500 is a good amount of money to bring for personal expenses.

▶ "Expect things to move slowly in Ecuador. The buses are usually late, and sometimes they do not come at all!"

▶ "Bring mosquito netting!"

▶ "Be ready to stand up for yourself—especially if you are a woman! Expect to be hassled and be ready to deal with it."

The Best + The Worst

👍 The ISP

👎 Seeing the rain forest being destroyed

👍 The Galapagos

👎 The boat during the Galapagos

👍 Staying with wealthy families

👎 Staying with wealthy families

👍 Just seeing the rain forest firsthand

👍 How the program combines science and culture

👍 Traveling in the Amazon, walking with the shaman

INDIA
PROGRAM

Todd Nachowitz/School for International Training

LOCATION: Various locations in India

HOST SCHOOL: School for International Training

DESCRIPTION: A fifteen-week study of India, focusing on its history, culture, and language

DURATION: Semester

COST: $8,500 (travel expenses to and from departure point not included)

FINANCIAL AID: SIT offers scholarships on a need or merit basis, and accepts federal aid and loans.

PREREQUISITES: None

COURSE FULFILLMENT: History, Religion, Politics, Hindi, Field Research

NO. OF STUDENTS: 14   M/F RATIO: 1/3

HOUSING: Hotels, hostels, on-site dormitories, and a two-week homestay in Udaipur

COMPUTERS: Not provided. Personal computers not suggested.

CONTACT INFORMATION
Admissions Office
College Semester Abroad
School for International Study
Kipling Road, Box DA1WA
Brattleboro, VT 05302
Phone: (800) 336-1616
Fax: (802) 258-3126
E-mail: 6424659@mcimail.com
WWW: Not available

Overview

"SIT opened up a whole new world for me."

Trying to study India is a task worthy of Hercules—its borders contain a sixth of the world's population, seven prominent religions, and sixteen major languages. India is also the largest democratic society in the world, and the tenth largest industrial power.

> *"It was crazy trying to navigate the streets, but it was the most exciting thing I've ever done!"*

Traveling around the northern reaches of India, from one of the most urbanized centers to some of the least, the SIT India program exposes students to a broad range of the problems and issues facing India today. With typical SIT grace and competence, the program provides students with the opportunity to examine the development challenges and progress in a very complex society.

The orientation takes place in the capital city of New Delhi, as do the next three weeks. These weeks are jam-packed with Hindi lessons and lectures for nearly seven hours a day, every day. The next month is spent in the state of Rajasthan, in Udaipur, a city that practically all of the students fell instantly in love with. Here the schedule is relaxed quite a bit, allowing more time for a student's own explorations and "wing-flexing." There is also a two-week homestay in Udaipur, an aspect of the program that students particularly praised. The last month is for the student's ISP, with participants traveling all over the northern and middle parts of India to conduct their research.

This is a program that immerses students in India, but also allows them a fairly secure lifeline back to American culture if they need it. The program takes care of you and coddles you a bit, perhaps more so than any other SIT program we've encountered. There is a strong structure that is enforced—there are always places you have to go and past students said there generally was at least one structured event each day. But, particularly in India, this is not such a horrible thing, and the students did not seem to mind it. There is still ample free time, and of course there's the ISP.

Environment

"I was walking around in awe most of the time."

When students first arrive in New Delhi, they are in for a shock. Not only is it one of India's busiest and biggest cities (third only to Calcutta and Bombay), but it is also, to Americans, completely foreign. Take New York City, leave roughly the same amount of people, take away the glitz, make the buildings smaller, add a lot more cows, a lot more poverty, a lot more temples, and have it be permanently summer, and that's pretty close to New Delhi. A few students remarked that they did not feel safe going out by themselves in the city, and even more remarked that New Delhi was not their favorite place in the world.

Udaipur, called the "City of Lakes and Palaces," is the next stop for the program. A much smaller city than New Delhi, the pace of the program and of life in general is considerably slower. Old palaces of Rajas (royalty) overlook several crystal-clear lakes that are interspersed throughout the city. The other parts of the city are comprised of beautiful, gleaming white buildings.

The streets of Udaipur are straight and narrow, and students claimed that the city was easy to navigate either by foot or by bicycle. Passing by elephants, monkeys, vendors, and people driving on the wrong side of the road were common sights as students biked to class. Though hot during the day, the air is dry and the nights are cool. As was mentioned before, students unanimously loved Udaipur.

Simply being in India is the hardest part of the program for Americans. Traveling on the SIT program exposes students to the extremes—from a metropolis like New Delhi to rural villages where the people have seldom seen Westerners. As one student said, "One night we were eating with royalty, and the next day we were eating food cooked over shit."

> *"You're challenged all the time, in some way."*

SIT helps out as best they can, and there are roughly fifteen other Americans going through similar feelings. One student summed up the impact the program has: "A year later, and I'm still thinking of India three times a day." It needs to be mentioned that none of the students would have rather done a different program.

Housing

"A lot of times we would watch the sun set over this sixteenth-century palace."

In New Delhi, the group stays at the local YMCA. There are the typical facilities that are found in YMCAs all over the world. They are just as clean and just as devoid of personality. "It was weird. Here we were in India and we were staying in a Christian Youth Hostel."

> *"It's a really comfortable program. My parents felt perfectly safe sending me on this program."*

In Udaipur, students stay in a family-owned hotel and share double rooms. Located near the Nathdwara, a sacred pilgrimage spot, the hotel clientele is made up of SIT students and Indian tourists visiting the shrine—providing SIT students with a fascinating living environment.

The homestay accommodations in Udaipur range from upper-class families with servants to middle-class artists who live in the seedier parts of town. A few students had such wonderful experiences on their homestays that they decided to continue their stay with them during their ISPs.

Academics

"I was really impressed with the diversity of the curriculum."

Covering everything from history to belly dancing to traditional medicinal techniques, the program gives students an enormous look at Indian life and society. While in New Delhi, the students are bombarded with lectures and language classes nearly every day, all day—all while trying to get a handle on a very different culture. Students

> *"Going abroad is so amazing, India is so incredible, I don't see how it could possibly go wrong."*

do have a little free time, and this is usually spent doing errands like buying Indian clothing, which you wear as much for the comfort as for the camouflage.

In Udaipur, however, the class schedule is relaxed considerably. The language class continues for another two weeks, at a slower pace, and then ends. The topical seminar class is held perhaps a few times a week. With so much free time, students have the opportunity to take up additional studies. Batik classes were popular for many, as well as traditional Indian music, dancing, cooking, and yoga. Students do, however, have to prepare for their ISPs during this time.

The students grumbled a bit about the structure of the academics, but when pressed admitted that it was probably the best way to do it. The reason for such a lopsided class schedule is simple—New Delhi has most of the resources in terms of lectures, materials, articles, libraries, and universities. Most of the people whom you would want to lecture on a particular relevant topic are in New Delhi.

WORKLOAD

By far the most strenuous time students have is in New Delhi. Classes start early in the morning, and last until mid-afternoon. In addition to lectures, students are trying to learn Hindi, one of the national languages of India. The class is made easier by the instructor, who, besides being enthusiastic all of the time, has in the past taken students out for tea, shopping, and even invited them over to her house. This class has a lot of memorization and occasional tests.

Students still, however, mentioned that it was a lot of work attempting to learn Hindi, in addition to listening to lectures every day, trying to see New Delhi, studying for exams and writing in their journals, and finding time for sleep. The work pays off, though, as most students feel fairly comfortable on their own after the language classes ended, and it helps to have the skill during the homestays. "Once that people learned you could speak Hindi they were much more receptive."

The bulk of the real workload is reading materials, in addition to the reading required before the trip. There are papers due each week, and a comprehensive test at the end of the first part of the semester on the lectures.

The journal for the field study class is particularly stressed on this program—students feel as if they are constantly writing in them. On the whole, this is a positive aspect, as it forces them to write down their thoughts and feelings all of the time.

LIFE AND CULTURE SEMINAR

The Life and Culture Seminar (the topical seminar) is broken up into four different topics. *History and Politics* cover aspects such as the Gandhi peace movement, as well as the roles played in the democratization of a colonial state. Covering the nation's development and the role of the government in its economy, *Geography and Economics* also covers issues concerning India's environmental resources. *Cultural Anthropology* explores the social customs and the issues concerning India's caste system. The *Arts and Humanities* of India are represented with visits from local artists and musicians who talk about their works and the influences of India upon the global art world.

INDEPENDENT STUDY PROJECT

The ISPs are conducted around the northern part of India, but students have ventured as far south as Bombay. Past projects include: *Traditional Cooking of India, Local Folklore and Culture, Health and Life Practices of Rural India, Different Schools of Religion in India, Sustainable Agriculture, Role of Midwives,* and the *Content and Methods of Rural Education.*

FIELD TRIPS

Lectures often turn into field trips as the group travels to wherever their lecturer works, be it a plantation or a newspaper office. More organized trips include visits to Ahmedabad and Sadra in the neighboring state of Gujarat, where students have the opportunity to visit institutions inspired by Mahatma Gandhi. Additionally, day trips to ruins or old palaces are common throughout. For

---

COURSES (1995)

Life and Culture Seminar
Methods and Techniques of Field Study
Intensive Hindi
Independent Study Project

---

the last week of the program, after students have presented their ISPs, there is usually a relaxing trip to the Taj Mahal, in Agra.

FACILITIES

There is little in the way of facilities—most people handwrote their ISP papers. Then again, little was needed. Students have all of the texts and handouts that they need, and there are no major papers besides the ISP.

Classes are held in a conference room of the YMCA in New Delhi and in a lecture room in the hotel in Udaipur.

Off the Track

While New Delhi has a pretty full schedule, students have more than enough time for their own explorations in Udaipur and during the ISP. Here's what happened to some students of the SIT India program:

Trying to find a thousand-year-old banyan tree was a memorable time for one student. She was in a jeep with seventeen other people, and they arrived in the dead of night. They couldn't see a thing—the only way they knew they were near was that they could hear the cries of the monkeys.

Visiting a local temple, a student witnessed a woman bringing her sick child to a healer. The healer and a few old men began ringing bells and chanting. The old men became so entranced that they began hyperventilating and flagellating themselves with chains.

One student's ISP took place in a very rural village—she stayed in a small hut with a large family and their cows. Since she was a medical student, she helped out the local doctor occasionally. She even helped deliver a baby with a midwife.

Jaisalmer, a town about sixty miles from the Pakistani border, entranced a few students. Built almost entirely out of sandstone, the buildings have detailed work and engravings that amazed the students. The city seems to rise out of the desert, appearing to those who approach it almost as giant sand castles.

A group of students took time out of their ISP time to go north for a camel safari. They traveled through the Thar Desert out near the Pakistani border. "It kind of was like an American rafting trip, except instead of boats and water, it was camels and sand." Traveling with five guides and camels for nearly a week, they would ride across the desert all day and then eat incredible well at night. The whole trip only cost them the equivalent of $30 each.

Advice and Warnings
from the Students

▶ "Don't bother with water purification tablets. They don't taste good and they don't really work."

▶ $500 was a good amount of money to bring for personal expenses.

▶ "Bring Tevas!"

▶ "If a man is bothering you too much, take off your sandal and hit him on the head with it. That's what I did."

▶ "Bring at least one pair of comfortable jeans, a Walkman with lots of tapes, and very little else!"

▶ "Bring pictures of your family back home—people love to see it!"

▶ "Bring your own books on India, so you can educate yourself while you're actually there!"

The Best + The Worst

👍 Just being able to travel around India

👎 New Delhi

👍 The Hindi class

👎 Being a *complete* outsider and not understanding anything that was going on

👍 Taking bike rides anywhere

👎 The poverty

👍 The food

👎 Getting sick in a rural village

👍 The homestay in Udaipur

👍 "Narrow it down to one thing? I can't."

KENYA COASTAL STUDIES

Nanci Leitch/School for International Training

LOCATION: Various locations in Kenya

HOST SCHOOL: School for International Training

DESCRIPTION: A fifteen-week study of East African society and culture, including language study

DURATION: Semester

COST: $10,300 (travel expenses to and from departure point not included)

FINANCIAL AID: SIT offers scholarships on a need or merit basis, and accepts federal aid and loans.

PREREQUISITES: None

COURSE FULFILLMENT: Rural Development, History, Politics, Religion, Swahili

NO. OF STUDENTS: 20   M/F RATIO: 1/7

HOUSING: Private houses and two homestays

COMPUTERS: Not provided. Personal computers not suggested.

CONTACT INFORMATION
Admissions Office
College Semester Abroad
School for International Study
Kipling Road, Box DA1WA
Brattleboro, VT 05302
Phone: (800) 336-1616
Fax: (802) 258-3126
E-mail: 6424659@mcimail.com
WWW: Not available

Overview

"I can't believe that people wouldn't go on this program."

Overshadowed by the more famous savannas and game parks, Kenya's coast nevertheless is a fascinating and beautiful area to visit, let alone have a chance to study. And why shouldn't it be? With an equatorial climate, stunning beaches, turquoise waters, and an exciting mix of people and cultures, the coast of Kenya is certainly an area that deserves more scrutiny.

Don't let the name of SIT Kenya's Coastal Studies program confuse you, though—students aren't concentrating on marine processes or studying the geology of Kenya. Instead, they are getting a broad view of Kenyan life and an introduction to East African society and culture. From the capital city of Nairobi to the small island of Lamu, students have lectures on all aspects of Kenyan life, receive intensive Swahili language study with personal tutors, participate in a two-week-long work camp and homestay in a rural village, and even have time for a safari at Maasai Mara national park, just to name a few of the features.

Beginning in Nairobi, the orientation lasts perhaps a week, and in this time students already are covering a fair amount of ground—from Nairobi the program quickly moves down to the port town of Mombasa, and then north to the coastal town of Malindi, where students are introduced to the marine and coastal environment of Kenya.

But students didn't feel the program truly began for them until they traveled to the small tropical island of Lamu, where they stayed for three weeks. Lamu is a predominantly Islamic island, and students may find that the program arrives around the start of Ramadan, the Muslim holy month. While this affords the students a chance to see a significant aspect of the culture up close and personal, it does effectively shut down the businesses of the town for its duration. In Lamu, students participate in the Life and Culture and Rural Development Seminar, as well as receiving intensive Swahili classes. To add to an already rich experience, each student has a personal tutor to help them along with the language.

After Lamu, the program moves on to a rural village (*"very rural,"* as one student said) outside of Nairobi for two weeks. Here, the program goes to work—literally. Students are in a sort of work camp, helping out with a few community service projects, as well as participating in a week-long homestay. The intensive language study and the Life and Culture class continues here, but it's not all hard work—the group is treated to a weekend off at a nearby resort.

The next two weeks are spent in Nairobi, where students participate in a second homestay, receive lectures for the Life and Culture Seminar, and prepare themselves for their ISPs. At the end of the time in the capital, the program travels to Maasai Mara National Park for a three-day safari. This is one of the highlights of the trip, allowing students to play tourist for a while before going on to their ISPs. After the safari, one week is also spent on the island of Zanzibar.

The last four weeks are dedicated to the ISPs, which take students all over Coastal Kenya.

Environment

"I had chickens running across me in the night."

When asked about the environment of the program, most of the students immediately started talking about Lamu. Obviously this was a place that nearly everyone loved and felt to be a sort of home, which isn't surprising, as the largest amount of time is spent in Lamu, and it's a fairly small island.

Lamu is a community that is more than one thousand years old, and it has a rich history of seafaring trade with the ancient civilizations of Arabia, Persia, China, and India. Situated north of Mombasa, Lamu's small size soon becomes apparent—there is only one car on the island, and that is used by the district officer. He doesn't have much use for it, except for a quick nap, as the few roads are a bit tricky to navigate. The preferred transportation is either walking, donkeys and carts, or sailing on a dhow (a canoelike boat with one sail). "You really can't help but see familiar faces when you walk through town," one student remarked. Evidently the SIT program is well-established in Lamu, and the residents are enthusiastic and friendly whenever a new semester pulls into town.

Lamu's architecture is heavily influenced by Islam, as that is the prevailing religion, and so most of the buildings are Arabic in style with cambered doorways and open-air designs. Patios, verandas, and balconies are everywhere, and students particularly loved sitting on their own balcony, staring at the ocean and listening to the callers announce evening prayer.

There isn't much to do in Lamu (that is, besides look at the cultural influences of a few ancient African and Middle Eastern civilizations), except taking walks by the waterfront or going to the only bar on the island, which is on top of the local hotel. The town is especially quiet during Ramadan, when devout Muslims are fasting and praying during the daylight hours. Once the sun has set, however, fast is broken, vendors line the streets, and the nights take on almost a carnival atmosphere.

In stark contrast, Nairobi is Kenya's capital and largest city, a bustling metropolis landlocked in the middle of the country. Students spend the second largest amount of time in the city, first with the orientation at the beginning of the program, then near the end with a two-week homestay.

Nairobi is Kenya's most modern city, but don't think it's going to be anything like Chicago. While the skyline *is* growing, there are still relatively few tall buildings. It's still crowded and noisy though, and students assured us that the mass transit system is always an experience. Small buses called *matatus* are used to get around, and it's not uncommon to see people clinging to the sides of them because the inside is jam-packed.

Because it's a big city, however, there are plenty of diversions. Ranging from world-class restaurants serving exotic game meats to dance clubs to museums and the theater, the students were always busy in Nairobi.

Like all big cities, Nairobi is more dangerous than most of the smaller towns around it, and students have to be careful when they're out and about. While none of the students we talked to had any problems, they all stressed that being cautious was a very smart idea.

Housing

"Living with the families was amazing, and Lamu is a very mystical place."

There is a range of accommodation throughout the semester, from resorts to mud huts. Beginning with Lamu, SIT rents two houses that students raved about. Both have ocean views and are open-aired, allowing cool breezes to blow in at night. It also, though, allows for local winged creatures to fly in whenever they feel like it. Students spoke fondly of a bat that would regularly visit them, which they appropriately named Mohammed. There were large shared rooms, as well as shared bathrooms. Three meals a day are served at the houses.

For the first week of work camp, the program camps out in a school/church, cooking and holding classes there as well.

"There are days when I would say, 'Why didn't I go to Europe?' But it was awesome."

But the following week is the one that stands out in students' minds. Paired in twos, they participate in rural homestays. Most stay in houses made of mud with thatched roofs, dirt floors, no plumbing facilities, and little inside besides one or two rooms for perhaps up to eight people. But the conditions were not foremost on the students minds, as they spoke of getting to know their families, singing songs with them, and dancing in the African night.

In Nairobi, students stay in the local YMCA during the orientation. When the program returns several weeks later, students have another homestay, this time for two weeks. These conditions are far more western, as most lived with middle- to upper-class Kenyan families. While the first homestay is an experience never to forget, the second allows for perhaps a closer bond with their host families. Many students spoke of going out with their adopted brothers and sisters and their friends at night and on the weekends. A stipend is given for two meals, and the third meal is supplied by the host family.

Academics

"Easily the most intensely educational four months of my existence."

What SIT offers in terms of academics is not really impressive until you think about all of the things students actually learn, do, and have available to them. There are the Life and Culture lectures throughout the program, covering everything from East African politics to Kenyan art. Students also are receiving intensive language training for nearly a month—with personal tutors during their time in Lamu. On top of this there is, of course, the

"You would have fifty experiences a day that you could write about."

Field Studies class (evidently stressed a bit more here than on other programs), and the ISP. Students are kept busy on this program, and academically stimulated.

In Lamu, the academics focus on the Swahili class. With classes in the mornings, the group is broken up into four different work groups and are taught round-robin style all morning with four language teachers. The groups meet with each teacher for about one hour and focus on a different aspect of the language. Most of the students thought Swahili was a beautiful language, and not a particularly hard one.

Normally students meet with their tutors in the afternoons for anywhere from one to two and a half hours, practicing their conversational skills. Many students also become good friends with their tutors. Almost all of the students whom we talked to said that they got to the point where they could speak Swahili well enough to hold a decent conversation. Occasionally, there were lectures in the afternoons for the Life and Culture class.

In Nairobi, the program has the resources to call in an impressive and sizable host of lecturers. Therefore, the majority of the lectures are held here, sometimes for up to six hours a

> *"You're constantly learning about the place where you are."*

day. Students did grumble a bit about being stuck in a hot room for hours on end with no fan. Fortunately, the program is only here for about two weeks. During this time students are also finalizing plans for their ISPs.

While the program goes to work camp, the academics are reduced to the Swahili lessons for the most part. The language teachers come along with the group, and classes are held only in the afternoons, so the group can work with the community as much as they can.

WORKLOAD

The students carry a fairly light daily workload, although there are the long-range projects that are inherent to any SIT program. In addition to occasional three-page cultural analysis essays, the Field Studies journal is taken rather seriously. Students must complete at least four entries a week, and they are checked regularly. There are also nightly Swahili assignments, but there is little in the way of written work for this, as a typical night's work involves vocabulary memorization. The bulk of the work comes later in the Independent Research Project, and students focus much of their free time to seek out contacts for their topic. There is a midterm in Nairobi, and a final examination in Zanzibar.

LIFE AND CULTURE CLASS

The Life and Culture class is generally divided up into four sections: *History and Politics, Geography and Economics, Social Anthropology,* and *Arts and Humanities.* Among others, typical lectures and discussions touch upon: the history of Kenya and the Lamu archipelago, nationalism in East Africa, national parks and wildlife conservation, economic and rural development in Kenya, marine ecology and conservation, Islam in Kenya, the population and demography of East Africa, Swahili culture and society, the role of women in development, traditional music in Kenyan life, Swahili architecture, and traditional and modern literature.

INDEPENDENT STUDY PROJECT

With three to four weeks to complete their independent research, students range all over coastal Kenya, from Mombasa to Lamu. Past projects include: *Beauty Secrets of Swahili Women, Traditional Islamic Music, Environmental Education, Coastal Archaeology, Rural Agricultural Development, Swahili Oral History, Islamic Education,* and *Traditional Boat Building.*

FIELD TRIPS

There are small field trips scattered throughout the program, ranging from excursions to the Gede ruins to snorkeling off the coast. There are also a few larger field trips. In Lamu, the program takes a weekend off and travels by dhow to one of the remote and practically deserted islands. Besides beautiful beaches, students have an opportunity to meet the residents of a small fishing village and camp out underneath the stars on the beach.

While at the work camp, the program again takes a few days off and goes to a resort, allowing students the chance to relax and "decompress" from the emotionally draining previous week. However, by far the most talked about field trip was the three-day safari before the ISP period. Camping outside Maasai Mara, the program takes walking tours of the area, talks to local Maasai, and also gets in some fantastic game drives.

Although the time in Zanzibar does have lectures for the seminar class, much of the time is spent sightseeing around the island nation, visiting sites such as old slave plantations and the rain forest. There is even some time for simply lounging on the beach.

FACILITIES

Facilities are practically nonexistent for the program, but none of the students could really think of a thing that they needed or missed. Readings are from photocopied packets, and papers are handwritten. While in Lamu, classes are held in the house where the group stays. There are blackboards, but little else. Lectures in Nairobi are held at the University of Nairobi, and SIT has the use of its own classroom.

COURSES (1995)

Life and Culture and Rural Development Seminar
Methods and Techniques of Field Study Seminar
Intensive Swahili
Independent Study Project

Off the Track

With a few weekends off in Lamu and Nairobi, as well as the ISP period, students had plenty of time for their own explorations and adventures. Here's what happened to some students of the SIT Kenya program:

The last night of the rural homestay was a highlight for several students. While sitting around a campfire, the homestay children spontaneously put on a show of their local dances and songs. Not to be outdone, the students taught them the Hokey Pokey in Swahili, which they had practiced in their language classes weeks before.

One student marveled at the coincidences that occurred on the program. For example, she was wandering around Mombasa, looking for an English translation of the Koran for her ISP. A man politely asked her what she wanted, then took her to his house to get a copy. He turned out to be the head of the Islamic Party of Kenya.

In their free time, a group from the program chartered a dhow and sailed to Kiwaiyu Island. There they relaxed on the bone-white beaches and swam in the clear waters that surround this uninhabited island. Unfortunately, on the trip back they ran aground on a reef and ended up being stuck out on the water for hours until they were rescued by a local fisherman.

One woman told us about the most physically challenging part of the trip for her—climbing Mt. Kenya. She and a few others took time off from the ISP period and went up to the summit of Kenya's highest peak. According to her, it was a good thing that they hired a guide to help them, as the trails were poorly marked, and every one came down with mild cases of altitude sickness. The view from the top, however, made all the difficulties worthwhile.

While investigating Tarab music, a mix of Swahili poetry and Islamic melodies, one student got to know the local musicians fairly well. During his research he met up with a group that played Tarab music at weddings, to which he was invited along. This gave him the opportunity to witness Muslim wedding ceremonies firsthand and to attend the receptions afterward.

Advice and Warnings from the Students

► "Don't bring a sleeping bag, it's too hot! Bring a couple of sheets instead!"

► "Get the shakes in Nairobi, they're amazing."

► $500 was a good amount of money to bring for personal expenses.

► "Don't bother with chlorine pills—you don't really need them and the program has lots of them from past students."

► "If you are looking to go to Europe, go to Europe. Because there are times on the program when you are not at all in the western world."

► "Remember that everything you bring you have to carry around, so pack light."

► "If you don't go now, you're not going to go when you're forty with three kids."

The Best + The Worst

👍 The friends made in Kenya

👎 Being viewed as "money"

👍 Learning Swahili

👎 The food was constantly fried

👍 Work camp

👎 Work camp

👍 "The constant excitement, the constant travel"

👎 Nairobi

👍 The coastline

👎 Eight-hour, hot bus rides

👍 The houses in Lamu

👍 The language tutors

TANZANIA WILDLIFE ECOLOGY AND CONSERVATION

LOCATION: Various locations in Tanzania

HOST SCHOOL: School for International Training

DESCRIPTION: A fifteen-week program covering the ecology and conservation of local wildlife, and its effect on the Tanzanian population

DURATION: Semester

COST: $10,303 (travel expenses to and from departure point not included)

FINANCIAL AID: SIT offers scholarships on a need or merit basis, and accepts federal aid and loans.

PREREQUISITES: Previous course work in environmental science, ecology, or biology at the college level

COURSE FULFILLMENT: Wildlife Ecology and Management, History, Politics, Religion, Swahili

NO. OF STUDENTS: 21   M/F RATIO: 1/4

HOUSING: Dormitories, mud huts, and a three-week homestay in Arusha

COMPUTERS: Not provided. Personal computers not suggested.

CONTACT INFORMATION
Admissions Office
College Semester Abroad
School for International Study
Kipling Road, Box DA1WA
Brattleboro, VT 05302
Phone: (800) 336-1616
Fax: (802) 258-3126
E-mail: 6424659@mcimail.com
WWW: Not available

Overview

"I want to go back."

Put the terms "Tanzania" and "Wildlife Conservation study" together and people have an instant image of themselves sitting in the Serengeti, watching lions, wildebeests, elephants, and impala. While SIT's Tanzania Wildlife Ecology and Conservation program *does* do this, it offers students so much more as well. The program covers the issues that are involved not only with the preservation of the herds and flocks of wildlife in Tanzania, but also with the necessary interaction between them and their human neighbors.

Besides safaris in Serengeti National Park, students receive intensive Swahili language training, study at the Mweka College of African Wildlife Management on the slopes of Mt. Kilimanjaro, and even participate in a three-week homestay in Arusha.

The program begins in Nairobi, but then quickly crosses the border into Tanzania for the typical week-long SIT orientation. At the start of the four-week stay in Arusha, the program camps at a compound/club called Klub Afriko for a week, allowing students to get acclimated to the program and the culture, and to start their Swahili classes. The next three weeks are spent in homestays, while lectures and classes continue at the club. Small field trips are also taken during this time to nearby nature preserves and parks, villages, and places of cultural and historical interest.

The small rural village of Olkokola is the next step for a week-long work camp. This stay is primarily a community service stop (helping implement irrigation, repairing houses, etc.), but students were unanimously overwhelmed at the amount they learned simply from being someplace so *completely* different from the U.S.

From Olkokola, the program moves up to Mt. Kilimanjaro, to study at the Mweka College of African Wildlife Management, the world's leading institution devoted solely to this issue. Students report this is where the issues of wildlife management are really first addressed and discussed. Students receive a week of lectures here by the top professors in the field, integrating intense classwork and small individual projects. The program then goes on its first major field trip to study a wildlife corridor called Kwakuchinja, between Lake Manyara and Tarangire national parks.

After this, the group visits other national parks for two weeks, hitting the big ones—Ngorogoro and Serengeti. In each location the program focuses on a different issue—for instance, the group may study wildlife ecology in the Serengeti, while concentrating on human and wildlife interaction in Ngorogoro.

The next three to four weeks are devoted to the students' ISPs, and students go all over Tanzania to conduct their research. The last week is spent back in Arusha, where students present their ISPs and receive their evaluations.

Environment

"I felt like I was constantly on my own personal Discovery Channel."

Since the program moves around a fair bit, the closest thing to a stable environment that students have is their four-week stay in Arusha. At the foot of Mt. Meru, Arusha has been described to us as one of the most beautiful towns in Tanzania, enjoying a temperate climate all year long. It is, however, very much a tourist town, since Arusha is the gateway to most of the more popular game reserves, including the Serengeti and Tarangire.

Divided into two sections by the Naura River, the town is a wonderful place for walking and exploring the sights. The main open market is the town's centerpiece, though, where everything from fruit to handicrafts are for sale. As for nightlife, there are a few local bars, a few good restaurants, and two discos that stay open late. However, most students are still too busy getting used to their classes, the group, and their homestays to have much of an active nightlife.

The program also spends a fair amount of time at the national parks, which really can't be described in a few sentences. The parks range anywhere from open savannas to forests. A common theme throughout all of them is the African sky—with no buildings or lights around, it is a constant 360° presence. Whether it was brilliantly blue during the day or "impossibly starry" during the night, students sighed a

"You can see the dawn of humanity right there."

lot when they spoke of their time in the wild. And, of course, you can't forget all of the wildlife sharing this scene with you. Without going into detail, students reported seeing everything they had ever heard or dreamed about, and then some.

Housing

"You stay in campsites so close that you can hear the lions roaring."

For the first week in Arusha, students are camping out at the campground near Klub Afriko. This was so they have the time to get better acquainted to their surroundings, bond with the group a little more, and get a feel for the town. The next three weeks, students were placed in homestays. The homestays seemed to vary greatly—from lower-middle-class to upper-class families. We talked to one student who stayed in a traditional Maasai compound, while another student stayed with a rather wealthy family, which she described as "kind of western."

The rural stay in Olkokola is perhaps just a tad misleading. The program *is* in a very rural village, complete with mud huts and no running water or facili-

"You wake up to Swahili spoken to you right off the bat."

ties. However, students are not participating in a homestay. Rather, the village vacates one of the huts for SIT's use, though students sleep outside as it is usually beautiful at night. Still, this is usually one of the highlights of the trip for students.

While at Mweka College, students are staying in dorm rooms, which they compared to U.S. dorm rooms. The added bonus of this is that Mweka is a very international school, and students have the opportunity to meet students from all over the world who are studying the same topic that they are. The time in the field is usually spent camping, which is not only a very romantic way to see Tanzania, but was unanimously a favorite part for the students.

Academics

"I was learning science the way I've always wanted to."

As with all SIT programs, the academics rely heavily on the main lecture series as well as the experiential field work. The Tanzania Wildlife Ecology and Conservation program investigates the issues surrounding one of the country's biggest trades: ecotourism. This is the main focus of the program—examining both the methods of maintaining the immense tracts of land set aside for national parks, and the issues and problems of the groups that live on or near them.

When the program reaches Arusha, the academics start off in full swing. Students work on their information-gathering skills and cultural sensitivity training in the Field Study class, as well as receive lectures for the Life and Culture class in the afternoons. The mornings are spent in the Swahili class, and students study the language nearly four hours a day, every day. This class proved to be very effective as well as fun, which is fortunate considering that students are placed into homestays a bit more than a week after arriving.

> *"I learned the language, lived with a family, and studied every imaginable view on conservation."*

The program slows down a bit in Olkokola, the site of their rural visit. There are few lectures here, although the Swahili class continues only slightly less intensely. Students are mainly working on a few community projects. After one week in Olkokola, the program travels to Mweka College of African Wildlife Management. Here they are lectured to by some of Tanzania's, and indeed the world's, experts in game reserve management.

The next two weeks are spent in the field at the various game parks of Tanzania. Students report that they received perhaps the most powerful and memorable lectures here, simply because they are in the field and seeing the very things they are learning about.

WORKLOAD

The workload is fairly run-of-the-mill SIT. There is the field journal that students are responsible for, which is periodically checked, and assignments for the Field Studies class, like interviews and observational reports. Additionally, there are a few three-page cultural analysis papers re-

> *"I spent a lot of quality time with my Swahili dictionary."*

quired. As the Swahili classes are focused on conversational skills, the workload for this class is primarily vocabulary memorization.

There are also small exams scattered throughout the semester, which surprised most students since it is not an intensely book-oriented program. Even more surprising is the fact that most people learned so much by SIT's hands-on method of teaching without even realizing it, and did quite well on the tests. While at Mweka College, students each have a "creatures" report due—a short paper on one of the national park's many inhabitants. There is a final comprehensive exam at the end of the program.

WILDLIFE ECOLOGY AND CONSERVATION SEMINAR

Titled *Wildlife Ecology and Conservation Seminar* (the topical seminar), this class is split up into two parts. The first is a short introduction to the life and culture of Tanzania—examining its history, political and economic issues, rural development, social anthropology, music and art, as well as geography. The second part is the main aspect of the class, and it covers the actual wildlife ecology and conservation problems and issues. It explores nearly every aspect, from an introduction to the ecological zones of Tanzania, to wildlife diversity and management. It also covers the impact of economic development and tourism on the natural environment and human settlements, and the management of national parks and reserves.

INDEPENDENT STUDY PROJECTS

With three weeks to complete their ISPs, students range all over Tanzania, and are even allowed to study in the game reserves, a privilege that the Tanzanian government does not readily hand out. Past projects have included: *Hunting as a Management Option, Traditional Maasai Stories, Wild Chimpanzees at Lake Victoria, Sustainable Agriculture, Women's Roles in Rural Reforestation, Flora and Fauna of Mt. Kilimanjaro, Ecotourism's Impact,* and *Poaching in Protected Areas.*

> *"I couldn't even have imagined a more amazing experience."*

FIELD TRIPS

While technically trips entirely of an academic nature, the field trips on the Tanzania program are perhaps some of the most exciting ones, not to mention longest, we have encountered. During the semester, the program visits Tarangire, Arusha, and Serengeti national parks, as well as Mt. Kilimanjaro, Ngorogoro Crater, and Olduvai Gorge. While these are all sites more commonly visited strictly for sightseeing, they are always supplemented with lectures from either the professors or scientists who have agreed to lend their expertise. Rest assured that students are learning far more on their visits than the average tourist.

> *"I would suffer a million times more to do it all again."*

As for pure recreation, students do have the opportunity to climb Mt. Meru, just outside of Arusha, and (attempt) Mt. Kilimanjaro while at Mweka College. Additionally, there are small trips taken spontaneously throughout the semester. For example, one semester the group took a camel safari for a night and a day in Arusha national park.

FACILITIES

The Tanzania program, like so many of the SIT programs, is minimalist at best in terms of facilities. Most of the time the classroom ends up being the largest room available. For example, at Klub Afriko, the program holds classes at the bar. At the other end of the spectrum is Mweka

> *"We were in the most capable hands we could have been."*

College, where students have access to the school's library and classrooms. As far as the rest of the program goes, there are no conveniences like computers and extensive research libraries available. Rather, students are constantly in the field and learning out-of-doors, and the best research material they have are the people they meet and their notes. To SIT's credit, the lecturers all sounded knowledgeable and fairly impressive, and no student we talked to felt as if they were in want or need of anything more.

Off the Track

While the schedule is fairly full most of the time, students do occasionally get a night off, and there is always the ISP time. Here are a few of the experiences of people on the SIT Tanzania program:

> COURSES (1995)
>
> *Wildlife Ecology and
>   Conservation Seminar*
> *Intensive Swahili*
> *Methods and Techniques of Field
>   Study*
> *Independent Study Project*

Being tall, female, and white made one student a constant center of attention. While in Olkokola one day, a woman started walking with her. The woman asked if she had ever had children and the student replied that she hadn't. The woman then reached out and grabbed one of her breasts saying, "Of course not. These are too small." On numerous other occasions people would also ask if her freckles meant that she was sick.

Camping out in the Serengeti is always an experience for students. Not only is it beautiful, it can be dangerous as you are occasionally in predators' territory. A few students heard sniffing outside their tent one night and were convinced it was hyenas, who had been around their campsite before. They grasped their flashlights and ripped open the tent . . . to see two cane rats jumping off the top and scurrying away.

While walking through the streets of Tanzania, Americans are often greeted with the cry of "Wazungu!" from the children who see them. This generally means "white person," and although it's much more genial and friendly than "gringo" is in Latin American countries, you will hear it *everywhere.*

While on his way to Zanzibar for his ISP, one student was stuck on a train for two days while a washed-out bridge was being repaired. He ended up eating pineapples and drinking water while the bridge was being fixed in the company of the other 800 travelers from the train. He found out later that if they hadn't made an unexpected stop they would never have found out about the bridge until it was too late.

Observing mating lizards was necessary for one student's ISP. She came across two outside a local post office, but, unfortunately, she had left her camera back at her hotel room! She took off down the road, returning to find that she had an audience of twenty or so laughing townspeople watching the crazy *Wazungu* take pictures of lizards.

Advice and Warnings from the Students

▶ "Be ready to be astounded, because you will be."

▶ "Women, be prepared to be a target!"

▶ "Bring something (like Kool-Aid) to mix with the water!"

▶ $500 to $1,000 is a good amount of money to bring for personal expenses.

▶ "Plan ahead for the fact that things often do not go as planned in Tanzania."

▶ "Really make an effort to learn Swahili."

▶ "Bring gifts for your homestay family and the other people you meet."

▶ "Bring good camping gear! You have access to all of the parks after the program is done!"

The Best + The Worst

👍 The ISP time

👎 You're always clustered in a group.

👍 The day that a student and her family finally understood one another

👎 Going from being with twenty people to being all by yourself on the ISP

👍 Swahili class

👎 Lariam! (one of the medicines used to combat malaria)

👍 Being with the group

👎 Work camp

👍 The game drives and all of the animals you get to see

👍 The ability that SIT had to handle any emergency situation

TIBETAN STUDIES

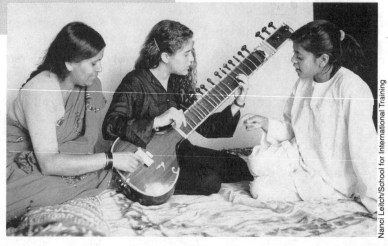

LOCATION: New Delhi, India; and Dharmsala, India, or Katmandu, Nepal

HOST SCHOOL: School for International Training

DESCRIPTION: A fifteen-week program examining the Tibetan people, their religion, history, and culture, including language study

DURATION: Semester

COST: $10,300 (travel expenses to and from departure point not included)

FINANCIAL AID: SIT offers scholarships on a need or merit basis, and accepts federal aid and loans.

PREREQUISITES: None

COURSE FULFILLMENT: History, Politics, Economics, Anthropology, Tibetan, Field Research

NO. OF STUDENTS: 22   M/F RATIO: 1/2

HOUSING: Hotels, hostels, on-site dormitories, and a five-week homestay in Dharmsala or Katmandu

COMPUTERS: Not provided. Personal computers not suggested.

CONTACT INFORMATION
Admissions Office
College Semester Abroad
School for International Study
Kipling Road, Box DA1WA
Brattleboro, VT 05302
Phone: (800) 336-1616
Fax: (802) 258-3126
E-mail: 6424659@mcimail.com
WWW: Not available

Overview

"It was the most powerful experience I've ever had."

Any program that is repeatedly granted a private audience with the Dalai Lama (His Holiness) catches one's attention. For the last thirty-five years, the Dalai Lama has led the nation of Tibet in exile, forced to flee their homes for fear of religious persecution from the Chinese government. Tibet has become, indeed, a nation without a country.

Focusing on an issue that many are ignorant of, or simply choose to ignore, SIT's Tibetan Studies program gives students a look at the religion, culture, history, and politics of the Tibetan people. The program offers so much—from a five-week homestay with Tibetan refugees to a week-long trek through Tibet or Bhutan to, yes, occasional private audiences with the Dalai Lama.

Beginning in New Delhi for a short orientation, the program then moves on to Dharmsala for five weeks, the seat for the Tibetan government-in-exile. Students' schedules are fairly full here, with the Tibetan language class and the Life and Culture seminar meeting five days a week, six hours a day.

The spring semester program usually coincides with His Holiness's public teachings, and classes are occasionally interrupted to attend a few of these,

"The Dalai Lama has got a great sense of humor.

or for such special occasions as the Dalai Lama's Oracle going into a trance. It is here that the group is usually granted a short audience with the Dalai Lama. Students also participate in their first homestay in Dharmsala. This was unanimously held to be an incredible experience, and many of the students go back to stay with their homestay families during the ISP period.

Moving on, the program travels to the city of Katmandu in Nepal for two weeks. Here, the language and lecture classes continue and students also finalize plans for their ISPs.

Just after the ISP period, the entire group goes on a week-and-a-half-long field trip to either Tibet (in the spring) or Bhutan (in the fall). This excursion is a highlight of the jour-

"You can't really plan things, because India doesn't happen that way."

ney, as very few Westerners are even allowed *into* most of the areas the program visits. The final month is dedicated for the ISP, with students going all over India and Nepal to conduct their research. The last week is spent in Katmandu where students present their ISPs, and SIT prepares them for the tough task of going home.

Environment

"Monkeys, street vendors, snake charmers, elephants—and that's just walking down the street."

Whether it's the fact that it's a center for a religion, or that it's just a delightful little town nestled into the foothills of northern India, students repeatedly spoke of "the embracing quality of Dharmsala."

It's a small town, with only two main dirt roads, and very community-oriented—most of the people in it are Tibetan and share a common heritage, culture, and experience in religious persecution. "After a while, you begin to recognize faces," one student claimed. For entertainment, students recalled a little movie house where someone had set up a TV, VCR, and wooden benches—and would charge seven cents for a movie.

Dharmsala is situated in some picturesque natural surroundings—nearly every student mentioned a particularly beautiful waterfall that was just

"If you can't adjust to all of the bizarre things that happen, it'll be hard."

on the edge of town. The weather is temperamental, as it "can be cold and rainy or 65 degrees and sunny." The students insist that every place in town was accessible by foot—this is made slightly less charming when you realize that to get practically anywhere you have to walk up a hill. Typical of towns in India, many of the roads are dirt and are a real mess in the rainy season.

Of course, the center of the town is the palace of the Dalai Lama. Several students recalled journeying daily up the hill to have tea at sunset and watching the devout pilgrims circumambulate the palace.

As for Katmandu, the capital of Nepal is a lot more westernized, offering everything that a student may need. This ranges

"It was the hardest academic experience I ever had; it wasn't 'Let's go drink across Tibet.'"

from fast food to a copy place that has a laser printer. There is even a golf course nearby. The people who students may encounter in

Katmandu range from mountaineers looking to scale one of the country's peaks to exiles from either Tibet or the 1960s.

Many students rent motorcycles and ride up into the hills around Katmandu to take in the inspirational views (something SIT strongly does not recommend because of the danger). Katmandu's weather is usually sunny and in the 80's in the spring, slightly cooler in the fall. Students should be flexible while packing—many felt that they had brought too many clothes for the Nepalese climate.

Housing

"I would rather spend time with my homestay family than with anyone else."

While in Dharmsala, students participate in a five-week homestay. Homes are simple there, and most of the homestays typically have two rooms—a room for cooking, and another room that acts as a living room-cum-bedroom. A few lucky students in the past got their own room, but this is very rare. Houses most of the time do not have indoor plumbing, but there is always a tap nearby for water.

Although these conditions may sound shocking to Americans, they are typical for India, and none of the students ever mentioned missing the conveniences of home. In fact, most grew rather wistful when talking about their homestay, and it was obvious that nearly all became very close with their adopted families. Students talked of cooking with their families, waking up early and going to the morning rituals with them, going to festivals, or simply playing with their adopted brothers and sisters.

In Katmandu there is also the added bonus of having an "SIT House." SIT gathers here for meetings occasionally, and students of the Tibetan Studies program often meet up with the Nepal program for a few days when their schedules coincide. This really is a "safe" area that students can go to, and there are a few rooms if they need time to themselves for whatever reason—there are even showers and western bathrooms available for those longing for the comforts of the West. One past participant told us, "It was a great place to be sick in, because you could go to the House and be sick by yourself in comfort."

Academics

"It was the opportunity to study a culture perhaps on the way to extinction."

Following the SIT credo of experiential learning, students have educational opportunities nearly unheard of for Westerners. Almost daily contact with Tibetan Buddhist nuns and priests, a possible audience with the Dalai Lama, lectures from people high up in the government, a field trip through either Tibet or Bhutan, and intensive Tibetan language instruction, to name a few. Of course, throughout the entire program SIT encourages students "to go and hang out in the town, and learn as much as you can on your own."

> *"It was wonderful working with the intelligentsia of the Tibetan community."*

The workload is fairly balanced out, and students thought the structure of the program worked well. While in Dharmsala, students receive three hours of language instruction, as well as two to four hours of lecture five days a week.

For spring semester students, there is the added bonus of being in Dharmsala for the Tibetan New Year, and for the Dalai Lama's public teachings. During the New Year there are no classes, just observational assignments for the Field Study class. The program also attends a few of the Dalai Lama's teachings in lieu of a scheduled lecture—but then again, what better lecture could be had?

While in Katmandu, the schedule is much the same, although relaxed a bit so students have more time to prepare for their ISPs.

A small note must be made about the academic directors of this program. They received some of the most consistent praise by students we have heard. The academic directors are obviously extremely knowledgeable about Tibet and "know everything and everyone." They also never seem

> *"The program was enchanting and fabulous."*

too busy to actually try to get to know the students, their interests, and how the experience is affecting them.

WORKLOAD

In addition to the normal SIT course work, there are usually three small papers due. These papers try to force the student to become more observant of what is happening around them, and so can be viewed as another stepping-stone to the ISP. They involve anything from interviewing homestay families about their religious practices to merely writing thoughts and hypothesis on peculiarities observed in Tibetan culture. One student said, "It was so amazing to be writing about what you're experiencing."

The Tibetan language study is a rigorous and constant part of the program. This is an exceptional class for students, and the instructors are excellent. There is a lot of memorization,

> *"It's hard to imagine a more intense and beautiful experience."*

and the added hardship of trying to learn the Tibetan alphabet. Tests are frequent, as are small assignments. But the hard work pays off, as most students feel comfortable holding a conversation in Tibetan after only a month of study.

LIFE AND CULTURE SEMINAR

The bulk of the academic program is contained in the Life and Culture seminar (the topical seminar), which consists of four different topics. *History and Politics* covers the aspects of the exile government, as well as the roles played by China and International Tibetan support groups. *Geography and Economics* considers the difficulties with the physical and political boundaries of the area and also examines the accessibility of the resources of the Himalayas and the responsibilities of the Tibetan government, and how this affects the speed of development. *Cultural Anthropology* explores the issues concerning the refugees and their Nepalese and Indian hosts. *The Arts* are covered through the investigation of thangka painting, poetry, and theater.

INDEPENDENT STUDY PROJECT

With four weeks to complete their independent research, students go all over India and Nepal. Past projects include: *Tibet in International Relations, Buddhist Nun Communities, Tibetan Medicine, Buddhist Mind Training, Tibetan Oracles, Tibet in Sino/Indian Relations, Western Practice of Tibetan Buddhism, Ancient Pilgrimage Sites,* and *Tibetan Women's Issues.*

FIELD TRIPS

To supplement the lecture series, the program also travels out of the cities to see various cultural sites and events. In the past, students also have been assigned the task of mapping ancient holy sites used by early Buddhists. Others mentioned trekking to holy caves where, in the early days of the religion, monks practiced asceticism.

Of course, the main field trip is the journey to either Tibet or Bhutan. This gives students the opportunity to, perhaps, see a bit of the "motherland" of what they have been studying for two months. The treks are described as simply fantastic. "We were climbing up a 16,000-foot pass guided by local porters and yaks

> *"I was the only Westerner in a room in an ancient monastery with 300 chanting monks."*

carrying our gear. We stopped on a plain with mountains on either side of us, a brilliantly clear night, and natural hot springs ten feet away."

FACILITIES

Although there aren't tremendous facilities, none is really needed. While in Dharmsala, students attend lectures at the Library of Tibetan Works and Archives, the Medical and Astro Center, the Tibetan Institute of Performings Arts, the School for Dialectics, and the various government offices in Dharmsala. This sounds like quite a bit, but one student compared the libraries to his high school library back in the States.

There are more facilities available in Katmandu, which is fortunate because this is the place that students really need them. As opposed to other SIT programs, students have the opportunity of using a computer center to type out their papers and even laser-print them.

COURSES (1995)

Life and Culture Seminar
Tibetan
Methods and Techniques of Field
   Study
Independent Study Project

Off the Track

Although students' schedules are fairly packed, there is a bit of free time, and there is always the month of the ISP for individual explorations. Here are some of the experiences that happened to students of the SIT Tibetan Studies program:

A two-year-old boy was the head of a monastery that was the site for one student's ISP. He, evidently, was the reincarnation of the founder of the monastery, and she was always a bit skeptical of this fact. However, when she went to say good-bye, he looked up from playing with his Matchbox cars, touched her head, said simply, "Stay," and went back to playing with his cars. She swears that when he touched her, she saw a vision of him as an old man.

A high school became a regular calling place for one student. He would stop by to do interviews for his ISP, but would always be lassoed in by the kids to teach the boys how to play basketball, and the girls the latest American dance moves.

While the group was meeting the Dalai Lama, one student unfortunately had a cold. He just could not stop sneezing. The Dalai Lama came up to him and started laughing. He said, "You sound like an old Tibetan man." The student laughed and began reaching for his handkerchief. "But," continued the Dalai Lama, "if you were really a Tibetan old man, you would reach into your pocket and blow your nose loudly in a dirty handkerchief."

The three-wheeled motor scooters used as taxicabs are everywhere in Nepal, and their drivers are always eager to get you to hire them. One night a student joked to a driver that he would only hire him as long as *he* could drive. The driver surprisingly agreed, but a few hectic minutes later they were pulled over by one of Katmandu's finest. He got taken to the police station, but a quick bribe settled everything.

Witnessing a "sky burial" was an arresting moment for a few students. This act is a traditional form of Tibetan burial and is very seldom seen. A lama cuts the body up, then takes it to a place he knows where vultures and buzzards will carry the pieces off.

While in Tibet, a few students visited a museum and spoke with two of the museum's guards. They turned out to be members of the Tibetan Underground and quietly told the students of their struggle against the Chinese. "I'm a monk," one of the men told them, "and I can't wear my robes for fear of being sent away. Don't forget what you have learned. Don't forget Tibet."

Advice and Warnings from the Students

▶ "Don't let the whole idea of bad water and malaria scare you away!"

▶ $650 is a good amount of money to bring for personal expenses.

▶ "Don't go if you can't deal with Asia. It won't be like home."

▶ "Travel is easy to do after the program ends. Take advantage of where you are!"

▶ "Take in as many of the Dalai Lama's public teachings as you can."

▶ "Bring Pepto-Bismol!"

▶ "Hurry up slowly. In Tibet, that means don't try to force things, just let them happen."

▶ "Don't be afraid to jump into a conversation and use your Tibetan!"

The Best + The Worst

👍 The Tibetan New Year

👎 New Delhi

👍 Trekking through Tibet all day and then making camp with the mountains behind, the plains stretching out in front, jumping into the natural hot springs, and then dancing and singing all night with the Yak herders

👎 It's a fairly expensive program.

👍 The academic directors

👎 Coming back home

👍 The homestay

👎 Freezing cold showers on a cold day in a monastery

👍 Trekking through Tibet

👎 Getting altitude sickness

School for Field Studies

General Description

"The quality of what you learn, the quality of SFS . . . What more can I say?"

In a world of increasing conflict between development and environment, The School for Field Studies (SFS) offers students a highly scientific approach to study some of the world's critical environmental issues. There are very few programs out there that offer science-related students a semester abroad while not sacrificing anything scholastically. SFS does a remarkable job at both, giving students an exceptional experiential semester, as well as retaining a high-level of academic quality. The School for Field Studies, over a span of fifteen years, has provided excellent experience-based education on environmental issues. They are the largest private institution addressing critical issues facing the world today. Although not an educational organization, their courses are accepted at the university level nationally. Like the School for International Training (SIT), SFS impressed us so much that we decided to include five of their programs.

The main focus of SFS programs is Environmental Field Studies, but topics for individual program range from Wildlife Management in Kenya, to Rain Forest Studies in Australia. A truly remarkable aspect of SFS is that students' research is not simply filed away and forgotten. Rather, the information gained through the projects is given to the local government for their use. Students can complete the semester knowing that their efforts were not just an academic exercise and that their findings will be put to practical use.

SFS programs are very similar in many ways, and in order to avoid repetition we will discuss the aspects that are shared by each.

Orientation

Once the students arrive, the first week or so is devoted to an introductory "minimodule," where they get an idea of how the classes are held and what is going to be required of them. At this time there is also an introduction to the basic methods of research techniques, statistics, and scientific writing. Additional program-specific topics begin in this period, such as language components, and historical, economic, and regional issues.

Academics

CASE STUDIES

The academic structure of SFS programs is unique and very effective. Instead of taking three classes with very different subjects, all three classes are grouped together under the theme of the program. This theme is examined in three or four "Case Studies." Each Case Study is a topic that all three classes simultaneously address. So, if you are in the Wildlife Ecology and Management program in Kenya, your first Case Study may be "How can local communities live with wildlife?" Your ecology course may travel to several different sites, assessing and comparing wildlife conditions. Your Socioeconomic course, in turn, may interview communities around these sites to ascertain their attitudes toward wildlife, and try to devise economic and cultural incentives to promote wildlife conservation. And so on.

An extremely strong majority of the students felt that this academic structure worked perfectly. Many even went so far as to say that it was the best idea for a structure they had ever experienced, as it focused on particular areas and was never too broad.

FIELD WORK

Another characteristic of the SFS programs is the heavy reliance on field work as a teaching tool. Usually a *third* of the time on SFS programs is spent in the field in some manner. This may mean actively participating in reforestation projects, or doing population counts of a sea lion colony. Unanimously, the students felt that this is what made SFS stand out, and that they learned much more by doing something than by reading about it. "It gives you actual field research experience while earning credits."

FACULTY

SFS programs generally are staffed by no less than four full-time professors, enabling the students to work in an atmosphere with a low student-faculty ratio. Faculty members often live on-site, and this allows students to have a relaxed and casual working relationship with their teachers. Professors become simply friends with more knowledge of the subject, and students may find themselves discussing ecosystems with them over a beer. All faculty have advance degrees in their field of study, and usually have a Ph.D., along with several years of field experience.

There are usually three professors and one field director. The field director's main job is to make sure the entire semester runs smoothly, but he or she also will teach a class periodically. Just as in the School for International Training, the field directors and professors have the ability to make or break a program. It is their attitude that will shape the tone of the program, and their willingness to listen and interact with the students that can either make a program a joy or a pain. There are also two (sometimes more) interns helping out with the program, who are usually alumni from previous semesters.

DIRECTED RESEARCH

The highlight for most students comes at the end of the semester, when they conduct their individual projects, known as Directed Research, or DR. Students plan and carry out an intensive study of a topic relating to the course's theme. Students conduct their research in groups as small as two, but usually no larger than six. Projects can either be chosen from a variety of preapproved research projects, or students can design their own, provided that it meets with the approval of the field director or a professor. Projects are eventually written up into a paper, ranging from twenty to fifty pages.

Generally, the last four weeks are devoted entirely to students' DR, although a few programs allow time for it throughout the length of the semester instead. Nearly all of the projects done by students of SFS programs involve the environment or the impact of development in some way, and some projects have been going on for years in order to compile a large, intricate database. These projects allow students to contribute their ideas and work to a large, ongoing project during their semester. Projects can be anything from designing an underwater snorkeling trail for tourist use to investigating flying fox colonies. As was mentioned before, the information collected on these projects is usually passed on to the local government for their use.

TESTS

Testing on the SFS programs is intensive, stressful, and, some even say, unfair. Exams for every class are typically held after each Case Study, and all are held on the same day. How does a four-hour essay-exam encompassing all of the material for every class sound? Students all agreed that this was a grueling process, but that after that week of stress, there were then two weeks without. While students didn't particularly like this setup, they agreed that it was the best way, given the structure of the rest of the program. A few programs have variations on this structure, with a midterm and a final instead of tests after each Case Study.

Group Living

An important aspect of the SFS experience is group living, and SFS purposefully does not make the accommodations glamorous. Don't expect a single, and count yourself *very* lucky if you have hot showers. Usually a bit isolated but located close to a small town, SFS centers are simply places to get away from it all and study the topic at hand. They can be anything—from converted hotels to old gaming ranches. While the centers *are* rustic, they have everything students need to live and do research in terms of things like libraries and dorms (some even go as far as having a volleyball court). They usually also have a fair amount of land around them, used for anything from experiments with organic farming to preservation of the land as it is. The goal is teamwork, and learning how to get along in a group situation. Students are eating, living, working, and studying with each other on a nearly twenty-four-hour basis. They come to depend on one another, and the conditions force them to learn how to compromise and express their own complaints.

Many things, both in and out of the field, need to be coordinated with other people. The tight living can be hard sometimes, but it seems like it is always rewarding. SFS keeps an eye on this situation as well—"house meetings" are usually held once a week to make sure everything is running smoothly and to see if there are any complaints. Students usually are also cooking one meal a day for the group, as well as cleaning their entire living area weekly.

COMMITTEES

Tying into group dynamics is the committee system, which all SFS programs have. Each student chooses to be on a committee with a theme to it—for example, the Student Affairs Committee makes sure everything runs smoothly in the group, while the Social and Sports Committee organizes group activities like weekly soccer matches or a Thanksgiving feast. Specific committees vary from program to program, as the students choose what kind they would like to form.

Community Service

While other programs may "take over a town" or even ignore the locals completely, SFS actively participates in the local community in some way. Whether this means doing a simple highway cleanup or actually organizing events for the entire town, SFS tries to maintain strong ties with the community they are in or near. This attitude often is infectious on the students, and many of our interviewees got involved in the community during their free time as well. Of course, the entire SFS program can be seen as a community service, as the research projects are aimed at improving the environment around the area while at the same time helping, or at least not hurting, the local economy.

Safety

While SFS does like to make students "rough it," they go to every length to ensure a safe semester. The programs have been established in the areas for years, and they know the terrain and country extremely well. During our research for SFS, we never heard any of the infamous "horror stories" that can plague semester abroad travel. Some of the students even felt that SFS goes a little too far, and that some of their rules were too harsh and restricted their freedom.

TROPICAL RAIN FOREST MANAGEMENT

Ed Stashko

LOCATION: Queensland, Australia

HOST SCHOOL: School for Field Studies

DESCRIPTION: A three-month study of the conservation and management of northeastern Australia's rain forests

DURATION: Semester

COST: $10,970 (airfare to and from departure point not included)

FINANCIAL AID: Scholarships and interest-free loans available to those who qualify. Federal aid and Stafford loans are accepted.

PREREQUISITES: None

COURSE FULFILLMENT: Ecology, Ecological Management and Policy, Field Research

NO. OF STUDENTS: 32   M/F RATIO: 3/7

HOUSING: On-site housing at SFS center

COMPUTERS: Provided. Personal computers allowed and recommended.

CONTACT INFORMATION
Admissions Department
School for Field Studies
16 Broadway
Beverly, MA 01915
Phone: (508) 927-7777
Fax: (508) 927-5127
E-mail: sfshome@igc.apc.org
WWW: Not available

Overview

"You could walk one minute and be in the rain forest."

Set idyllically on the edge of an Australian rain forest, students on SFS's Rain Forest Studies program can wake up to the cries of king parrots, have breakfast overlooking the mist-covered forest, study reforestation processes in the morning, and then hike in the afternoon in search of a few of the rare mammals and plants found only on the Australian continent.

The focus of the program is to find alternatives for the conservation and management of Queensland's rain forests that are scientifically sound, culturally acceptable, and politically and economically feasible. SFS handles itself with its usual flair, combining academic excellence with practical field work in a truly wonderful setting.

The program is situated at the SFS Center for Tropical Rain Forest Management for the duration of the semester. Located on the edge of a rain forest preserve (a few hours away from Cairns), students are working on methods of maintaining the existing growth, and encouraging practices that aid the revitalization of new vegetation. They are studying in some of the last rain forest growth of its kind, while learning the issues regarding its preservation. The program is not entirely focused on rain forest vegetation, however, as students can study such mammals as the cassowary (a six-foot-tall flightless bird) and even work on projects in wetlands.

The north of Queensland has been called the most beautiful area of Australia, and SFS's center is within easy driving distance of both lush rain forest, impressive waterfalls, beautiful beaches, and the Great Barrier Reef. Field trips are taken several times a week, and there are also a few weekend trips designated for field work. There is a four- to five-day break in the middle of the program, allowing students time on their own to do anything from scuba diving to a safari into the Outback.

Environment

"The moon was so bright, sometimes I could see colors."

Life in the rain forest is not a Fantasy Island vacation. Prepare to be almost constantly wet, hot, and have mud smeared up to your waist from the day's hike. It will take some getting used to, especially when you discover that although the washing machine works just fine, finding a day with enough sunshine to dry your clothes takes a lot of patience.

But we heard no real complaints from the students. Instead, we heard countless descriptions of waking up to a chorus of birds, of the bandicoots (a bit like a possum crossed with a racoon), which would bravely steal food off the veranda, the small kangaroos that were always around camp, and of taking short hikes into the surrounding forest and

> *"I started hiking in the best place on earth, and now everything pales in comparison."*

then running back to professors with a new discovery. The center is situated on 150 acres of protected rain forest, with fruit trees scattered throughout from some long-forgotten farm.

Besides the center, though, there is very little around. The nearest town does not have much—a post office and a bank are the luxuries it offers. It does have a weekend farmers/flea market that students would occasionally go to, and the town also holds "bush dances" (the equivalent of square dancing in America), which nearly every student mentioned as an enjoyable experience. Typical of Australia, the locals are all extremely friendly—especially since they are all familiar with the program and love the opportunity to talk to the new "Yanks."

Students' days are filled with classes, meals, field trips, and then reading and homework at night. Living in the rain forest allows students to look up from the pages of their books and gaze out at what they're studying. With their free time, students can go on walks or runs along the paths that are scattered about the forested areas. Occasionally, students can convince an intern (which doesn't require much) to drive a few hours to catch a movie in Cairns, or to go off to one of the many waterfalls nearby for a quick swim. Volleyball is the sport of choice at the center, as students in the past constructed an excellent court. There is also the weekly "barby" (BBQ to Americans), and the big cook-out attracts some of the locals as well.

COMMUNITY SERVICE

SFS puts a lot of emphasis on returning the local population's typical generosity. While this program is a bit more isolated than other SFS programs, it makes an effort to become involved. During one semester, students got involved in a local organization called TREAT, which raises and plants seedlings in the protected rain forest areas. The program also organizes a day trip for local elementary children to the center, to teach them a little about their environment and how to protect it. At the end of the semester, the program holds an open house, to which the entire town is invited to come and hear presentations on some of the projects the students have completed. Students also participate in such simple yet necessary activities as highway cleanups.

Housing

"It's group living with a capital G."

The center has two parts to it: the main building and the cabins. The main building is on top of a small hill, allowing a view of the forest it sits astride. A short path leads down from the main building to the cabins that are nestled into the rain forest itself. Also below the hill are a shade house (where the seedlings for the reforestation plants are), a house garden, and the volleyball court.

In the main building there is the kitchen, the library, the computer room, offices for the faculty, and a living space with lots of large beanbags, a dartboard, and even free weights. The program usually has its meals outside on a large veranda, which wraps around the building.

The cabins hold eight people and are usually separated by sex, although it depends on the male/female ratio. Each person

> *"The place is so beautiful and you learn to live so simply."*

gets a cot, a shelf, and a small space for clothes and personal items. The cabins tend to have minor inconveniences, such as mice, mildew, or simply smelling a little. The lights of the cabin are in the precarious position of being solar-powered, although students said that they were never on long enough to drain the batteries.

While the cabins are Spartan and damp (what's not damp in a rain forest?), students insisted that they are hardly ever used except to sleep in. One thing they have in their favor is beautiful views, as nearly everyone fondly recalled watching the sun set over the rain forest from the porches. The bathrooms and showers are shared in a separate building. The showers are cold water only, unless some early riser takes the time to light a fire under the water heater (apparently, few people do).

Food seems to be no problem and in plentiful supply. Students prepare breakfast and dinner for the group on a rotating schedule, which some found to be a new experience: "It was

> *"You get very unconscious of self—half the people didn't wear underwear after a while."*

fun, but it was a pain to cut up thirty onions for a stew that feeds forty." Meals always have a vegetarian option. To allow students the time to have a large amount of research time, the interns make lunch, which is usually sandwiches.

Academics

> "It was very challenging stuff to learn, but you learn so much."

Typical of SFS, this is by no means a party program. It is incredibly work-oriented, and the atmosphere condones this perfectly. Besides living in the very ecosystem they are studying, students are living in close quarters with their professors. Not only is the learning at a more personal level, but it also leads to more discussions over dinner about

> *"It's not a bunch of hippies living out in the rain forest smoking pot—it's extremely challenging."*

rain forest issues than students would normally have at their home universities.

Though the days vary, there is a routine to the program's schedule. A typical day has classes from 9:00 A.M. until 12 noon. The afternoons are slated for field trips, or sometimes an-

> *"Out of the university classroom setting and into the field!"*

other lecture by visiting scientists. As one student said, "First we read about a subject, then we heard a lecture on it, and then we went into the field and actually saw or applied what we learned."

The last four weeks are devoted to the Directed Research project. Occasionally during the semester, longer field trips are planned, or community service events such as a highway cleanup.

CASE STUDIES

Case Study #1: "What Are the Most Viable Reforestation Strategies for Patterson Creek?" The goal of this first Case Study is to understand the role that reforestation can play in restoration, wildlife conservation, and watershed protection.

Case Study #2: "How Can Cassowaries Be Conserved and Managed on the Atherton Tableland?" These large (typically six feet tall), flightless birds are rarely seen these days. They are poorly researched in all areas, and this second study has students trying to fill in the missing data for its range, habitat needs, food sources, etc., as well as devise stages of a management plan for cassowaries to be submitted to the Conservation Research Center in Cairns.

Case Study #3: "Are Agroecology and Food Production on the Tableland Sustainable and Compatible with Rain Forest Preservation?" Examining land-use patterns, optimal-use models, and both conventional and alternative low-input systems (organic farming, permaculture, and integrated pest management), students will evaluate sustainable methods of food production that have a low impact on the rain forest.

WORKLOAD

Although there is much more in the way of experiential learning, the workload, considering the amount of time spent in the field, is considerable. Students have to learn the names of all the local plant and animal species, as well as their scientific names, and they are tested on this knowledge. At the end of each Case Study, students are assigned papers on them, in addition to their exams. These are a bit like mini research papers—they have a hypothetical problem and are required to come up with a solution. The main workload is reading, as there is a packet of reading materials assigned each week.

DIRECTED RESEARCH

The last four weeks are dedicated to the DRs, and have students ranging all over the local area and surroundings. Past projects included: *Bird Nesting in the Wetlands, Creek Invertebrates, The Impact of Ecotourism, Sustainable Gardening, Flying Fox Colonies,* and *Cassowaries.*

"It's something that college students don't usually get to do."

FIELD TRIPS

As was mentioned before, field trips are stressed for experiential learning and occur at least three times a week. Field trips visiting local scientists for the purpose of examining their research happen quite a bit, as do trips to nearby rain forest locations for "learning hikes." The largest field trip enthusiastically mentioned was the trip to nearby Mission Beach, site of one of the few cassowary management areas. Here, students learned and helped out with the research of the possibly vanishing species.

> **COURSES (1995)**
>
> *Rain Forest Ecology*
> *Principles of Forest Management*
> *Environmental Policy and*
> *   Socioeconomic Values*
> *Directed Research*

The program usually schedules a few days during the last week for a large, purely recreational trip. Past programs took the entire group on a two-day trip into the Outback, where the most stressful activity they had to do was look up at the stars.

FACILITIES

Despite its remoteness, the center has more than an adequate amount to offer students in terms of facilities. It has a small library with all the DR papers from previous semesters on file, as well as a good amount of scientific texts and articles relating to topics that are taught during the semester. There are adequate computers that are always available for student use, and in "crunch time" the faculty usually allow their computers to be used as well. The program has vans for most of the field trips, and a Land Rover to journey into the roadless areas.

Off the Track

Although there isn't a tremendous amount of free time, students always have Sundays off, and an occasional afternoon or night, as well as the four- to five-day break in the middle. Here is what happened to past students of the SFS Rain Forest Studies program:

Visiting a colony of flying foxes was a highlight for a few students. They arrived at the observation platforms right before dusk, as the foxes are nocturnal. The sky was still orange and purple from the night's sunset, when the foxes suddenly filled the sky, blacking it out.

One of the best days for a student was the first time the group went into town. The weekend market was just starting, and she strolled about, buying mango ice cream and lime. Later that night she went to her first "bush dance" and felt immediately welcome by all the locals. To top the night off, on the way home the group took a midnight swim in a nearby waterfall before getting home, exhausted.

Spring (or fall) break afforded the best opportunity for the students' own adventures. Some went to the Great Barrier Reef to learn to scuba dive, while others camped out on the remote tropical islands that are plentiful on the northeastern shore of Australia. A few took safaris into the Outback, visiting Ayers Rock, the Olgas, and Kings Canyon, while one student ended up taking horse-riding lessons from a former Australian Olympic athlete whom she had met at the weekly barby.

Everyone from this program said that the one thing that stuck out in their minds was going to see the cassowaries. Ironically, practically no one saw them. On the last day, though, a student who was studying them for his Directed Research came across a mother and chick. A cassowary has the strength to disembowel a person when it is angered or defending its young, and can grow to be up to six feet tall. He said that seeing the bird then was about as frightening and as exhilarating an experience as he had ever had.

The first few weeks were tough on one semester's group, as they had fourteen inches of rain over a period of twenty days. One student said that there was a time that it rained for seventy-two hours straight. "It was the kind of rain where you're thinking, 'Quick, I have to build an ark and save two of every species in the forest!'"

Advice and Warnings
from the Students

▶ "Bring a sweatshirt, clothes that don't mean a lot to you, and something that will make you look a little civilized."

▶ "Most things are going to mold if you go in the wet season."

▶ "Bring bug spray and suntan lotion!"

▶ $1,000 is a good amount of money for personal expenses (includes travel money as well).

▶ "Remember—there are a lot of bugs, you need repellent, there are leeches, and you can get sunburned. If you can't deal with any of these, don't go."

► "Be prepared to give up a little bit of your personal space."

► "Bring lots of sunblock, good raingear, and always carry it with you!"

The Best + The Worst

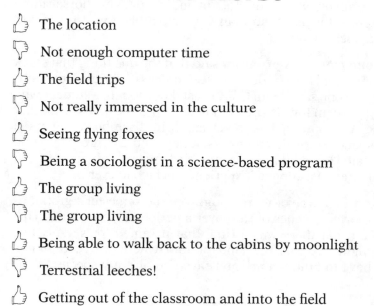 The location

Not enough computer time

The field trips

Not really immersed in the culture

Seeing flying foxes

Being a sociologist in a science-based program

The group living

The group living

Being able to walk back to the cabins by moonlight

Terrestrial leeches!

Getting out of the classroom and into the field

MARINE RESOURCE MANAGEMENT

LOCATION: Turks and Caicos Islands, British West Indies

HOST SCHOOL: School for Field Studies

DESCRIPTION: A three-month study of the issues of Sustainable Development in a marine environment

DURATION: Semester

COST: $10,970 (airfare to and from departure point not included. Scuba equipment not provided)

FINANCIAL AID: Scholarships and interest-free loans available to those who qualify. Federal aid and Stafford loans are accepted.

PREREQUISITES: Scuba certification is required. Students must provide their own equipment—tanks and weights can be rented on site.

COURSE FULFILLMENT: Marine Ecology, Resource Management and Policy, Field Research

NO. OF STUDENTS: 32   M/F RATIO: 3/7

HOUSING: On-site Housing at SFS center

COMPUTERS: Provided. Personal computers allowed and recommended.

CONTACT INFORMATION
Admissions Department
School for Field Studies
16 Broadway
Beverly, MA 01915
Phone: (508) 927-7777
Fax: (508) 927-5127
E-mail: sfshome@igc.apc.org
WWW: Not available

Overview

"How many people spend three months on an island diving?"

The Turks and Caicos Islands are hard to find on a map. Nestled in between the Dominican Republic and the Bahamas, these small islands are paradises just recently being discovered by the "outside world." From the air, they appear among patches of green and turquoise—evidence of the remarkably pristine coral reefs that are so plentiful in the area. The waters, and the islands, are as yet supremely untouched.

In these waters alone, 40 species of corals and 100 species of fish have been identified. SFS's Marine Resource Management program seeks to assist in developing culturally acceptable, scientifically sound, and economically and politically feasible recommendations for the sustainable development of the marine resources of the islands. The program looks at such critical issues as tourism and its effects on the marine environment, as well as sustainable levels for lobster and conch harvesting.

The Center for Marine Research Studies is located in a former hotel on South Caicos Island. Set on a small bluff overlooking both beautiful turquoise waters and the only town on the island, Cockburn Harbor, students are immersed completely in the environment they are studying. It is not a particularly hard environment to become immersed in—with the tropical days and nights and the constant presence of the Caribbean waters, very few students want to leave. As one student said, "I'm trying to figure out how to get back."

For the first half of the semester, students split their time between classes and field work. Scuba plays a large role, and students have the opportunity to dive nearly every afternoon to conduct their research (snorkeling is also an option). During the second half, the majority of time is devoted to the Directed Research projects, although classes are still held on a lighter schedule. Students technically have the weekends off, but there is usually a field trip planned on Saturdays. There is a five-day break in the middle of the program.

Although students come away from this program singing praises for South Caicos's waters ("They are the most beautiful, its coral reefs the most untouched and undisturbed, and the visibility some of the best anywhere on earth"), they strongly remind potential students that this program is not a dive vacation.

Environment

"Every day you are seeing the most beautiful things you have ever seen."

South Caicos Island is decidedly Caribbean—the people are friendly, the days are hot, the nights are warm, and the water seems to come in a million shades of blue. There is not much to do on South Caicos, and that perhaps only adds to the attractiveness of the location. When students aren't in class, or studying, or diving, the small town of Cockburn Harbor is nearby.

The local islanders call themselves "Belongers," and most of them live in Cockburn Harbor. The island's population is no more than a thousand, and it's not hard to get to know the faces around the dock. Students can find most anything they need in town, although items like batteries and film are very expensive. One student described town as "three grocery stores, seven churches, and ten bars." The bars are popular with everyone—locals, students, and professors (although students never drink if they are diving the next day).

The center fits into the environment perfectly. It is a rustic hotel built in the Caribbean style, so the trade winds can blow through the open architecture and act as a natural air conditioner. Nearly every place in the center has an ocean view, although the long front porch/patio was a favorite place to watch the sunrise, or to get some reading done. Good snorkeling reefs are right offshore, while great snorkeling reefs are only a short swim away. Four- or five-hour snorkeling expeditions are not uncommon activities.

"The diving was beyond belief."

Then, of course, there are the reefs the program goes to dive on. Since tourism has not reached the frenzy it has on islands such as St. Thomas or Jamaica, they are wonderfully unspoiled and in near-perfect condition. Nearly all of the reefs that students visited ("too many to count") were alive and thriving. They are also largely unexplored. For instance, one student remembered doing a great dive and then asking what the reef was called. The instructor shrugged, said it wasn't, and suggested that *she* name it.

COMMUNITY SERVICE

This is one of the most community-involved programs we have come in contact with. Not only does the school have organized events for the entire community that students are required to do, but students also often become so enthusiastic that many start their own community projects as well.

First off, the center organizes an event called "Sea Day," and it invites all of the children of the area to come and learn about their marine environment. Students have to design and present an exhibit for the youngsters on an aspect of the marine ecosystem they have been studying, and everyone we spoke to loved doing so. There are also the typical SFS cleanup drives, and students get to know people in the community through interviews, which they have to do as assignments for their socioeconomic class. Last year, one semester organized a conservation forum for the entire island chain of the Turks and Caicos Islands, and SFS is continuing this tradition.

On their own, the students have been just as impressive. Some cleaned up the local soccer field and erected permanent goals, others taught swimming or marine biology classes to elementary school students, while still others organized an Easter egg hunt for children. Many students participated in a local soccer league and played once a week.

Housing

"It was rustic, but it was home."

The center, while a bit old and worn, still serves the program well. It has an excellent location and gorgeous views, as well as being isolated enough so that students aren't distracted from their studies. Typical of SFS, the program tries to be very conservation-minded, and a rainwater catchment system is the sole provider of water (which is very precious on the island).

There is a library, a computer room, a kitchen, a classroom, study areas, a dining area outside under awnings, an area with games (darts, etc.), a front porch/patio, and a pool that is never filled (it's not needed, what with the ocean right there). Students share rooms with three other people, and all rooms come with *"Nothing was private."* their own bathroom and much-needed ceiling fan. The showers are cold water only, and students are encouraged to use them sparingly. There are laundry facilities, but, to conserve water, students are only allowed to use the washing machine once during the entire semester. After that one time, students must grab the washboard and head for the ocean.

The weekly SFS meetings are taken very seriously on this program, and students said that the faculty and staff were always very receptive to whatever problems they had with the program.

> *"You live with three other people in a small room with cockroaches."*

During student meetings, tradition dictates that a spoon is passed around, and whichever student holds the spoon is allowed to complain, lecture, or make suggestions uninterrupted.

FOOD

There is a cook who works full-time at the center, except for Sundays when the students cook. The menu usually has American-style dishes, as all of the food comes in from Miami. Some students felt that the meals got a bit repetitive at times, but if there was a consensus on a particularly unpopular dish, that dish was changed. Pork is a staple for many of the meals, but there is always a vegetarian option.

Academics

> *"It may be two weeks or two months, but you'll look back and realize how much you learned."*

Given the tropical location, there is the inherent danger that students, as well as the professors, may be less than willing to fully commit themselves academically, and instead try to work on their tan or go for a snorkel. The nature of the program, however, demands intensity, as students are constantly surrounded by the topic at hand. Whether it is in a class receiving a lecture, in a bar talking to a fisherman, at dinner arguing with a professor, or diving and conducting research, students are soon completely absorbed in the topic of marine resource management.

The aspect of having the professors live on-site greatly increased the interest in the program's topic for the students. Since they are with their teachers on a twenty-four-hour basis,

> *"The faculty brought a wealth of knowledge and personal experience."*

the professors became much more like enlightened friends than distant lecturers. Students said that they would talk about marine resource management all the time and anytime, and the professors were just as willing as they were.

Like most SFS programs, there aren't really typical days with set schedules. Generally, during the first half, there are two or three hour-long classes in the mornings, and the afternoons are dedicated to field work. Field work on South Caicos usually means collecting data via scuba diving or snorkeling, or a field trip. Students do not have to dive if they don't want to, but everyone we talked to said you were crazy if you didn't.

The evenings are free, but some are reserved for guest lecturers, presentations, or workshops, and a mandatory statistics class meets once a week (to brush up on analytical ability). Classes meet five days a week, and a field trip is usually planned on Saturdays.

The second half of the semester is really for the Directed Research projects, and students usually are given three to four weeks to dedicate their attention to them. Classes are still held, although only sporadically.

CASE STUDIES

Case Study #1: "What Can Be Done to Minimize Threats to Local Reefs?" The encroachment of development threatens the local ecosystems with pollution, boat traffic, overfishing, and tourism. Students hear from local environmental experts and members of the fishing industry, as well as receive hands-on experience in the field.

Case Study #2: "What Is a Sustainable Level of Lobster and Conch Harvesting?" These crustaceans are the main source of income for the island of South Caicos, and the decrease of their populations due to overfishing would hurt both humans and crustaceans alike. Students investigate methods of stock enhancement and the viability of catch restrictions and other controls. Field research again plays a large role in the examination of this topic.

Case Study #3: "What Is the Potential for Fin Fish Fisheries?" Considering the future of the fishing industry and the viability in sustainable crops of lobster and conch, this study looks at the alternatives in harvesting certain fish species. Through interviews with local fisherman and field research, students evaluate the potential for fin fish harvesting.

> *"The Case Study structure is the best way to learn."*

Case Study #4: "Tourism: Economic Salvation or Environmental Disaster?" The final module explores the issues of implementing tourism into the area, without endangering the marine ecology of the islands. In addition to field research, students hold a mock tourist development conference with the local tourist board and area businesses to determine the best ways to implement ecotourism.

WORKLOAD

This program keeps you busy. Classes are a solid hour, and most students take constant notes. In the afternoons, students conduct research that they know is vital for them to complete their DR. In the evenings, students try to complete all of the reading assigned, which is a considerable amount, or attend the statistics class.

Additionally, students are required to keep a field notebook, which is more of an observational diary than a scientific record.

> *"The tests are marathons."*

Nevertheless, most students work assiduously at compiling every new coral or organism they had seen that day in their notebook, which was checked and graded. For the socioeconomic class, students have four papers to complete, due at the end of each Case Study. Students must also prepare an exhibit for Sea Day, complete their DR papers (which can be upward of fifty pages), and take a four-hour exam at the end of every Case Study.

Small assignments are given out periodically, such as finding something wrong with the island's conservation plan, and coming up with a plan to fix it. Students are also expected to know every type of coral and fish in the waters surrounding South Caicos, and are tested on this knowledge.

DIRECTED RESEARCH

The Directed Research component starts out slowly and finally gives the entire program over to research for the last three to four weeks of the semester. Not all students had underwater-related topics, as some worked with the fishing industries, or used boats to do transects (a navigational technique used mainly for population counts) of larger species. Others, though, would dive daily. Topics related to the impact of tourism and the future of management of the local fishing industry. Projects included: *Designing an Underwater Snorkeling Trail to Lesson Tourist Impact on Reef Areas, Study on Repopulation of Queen Conch Colonies, Writing a User Guide to the Harbor for Tourists,* and *The Viability of a Fin Fish Industry on South Caicos.*

FIELD TRIPS

Every Saturday usually has a field trip scheduled. These are a combination of labs and cultural visits. The program may visit conservation problem sites such as the local dump or go and look at a local school to see how the education system is run on the island. Some field trips are

> *"SFS did above and beyond what they were supposed to."*

scheduled purely for pleasure, and students occasionally have the opportunity to camp out on uninhabited islands (where the professors are reputed to let their hair down as much as the students).

There is usually one weekend trip a semester. A typical destination is Grand Turk Island, where students get the chance not only to relax and see the sights, but also to soak in the culture and maybe even visit the marine biology museum. One semester the students were allowed onto a Greenpeace ship (due to SFS's conservation-minded reputation), anchored off the island.

FACILITIES

Facilities are completely adequate for the program, although students expressed the desire for more computers. The five they have are state of the art, with word processing as well as statistical software, but waiting to get to use one is commonplace. Library facilities at the center are limited, and there were occasions in the past when students could not find the materials they needed for their DR paper. There are five midsize motor boats for the program, although students are not allowed to pilot them due to liability reasons. There is a commercial air compressor for filling the center's tanks, and weights are also available. All other scuba gear, however, is the responsibility of the student. Students recommend bringing all of your own equipment, except for tanks which can be rented while down on the island.

> **COURSES (1995)**
>
> *Tropical Marine Ecology*
> *Principles of Resource*
>   *Management*
> *Environmental Policy and*
>   *Socioeconomic Values*
> *Directed Research*

Off the Track

Students have Sundays, many of the evenings, and a five-day break in the middle of the program for their own explorations. Here is what happened to some students of SFS's Marine Resource Management program:

Scuba diving was by far the most talked about activity for the program. Students eagerly related any and all diving stories to us, ranging from naming reefs to encounters with whales! A few people mentioned doing one particular "wall dive," which entails swimming adjacent to a wall of coral and not trying to go to the bottom. That would have been particularly hard, as they were swimming near the continental shelf and the bottom was thousands of feet below.

The local bars were frequented by professors and students alike, although hardly ever to drink if students wanted to be able to dive the next day. Instead, it was a way of winding down and getting to know the professors, and one student was amazed that she would blow off her work in order to meet her professor at the bar. It was also a great way to meet the locals and to fit in more with the community. Favorites included the Pool Bar, where you guessed it, people played pool, the Chicken Bar, where people ate chicken, the Little Blue Bar, and the Getaway Bar.

One student told us that her favorite dives were at dusk, when both the night and day creatures were out. This is one of the main feeding times as well, and she said that this is a prime opportunity to see the bigger fishes in action.

About half a mile down the beach sat an abandoned building called Highland House, which stands at the top of a cliff. Here daring souls would leap off, into the surf below. Just offshore, there was a maze of tunnels through the reef, accessible with a snorkel.

One semester almost all of the group went to the Dominican Republic for the five-day break. One group rented jeeps and merengued their way around the country. The other group reportedly went to almost every bar on the island and slept where they landed. Apparently, the trip to the "DR" has been done by students from the Caribbean program for years. This is no surprise as there is plenty to do, the country is clean, and the people are friendly. Most important, traveling there is cheap, with hotel rooms at about the equivalent of $5.

Advice and Warnings
from the Students

▶ $800 is a good amount of money to bring for personal expenses.

▶ "Definitely, definitely be certified for scuba beforehand."

▶ "Bring a laptop computer if you have one!"

▶ "Personally, I thought the books were a waste of money since we hardly used them."

▶ "Bring a wet suit, so you won't have to do more laundry, and a dive watch, which you use all of the time."

▶ "Don't bring any clothes you care about."

► "Bring a fan—a fan was key to have."

► "You should be able to subjugate your needs for the good of the group."

► "Bring more T-shirts than it says to."

The Best + The Worst

👍 The diving

👎 The courses occasionally overlapped.

👍 The Directed Research projects

👎 Not culturally immersive enough

👍 Hanging out with the professors

👎 "There wasn't a worst!"

👍 Learning so much about marine biology

👎 The group meetings

👍 The location

👎 Cockroaches in the room

👍 Knowing that your research will be put to use

👍 Naked dives

STUDIES IN SUSTAINABLE DEVELOPMENT

Meghan Kelley

LOCATION: Atena, Costa Rica

HOST SCHOOL: School for Field Studies

DESCRIPTION: A three-month study of sustainable development practices in Costa Rica

DURATION: Semester

COST: $10,970 (airfare to and from departure point not included)

FINANCIAL AID: Scholarships and interest-free loans available to those who qualify. Federal aid and Stafford loans are accepted.

PREREQUISITES: Applicants must have completed a college level course in Ecology, Environmental Studies, International Development, and Spanish before participating.

COURSE FULFILLMENT: Tropical Ecology, Resources and Sustainable Development, Field Research

NO. OF STUDENTS: 32   M/F RATIO: 3/7

HOUSING: On-site housing at SFS center and two-day homestay

COMPUTERS: Provided. Personal computers allowed and recommended.

CONTACT INFORMATION
Admissions Department
School for Field Studies
16 Broadway
Beverly, MA 01915
Phone: (508) 927-7777
Fax: (508) 927-5127
E-mail: sfshome@igc.apc.org
WWW: Not available

Overview

> *"Hands-on learning, the staff is awesome, and the subject matter is amazing."*

Costa Rica is famed for its natural wonders. Inside its borders lie cloud forests, rain forests, volcanoes, mountain plains, fantastic beaches, 6,000 plant species, 500 species of butterflies, and 800 bird species—all in a space the size of West Virginia. It's bordered on two sides by water—the green, hilly terrain seems to tilt from the Caribbean Sea in the east to the Pacific Ocean in the west.

Yet Costa Rica's natural resources are at a precarious point in time. Although an impressive 27 percent of its land has been set aside as protected areas, outside these areas deforestation rates are among the highest in the world. The struggle to preserve the country's beauty is coming into growing conflict with people's desire for First World–style prosperity, as well as an increasing need for productive agricultural land. SFS's Sustainable Development Studies program uses small communities as operational units and tries to develop sustainable management models that are socially, economically, and culturally feasible.

The center is located in Atenas county, in the small town of Barrio Los Angeles, about 40 kilometers northwest of San Jose. The center is in the typical SFS nature-oriented style—the

> *"If you go abroad for one semester in your life, it should be great—this is."*

main house is perched on a small cliff overlooking the farming valley below, volcanoes are visible in the distance, and there is even an open-air classroom where students can be distracted by the native birds playing in the trees. There is hardly any time for daydreaming, though—this is one of the most time-consuming programs we've encountered.

The days typically begin at 6:00 A.M. (to the crowing of the center's roosters), and there is

> *"If it hadn't been so intense, we would never have learned what we did."*

usually something to do until 9:00 P.M. (although there is a two-and-a-half-hour siesta every day). In addition to up to four lectures every day, students are spending a few days a week on field trips. This is, after all, SFS—one-third of the time is spent in the field, visiting such places as mangrove swamps, organic farms, and the Dole pineapple plantation. At the end of each Case Study, the program also takes a four-day trip to research areas like a biological preserve in a cloud forest. The last four weeks are dedicated to students' Directed Research projects.

For the first six weeks there is also a nonintensive Spanish class to beef up students' conversational skills. Students have one day off a week, and there is a five-day break in the middle of the program.

Environment

> *"We taught them how to recycle, and they taught us how to dance."*

Interestingly, most people who we interviewed for this program went to Costa Rica thinking it was going to be much more underdeveloped than it turned out to be. Students felt that Costa Rica was far along in the benefits of the Age of Technology, complete with an easy, comfortable, and affordable public transportation system, a busy yet friendly capital of San Jose, and a remarkably well-educated population. Add some stunning natural resources to this, and it's no wonder why students fall in love with Costa Rica.

However, it's not a complete paradise quite yet. It is still largely an agricultural-based economy, and most of the land that is not devoted to urban areas is for private farming. The standards of living are well below the U.S., and the per capita income is only $2,000 (as opposed to $16,000 in the U.S.).

As for the town Barrio Los Angeles, one student echoed everyone's comments perfectly—"I had visions of going down into this primitive village, but that's not it at all." The town, while very small, has everything you need, although not every brand. There are a few bars and small restaurants here, and an open-air market. For those who need more than a small town, San Jose is only a short, cheap (less than $1!) bus ride away. Students thought that the people of Costa Rica were the friendliest they had ever met, and no one felt unsafe walking the city streets.

Mixing with the people of Barrio Los Angeles is common, and, among other things, students usually form soccer teams to compete with the locals (they

> *"There is so much to learn, do, and see!"*

always get creamed). Soccer in Costa Rica, we're told, is third in national importance only to family and church. Dancing is also a national favorite, and many students take every opportunity to practice their new skills at merengue and samba. The traveling discotheques that roll into town are extremely popular—they're much like a circus, complete with rides, games, and, of course, dancing. Some people also love to go to the Saturday-night bingo game, which everyone in the program is always invited to.

The program visits Costa Rica in its two seasons—wet (fall semester) and dry (spring semester). Most people who went during the dry season thought that people who went during the wet season were nuts, and vice versa. Actually, both seasons sound pretty good to us.

During the dry season, expect brilliantly clear days with temperatures in the mid to upper 80's. Most people took advantage of the warm, clear nights to sleep in their hammocks out on the vista that overlooks the valley. The wet season is much like the dry, except that the temperatures are ten degrees cooler, and it evidently rains every day from three to five P.M. ("a warm hard rain that's perfect for playing in.") After the rainstorm, students swore there was always a gorgeous rainbow, and that the nights were beautiful, with only a few rainy ones.

COMMUNITY SERVICE

This is *the* most community-centered program we've encountered. SFS goes to great length, to be an active part of the small town they're located in. English classes, soccer games, BBQs, Earth Day fairs, community cleanups, and recycling programs are just a few of the projects that SFS organizes. As a result, the locals usually greet SFS students with open arms—much to the surprise of the students.

> *"You're there for such a short time, so why not do everything do can?"*

Neighbors and residents commonly invite students to dinner with them, friends are made in the local bars, and practically everyone wants to teach the new Americans how to merengue or samba. There is also a weekend homestay opportunity, which allows students to experience how Costa Ricans live firsthand. As an added bonus, all of these activities are extremely helpful in improving students' Spanish skills.

Housing

"I got stung by a scorpion—I wouldn't want to do that again."

Perched above mango, papaya, orange, lemon, and avocado farms, the center is in one of Costa Rica's largest valleys. It's based in the farming locale of Barrio Los Angeles for good reason—the topic of sustainable development can be studied right in their backyard. At "the end of the road" from the town, the center is comprised of a main house, a dormitory, a vista (patio), an open-air classroom, and even a pool.

The main house is evidently very nice, and it holds a well-stocked library, computer room, lab, kitchen, faculty housing, and living space where class can be held if the weather outside is uncooperative. The dormitory that students live in is actually a refurbished old chalk factory. There are five rooms that students share, all with bunk beds and mosquito netting. There are two shared bathrooms for men and women.

"You live with your professors as one cohesive unit."

There's no hot water, but there *is* a washing machine that students can use at their whim (a luxury for SFS programs), and plenty of electricity (another luxury). There are, however, lots of creepy crawly things (like frogs, iguanas, and scorpions), and those people who are a bit squeamish should think twice before applying. Also, the only telephone available is the one in town.

By far the most talked about aspect of the center is the vista, which not only offers a gorgeous view of the valley and the volcanoes beyond, but also has places for students to hang their hammocks (you can buy one very cheaply in town). One student discovered this early on, and made the mistake of telling everybody else about it—soon there were at least ten or twelve people sleeping out there every night. This is also the location for any BBQs that the students decide to hold.

There is also a small garden plot that is generally for Directed Research projects, and another plot with vegetables that the program keeps going year round. There is a 10:30 P.M. curfew for most nights, midnight for the night off. This rule is in effect for reasons of general safety, and for the fact that even one taxi coming back late will wake up all of the dogs in the neighborhood, who in turn will wake up all of the neighborhood with their barking.

FOOD

Costa Rican food is typically rather plain, but there is tons of fresh, succulent fruit available. Vegetarians will have no trouble here, as most of the meals are vegetarian anyway, and are only occasionally spiced up with locally raised meat or poultry. Most students described the food simply as "beans and rice, beans and rice, beans and rice," although they admitted it did taste good, and there was plenty of it. The program hires two cooks for most of the week, but students are responsible for their own meals during their day off.

Academics

"Free time? What's that?"

Everyone mentioned the rigorous schedule of the program. Past years' students had complained of a lack of academic rigor, and SFS has more than made up for their previous lapse. Almost every angle of sustainable development is looked at, from small organic farms, to cooperatives, to multinational corporations—examining not only which systems work, but also those that don't. To our surprise, no one really minded this pace, and most praised the academics and professors as being exemplary.

A typical day is as follows: students get up with the roosters at 6:00 A.M., have breakfast at 6:30, and have the first lecture from 7:30 to 9:30. On field trip days, the lecture is related to the site. Otherwise, there is a second lecture until lunchtime, at noon. Afternoons are generally pretty hot, so siestas are scheduled from 12:00 to 2:30 P.M. After this, the schedule involves either Spanish language study, a field exercise, or a lecture, until 4:30. The students then have a bit of free time until dinner at 6:00, with a lecture or presentation usually scheduled for 7:30 to 9:30. Some days, however, are spent entirely at a field site.

Add this schedule in with community projects and other work, and students are really busy. As one student said, "If you could find an hour or two to read or something, you felt really lucky." Students have one day off a week. The last four weeks of the program are dedicated to students' Directed Research projects.

CASE STUDIES

Case Study #1: "Do the current management and design of Costa Rica's protected areas effectively meet the goals and objectives of conversation?" In this first Case Study, students investigate the methods of Costa Rica's land management. With field trips to some of the country's protected areas, the group evaluates them against the requirements for sustaining key members of the ecosystems necessary for its collective health and survival.

> *"Costa Rica is far ahead of its neighbors in conservation, but well behind the U.S."*

Case Study #2: "How can agroecosystems promote sustainable management in Costa Rica's protected zones?" In this section, students employ field techniques to determine the quality of local land-use methods and choices, and to determine alternatives to the more conventional practices.

Case Study #3: "What are the impacts of foreign direct investment and sustainable entrepreneurial models?" Traveling to different ecological zones

> *"It's a field study approach to science."*

within Costa Rica, students examine several multinational companies, as well as grassroots businesses. This study focuses on ecological stability and the success of such operations, as well as their impact on the culture. Students also examine the environmental and economic factors involved.

WORKLOAD

The work required for this semester is no more difficult than other SFS program, it's just the pace of the program that makes it rigorous. Students have to make time for the reading that is expected of them, and many students who have a limited background in the areas of study may find themselves staying up late to review journal articles. There are papers and tests for each Case Study, so there is roughly one test and one paper every three weeks. As always, the directed research paper at the end is the crowning achievement, scholastically, for students.

DIRECTED RESEARCH

Although a few projects necessitate starting before the allotted time for DRs (i.e., planting a crop), most students do their projects solely in the last four weeks. Projects vary greatly, although most are conducted in and around Atenas. In the past, students have covered *The Demographics of Medicinal Plant Use, Equity in Land Tenure, Integrated Pest Management,* and *Pesticides and Their Use in Costa Rican Agriculture,* among others.

FIELD TRIPS

According to the students, one of the most remarkable aspects of this program is the range of ecosystems it visits. Since Costa Rica protects such a large amount of acreage from development, the program has the opportunity to do research in most of the ecosystems in the area. Students travel extensively throughout Costa Rica, exploring cloud forests, mountain plains, and mangroves, as well as other ecosystems in the transition between wet and dry forest climates. The program also visits business sites ranging from experimental mangrove charcoal operations, to women's cooperatives, to large-scale fruit production sites such as the Dole and Chiquita companies.

COURSES (1995)

Tropical Ecology and Sustainable Development
Sociopolitical Systems and Sustainable Development
Economic and Ethical Issues and Sustainable Development
Directed Research

FACILITIES

The facilities work for what students need. The library is well stocked with books and journal articles on all of the topics. The lab is reported to be a little skimpy but adequate. The worst reviews, however, are for the computers. They are a bit old, and there are only five of them. When papers are due, students must squeeze in every bit of time possible on them. One student would wake up at 4:00 A.M. just to be able to work on one. However, no one *really* complained about this, as the computers adequately provided for their needs. There are two vans that transport the program to all of the field sites.

The most talked about facility is the open-air classroom, which allows students the chance to be continually outside in the beautiful weather.

Off the Track

Although the schedule is packed most of the time, students do have one day off a week, a five-day break in the middle of the program, and, of course, many students elect to travel afterward. Here is what happened to some students of SFS's Costa Rica program:

Camping in the wet season is something Costa Ricans simply don't consider. So it is not surprising that a few students on one fall semester had to convince a ranger for a half hour that they really *did* want to go into the national park and camp. The students had the entire park to themselves, in, they insist, the only weather to truly see a rain forest. They were covered in mud, were sucked dry by mosquitoes, and loved every minute of it.

Traveling after the semester ends is a common adventure for students on this program. It's extremely cheap—hotels can cost around $3 a night, and meals (of beans and rice, of course) cost less than $1. Students are also located near some spectacular scenery, besides the beauty of Costa Rica—the rest of Central America, and even all of South America, is just a short trip away.

Of all the things to do in Costa Rica, one student recommended doing what he did—hike up the country's highest mountain. The trail leads hikers up through rain forest to the summit. There, at 12,000 feet, both the Caribbean Sea and the Pacific Ocean are visible on a clear day.

A group of students decided to go see the wonders of the Caribbean coast. Taking the bus from San Jose, they traveled to the eastern shore, where they camped out on black sand beaches, drank fresh coconut milk with rum, and went nude bodysurfing at midnight under a full moon.

Traveling along the coast, a pair of students befriended a few fishermen. They hung out by their boat, talking until dark, until one of their newfound friends invited them to his home. They jumped in the boat and traveled in complete darkness on the water, navigating by compass alone. They ended up in a tiny fishing village, where they feasted on the day's catch.

Advice and Warnings from the Students

▶ "Bring a raincoat."

▶ "People like to dress up more in Costa Rica, so bring one or two nice outfits."

▶ "Bring a laptop if you have one, but remember that if you travel afterward you have to lug it around!"

▶ $600 is a good amount of money to bring for personal expenses (*besides* traveling afterward).

▶ "Really brush up on your Spanish before you go—it helps so much."

▶ "Bring mosquito repellent."

▶ "Bring camping gear for traveling afterward."

▶ "A radio is key to have if you like music."

▶ "If you go in the wet season, bring warm-weather clothes that you don't care about."

▶ "Bring a Crazy Creek chair."

The Best + The Worst

👍 The community involvement

👎 The lack of free time

👍 The experiential learning

👎 Very tight living conditions

👍 The staff of SFS

👎 The computers

👍 The national parks and reserves

👎 The monotony of the food

👍 The content of the academics

👍 Sleeping out under the stars on the vista

👍 Learning to samba!

WILDLIFE ECOLOGY AND MANAGEMENT

Michelle Gadd

LOCATION: Outside Nairobi, Kenya

HOST SCHOOL: School for Field Studies

DESCRIPTION: A three-month intensive examination of the issues in Wildlife Management and Conservation

DURATION: Semester

COST: $10,970 (airfare to and from departure point not included)

FINANCIAL AID: Scholarships and interest-free loans available to those who qualify. Federal aid and Stafford loans are accepted.

PREREQUISITES: None

COURSE FULFILLMENT: Ecology, Wildlife Management and Policy, Field Research

NO. OF STUDENTS: 32   M/F RATIO: 3/7

HOUSING: On-site housing at SFS center

COMPUTERS: Provided (laptops). Personal computers allowed.

CONTACT INFORMATION
Admissions Department
School for Field Studies
16 Broadway
Beverly, MA 01915
Phone: (508) 927-7777
Fax: (508) 927-5127
E-mail: sfshome@igc.apc.org
WWW: Not available

Overview

"Come expecting to learn a lot, to see a lot, and to take a lot of pictures."

Where else can you have your class interrupted because a few eland gazelle are walking through campus? This actually happens at the Center for Wildlife Management Studies.

Kenya's wildlife is perhaps the most famous wildlife in the world. Students who grow up watching *National Geographic* specials dream of one day visiting the great Serengeti and seeing the astonishing variety of animals face to face—from zebras and antelopes to elephants and lions. Kenya has entranced writers like Hemingway and Markham, and movies such as *Out of Africa* have captured the imagination of millions.

However, Kenya has an increasing conflict of interests. With the largest population growth rate in Africa, Kenya's arid land is hard put to produce enough food. Land usable for agriculture is of tremendous importance, forcing massive relocation of Kenya's leading economic boon—the wildlife. SFS's Wildlife Ecology and Management program strives to develop scientifically and environmentally sound, and economically and culturally appropriate, plans for managing Kenyan wildlife.

Perhaps the most rustic of the SFS programs, students may wake up to see a giraffe calmly eating the thatch off their hut. The Center for Wildlife Management Studies is simply a main building, student and faculty bandas (traditional thatched-roof huts), outhouses, and an open-air shower. Set on the high plains in the middle of an eighty-one-square-kilometer experimental gaming ranch, animals are free to wander in and out of camp at their whim. Students are quite literally surrounded by what they are studying. Safety is not a problem, though—there are no predators on the ranch.

"It's the best thing I have ever done academically."

For the first half of the semester, the schedule is fairly fixed. Students have up to three seventy-five-minute-long lectures in the mornings, while the afternoons are reserved for Directed Research field work. Evenings usually are for catching up on assigned reading, but there are occasionally classes, guest lecturers, or presentations scheduled. The second half of the semester is devoted more to Directed Research, but classes are still held sporadically.

However, nearly a quarter of the time is spent out on field trips, visiting Kenya's famed game reserves. The program takes three one-week excursions to Amboseli, Maasai Mara, and Tsavo national parks. While students *are* being treated to incredible safaris, they have the added bonus of being there as students, not as tourists. Lectures continue

> *"You learn so much without realizing you're learning."*

while on safari, with a portable blackboard and the savanna as the classroom. Additional field trips to other conservation sites are taken, such as Lake Nakuru, and places of cultural interest, such as Maasai villages.

Students have one day off a week, and there is a week-long break in the middle of the program.

Environment

> *"I woke up several times at night to the roaring of lions."*

Students said that nearly every day a new animal would stroll through campus—usually during classes. Eland and Grant's gazelle, wildebeest, zebra, impala, and fringe-eared oryx all roam freely on the ranch. However, the most frequent visitors to the center were the gentle giraffes, coming to snack on the compound's acacia trees.

The center is on a ranch called Game Ranching Ltd., about an hour south of Nairobi. The ranch is experimenting with indigenous grazing animals as an alternative food source, which fits in nicely with the program's theme. The ranch not only provides the site for a few interesting field trips, but also some of the program's food (discussed later in the "Food" section, but you do get to eat most everything you see on safari).

The ranch, as well as the program, employs local Kenyans from several tribal groups, including the famous Maasai. Since the program has no official Swahili language component, students said that they learned the language by just hanging out with the employees, as well as getting one or two of them to teach an informal class. This is also the students' main opportunity to experience the culture of Kenya, as the ranch is fairly isolated.

As was mentioned before, students are *really* surrounded by what they are studying. They can wake up in traditional ban-

> *"It was better than I ever imagined."*

das and go jog on either the two-kilometer or five-kilometer path, stopping occasionally to watch a herd of wildebeest, or to avoid a giraffe. The landscape of the ranch has a bit of everything—the rolling savannas dotted with acacia trees, and the small clustering of shrubs and trees, merely referred to as "the bush." The days are hot, with temperatures usually in the high 80's, while the nights are cool enough to merit long pants and a sweater. Of course there is the African sky, the unique aspect of having days and nights nearly equal in length, and sunrises and sunsets of unbelievable beauty.

Students have one day off a week, and most used this day to go into Nairobi, only an hour away by Land Rover. Nairobi is Kenya's capital and largest city, and although it doesn't approach the magnitude of London or New York, it is certainly a bustling metropolis. There are plenty of distractions and ways to unwind for students, from restaurants to theaters to discos. Of course, there are the more practical things as well, such as banks, grocery stores, and post offices.

COMMUNITY SERVICE

This program has the least amount of community service of any SFS program, although we were tempted to say there was none at all. However, there are small projects such as experimenting with local groups in alternative energy sources (like solar energy). Students also have the chance to get to know the employees of the ranch rather well, either at weekly soccer matches or when just trying to learn Swahili. But this is not a very community-oriented program, which is understandable, as there isn't really a large community around them.

The best thing that SFS does on this program, clearly, is the actual research. The results from SFS's research could help not only the wildlife, but all of Kenya as well.

Housing

"SFS couldn't have picked a better spot to be in."

The center has little to offer in the way of conveniences—the bathrooms are outhouses, the housing is huts, the telephone works sporadically, and electricity is only a recent addition and is turned off at night to conserve power. This, however, is the charm of it, and students fondly remembered reading by their oil lamp, listening to the evening noises of Africa. They did, though, have to periodically brush beetles off their books.

Students are housed in bandas, which are traditional thatched-roof huts that hold four people. Inside are four beds, four drawers, four oil lamps, and nothing else. The design of the hut allows it to be cool during the day and warm at night. Rather than missing the comforts of western architecture, most students loved the huts.

> *"Shower day was a special day."*

The main building is of open-air design, and has a lecture hall, offices, library, reading room, kitchen, and a dining pavilion. There is also a sand volleyball court that is put to frequent use. The outhouses are nicer than regular African outhouses—at least the holes have porcelain seats. There is a "shower area," with a screen and a solar-heated bag of water attached to a pulley. If a shower is needed, a student merely has to fill the bag and hoist. Laundry facilities are nonexistent, and students soak their clothes, scrub, rinse, and then hang them out to dry.

> *"It turned out to be the adventure I thought it would be."*

While in the field, the program usually camps outside of the game reserve they are visiting. This is unusual in itself, as camping permits are extremely hard to come by. Most students agreed that this was one of the best parts of the trip—going to sleep and hearing the hyenas bark, or waking up to a lion's roar.

FOOD

Food at the center reflects the work done at the ranch, with a lot of meat in the menu. When the students aren't sampling gazelle, giraffe, or zebra ("Gazelle tastes too much like horse"), the menu usually has pasta, rice, and American standards like peanut butter and jelly. Although there is usually some kind of vegetarian option available to students, many of the vegetarians we interviewed opted to try the game meat in order to "get the whole experience." The program also tries to have as much fresh fruit and vegetables as possible, and many of the students mentioned the quality of the pineapples and avocados as "to die for."

There is a full-time cook employed at the center, but students are responsible for preparing dinner.

Academics

> *"It's not a safari tour—it's the hardest academic semester I've ever had."*

Although the program is not terribly "homework intensive," students are almost constantly in the field, participating in all manners of research. Whether it is during their Directed Research, a safari, a cultural visit to a Maasai village, or conducting a general experiment for SFS, the education on this program is truly hands-on. Add this to the fact that some students elect to sacrifice their days off to work on their DRs, and it shows that students are not only extremely involved in the program, but working hard.

During the first half of the semester, the days follow a pretty regular routine. The mornings are devoted to classes, while the afternoons are laid aside for field research. Most students can complete their research on site during these hours, although a few may be studying nocturnal life and must do their work at night. Interspersed throughout, however, are the week-long trips to the game reserves. Looked at as a whole, students are spending a few weeks at the center studying a particular topic, then traveling into the game parks to observe what they had learned about.

The last half of the semester is designated mainly for the DR projects, although classes continue at a lesser rate, as well as small field trips. Overall, evenings are usually free, but there are sometimes guest lecturers (while in the field, especially) or presentations scheduled. Guest lecturers include some of the top minds in wildlife management, ranging from wardens of national parks (who would be *impossible* to get to see through normal channels) to spokespeople for the World Wildlife Federation.

Classes meet six days a week at the center, and there are a few classes while in the field, as well.

CASE STUDIES

Case Study #1: "How Can Local Communities Live with Wildlife?" As an introduction to the area and the issues concerning wildlife management, this segment looks at the problems of converting public land to private use, and the encouragement of agricultural land usage. Students will conduct population counts and habitat assessment in order to determine the effects on animals as their natural habitat becomes reduced by development.

Case Study #2: "What Are the Most Viable Strategies for Managing Elephants?" In this study, students look at the management methods concerning elephants in the country's game reserves. Topics investigated include comparison of a "hands-off" approach to elephant management to population culling, as well as the issues surrounding the ivory ban and its repercussions on the local economies.

Case Study #3: "What Are the Impacts of Commercializing Wildlife?" Focusing on the concepts of game ranching, this segment looks at the inherent problems that face this idea for an indigenous, alternative food source. The reintroduction of native wildlife species as a food source has had a slow acceptance by the people of Kenya. Students study the tribal prohibitions of eating wild animals, as well as look at the management techniques of running a game ranch. The students investigate attitudes of local residents toward alternative foods, as well as looking at the benefits of eating game meat over more commonplace produce, such as beef and chicken.

WORKLOAD

Although there is little in the way of "normal university homework," students are certainly not goofing off. When they are not in class, they are out in the field, conducting their research. Up to five hours a day is spent in the field, and students receive incredible firsthand knowledge of how field research is conducted. During the evenings, students are studying and catching up on readings assigned for their classes. There are a few short cultural analysis essays due, and students must be able to identify all the animals in the area, and are tested on this knowledge. There are, of course, also major tests after each Case Study is completed. Meetings are held periodically so that students can present how their research is going, and keep the rest of the group informed.

DIRECTED RESEARCH

Almost from the beginning, students are researching their projects each afternoon. The research sites are typically at the ranch itself, as a wide variety of wildlife is present—except predators. Many of the projects focus on the aspects of commercialization of game animals, and methods of sustainable management. Past projects have also included research into *Giraffe Height and Its Relation to Feeding Habits, Nocturnal Spring Hares,* and the *Role of Scavenger Birds,* such as vultures.

FIELD TRIPS

Besides the three one-week field trips, there are small excursions taken throughout the semester. Past locations included Lake Nakuru, Kitengela Conservation Area, and sites of cultural interest, such as Maasai villages. Students also participate in a rural home-stay for a night while visiting a local tribal village.

FACILITIES

In keeping with the rustic theme of the program, there is little in the way of facilities. The library is small, but adequate for what students need to get done. Besides very recent journal and scientific articles, past Directed Research papers are also on file. The computers are laptops and there is a laser printer, but there is no separate computer room. Typical of SFS, students complained that while the com-

> **COURSES (1995)**
>
> *Techniques of Wildlife*
>   *Management*
> *Wildlife Ecology*
> *Environmental Policy and*
>   *Socioeconomic Values*
> *Directed Research*

puters were usually adequate, during "crunch time" a few more would have made things much easier.

Off the Track

With only one day off a week and a five-day break in the middle of the program, students have very little free time. However, they still found time to have their own adventures. Here's what happened to some students of SFS's Wildlife Management Studies program:

> *"I can't think of anything I'd change about it."*

By far, the safaris were the most talked about experiences of the program. Too many fascinating things happened to mention all of them, but how would you like to notice that while the professor is writing on the portable blackboard, a pride of lions had just moved to a tree one-half kilometer away? Or to be chased in your Land Rover by an angry bull elephant? Or to watch the hippos frolicking in the water, or to see a cheetah make a kill, or to shoo the baboons away from camp?

One intern was lent an African hawk eagle by the ranch's falconer for the semester, because of his interest in birds. This bird had been raised in captivity, and hand-fed its entire life. A student was talking to the intern and a friend about finding out if the bird knew instinctively how to hunt. The three of them went out at night—the intern driving, the friend with the eagle on his arm, and the student using a spotlight to find rabbits. A rabbit was spotted, and the bird took off immediately, flying right in the beam of light toward its first prey.

The roads in Kenya are really wild. Despite the fact that there are no speed limits or well-defined traffic laws, the roads themselves are in terrible shape. Added to this are the hundreds of buses that careen their way down through the country at top speed. One student told us about his bus trip to the coast during his semester break, where he shared the trip with about twenty Muslims. Apparently they were snacking on a root that has effects like amphetamines. "So there we were, *hauling* down the road in the middle of the night—with no headlights."

Wildlife was constantly walking through the campsite, and would do so at any time of the day, even at night. One student woke up in the middle of the night and stepped out of his banda to "go answer the call of nature." He was totally shocked when he walked right into the leg of a giraffe. The twenty-foot-tall animal looked down and regarded him for a moment, then resumed eating the leaves off a nearby tree.

While hitchhiking on their spring break, two students got a ride from a local man in a Land Cruiser. They hadn't gone a mile when the engine suddenly stopped. When they lifted the hood, they found that the battery cables had burned through. To remedy the situation, they drove down the road with one person sitting on the wheel well, holding the cables onto the battery terminals. Since the hood blocked the driver's view, the other student hung out the passenger side door, yelling to the driver, "Go left—no, go right!"

Advice and Warnings from the Students

▶ "Bring dark T-shirts, because white ones will be filthy all the time!"

▶ "Take every opportunity possible—don't wait for them to push you to do things!"

▶ "Bring sunscreen and iced tea mix!"

▶ $700 to $800 is a good amount of money to bring for personal expenses, including travel money.

▶ Although a typical visa issued for Kenya is six months, students reported having theirs cut in half by custom officials while entering the country. Effectively, this reduced their visa to three months, and they had to get new visas! Watch out and don't let the officials do this!

▶ "Take an intensive Swahili course before you go."

▶ "Try to find your own plane reservations—the group ticket is not necessarily the best way to go."

▶ "Bring a good camera—it's worth it."

The Best + The Worst

👍 The safaris

👎 Lack of communication with the main SFS office

👍 Sampling the game meat

👎 The academics are tough!

👍 Learning about wildlife management

👎 Lack of privacy

👍 The professors

👎 Lack of computer time

👍 Just being in Kenya

👍 The bandas!

ISLAND MANAGEMENT STUDIES

LOCATION: Ulimang, Babeldaub Island, Palau

HOST SCHOOL: The School for Field Studies

DESCRIPTION: A three-month study of Island Management problems and practices in Palau

DURATION: Semester

COST: $10,970 (Airfare to and from departure point not included. Snorkeling equipment not provided.)

FINANCIAL AID: Scholarships and interest-free loans available to those who qualify. Federal aid and Stafford loans are accepted.

PREREQUISITES: none—although scuba certification is suggested for trips during the midterm break

COURSE FULFILLMENT: Tropical Ecology, Resource Management and Policy, Field Research

NO. OF STUDENTS: 32   M/F RATIO: 3/7

HOUSING: On-site housing at SFS center

COMPUTERS: Provided. Personal computers not recommended.

CONTACT INFORMATION
Admissions Department
School for Field Studies
16 Broadway
Beverly, MA 01915
Phone: (508) 927-7777
Fax: (508) 927-5127
E-mail: sfshome@igc.apc.org
WWW: Not available

Overview

"It's wonderful! You're completely immersed in the topic and the culture."

When students tell people they just spent a semester studying in Palau, the most common reaction is, "Where?" Located 200 miles west of the Philippines and 200 miles north of New Guinea, it's no wonder the island nation of Palau is not high up on the recognition scale. It is, indeed, an isolated paradise—lush rain forests, pristine coral reefs, dense mangroves, and remote hamlets dot the 200 or so islands of Palau, which are inhabited by only 16,000 people.

However, this South Pacific island chain won't remain isolated for long—the country is at the start of a booming ecotourist trade. SFS's Center for Island Management Studies program studies the issues surrounding the economic development on the terrestrial and marine environments, and strives to help conserve the natural resources and ensure the fair distribution of the economic benefits to Palauans. The possible onslaught of tourism also brings other concerns—what to do about the limited availability of resources (food, fuel, etc.), and options for increased waste disposal.

"You learn something in class, and then go and look at it."

This is a young program, having had its first semester in the spring of 1995. However, it is an extraordinarily strong one regardless of its age, and SFS has the background and willingness to change and fix any problems that may arise. Indeed, most of the problems we heard of in our interviewing process had already been fixed by the time we talked to SFS. And, as past students said, "What other program does something like this?"

Located at the narrowest point on the main island of Babeldaob in the state of Ngaraard, the Center for Island Studies resides in the small village of Ulimang. The village is indeed small—SFS's presence doubles the population each term. However, the village soon becomes very much of a home away from home for students—with white sand beaches, turquoise waters, and extremely friendly and receptive villagers, it's not hard to see why.

The days start off delightfully—most students recall waking up to the Palauan national anthem being sung by the schoolchildren at the elementary school. The pace of the program is hardly lax, though—students typically receive three to four lectures a day, including two to three field trips a week to places such as breathtaking waterfalls and the farms around the capital city, Koror. The last four weeks are devoted to students' Directed Research projects. Students have one day off a week, and there is a week-long break in the middle of the program.

Environment

"It's the most beautiful place on earth."

There is a different pace to life in the South Pacific, and little to remind one of fax machines, cordless telephones, or traffic jams. On the small islands that are scattered throughout the coral reefs, the men travel out to sea to cast their nets, and the women tend the patches of

> *"Wherever you look it's green and blue and full of life."*

earth devoted to raising taro (a plant with an edible tuber root that is in wide use on Palau). Life here, for big-city Westerners, is deliciously simple.

Palau only received its independence in October 1994, and before that had seen a long line of occupation—from the Spanish in the 1500s, to the Japanese during World War I and II, and finally to the United States. The Japanese influence can be seen in Palauan homes—tatami mats are used for sleeping, and people must take their shoes off before entering. The islands still, however, retain their simple South Pacific airs.

Indeed, the island of Babeldaob has yet to have a road that connects all of the towns that dot the coastline (one is planned, and currently under construction). The standard way to get from town to town is by boat. The capital of Koror has perhaps five or six grocery stores, a few resorts, a variety of restaurants, a few nightclubs, and a population of about 12,000. But as one student said, "Compared to Ulimang, it's a bustling metropolis."

Ulimang, located twenty miles north of Koror, is small by practically any standard. The town holds little more than twenty homes, an elementary school, and a small store that sells handmade potato chips, soda, beer, and vodka. There are no telephones, except for one that is kept for emergencies only, and mail arrives about once a week with the boat that goes to the market in Koror. The town is not completely rustic, though—there is a generator that supplies power from 6:00 P.M. to 6:00 A.M. (so many of the homes have TVs and stereos), and there are even a few flush toilets.

By far the most talked about aspect of the environment, though, is the water. An offshore reef leaves a turquoise lagoon that rings the entire island, and protects miles of coral reef in water that is sometimes no more than ten feet deep, and as warm as bath water. The waters around Palau hold 625 species of coral, 1,400 species of fish, and everything else you would want to see, including sea turtles, sea grass (the only ocean sea grass in the world), giant clams, manta rays, dugongs, and sharks.

> *"I wanted to go someplace remote where I could make a difference."*

COMMUNITY SERVICE

We would be hard pressed to find another semester abroad program so integrated into its environment. Students told us stories of how warmly they were welcomed into the local culture; how curious, friendly, and open the villagers were. Pickup games of volleyball, soccer, and basketball are common everyday, and SFS occasionally holds bonfires (to the bemusement of the villagers, who wonder when the food is going to show up). Students also sometimes go fishing with the villagers, even though there's a joke going around that "whenever an American steps on a boat, the fish go away."

> *"It's just as much an experiment for the town as it is for the students."*

In terms of community service, we found that the students did more on their own than with SFS—students in the past even organized an English class for the elementary children (English is spoken by most Palauans), and movie nights. Past SFS projects include painting trash cans with the elementary school children and placing them around the village to encourage proper trash disposal.

> *"We were the kids' best friends for four months."*

Housing

> *"There are no nightlights, no street lamps, the bathroom is an outhouse, and you shower in cold water—you'll love it."*

When the research was done for this book, the housing for Palau was still being worked out. The previous semester had been located right in the middle of town—but students and SFS felt that both their impact on the village, and the fact that they were always "in the spotlight," made things a bit uncomfortable. Being almost completely immersed in the village can have a downside as well, as a few students occasionally felt as if they were "living in a fishbowl." SFS was in the process of constructing four rustic cabins as student accommodations. The cabins were planned to be a few hundred yards from the village, close to the water, surrounded by coconut groves, and built with porches. Eight students will live in each cabin, and share bunk beds. SFS is also planning on having rechargeable solar packs, so the computers and fans can be run during the day. Like the other SFS programs, toilet facilities are outhouses, and showers are cold water only.

Regardless of the setup, students will enjoy waking up and being a short walk away from the village, white sand beaches, and clear waters.

FOOD

Life on an island has many relaxing advantages, but one of the biggest drawbacks is the limited variety of food. Most of the food in Ulimang must be shipped in from Koror. As a result, many of the meals revolve around dry and canned goods, and what the market in Koror has available (things like finger bananas, papaya, and breadfruit are common). Meals also are centered around fish, but that's actually a nice bonus—it's *completely* fresh, practically right out of the sea and onto your plate. As one student said, "I had fish once I got back in the States, and I said, 'This isn't fish!'"

Students cook all of their own meals except for once a week, and everyone is assigned to a "Cook Crew" shift that prepares all of the meals that day. Once a week, however, women from the village take turns providing for the group. This meal is a favorite of students, as the meals are usually excellent and give a real sampling of the local fare. It is also yet one more opportunity for the group to mix with the villagers.

Academics

"You're living what you're learning."

Studying complex social, economic, and environmental issues on an isolated South Pacific island may seem to be an oxymoron. There is the inherent danger of Pacific Paralysis—the state attained when you are less than willing to fully commit yourself academically, and instead go for a swim or laze on the beach. The nature of the program, however, demands intensity, as students are constantly surrounded by the topic at hand. Whether it is in class receiving a lecture, on the beach talking to a fisherman, at dinner arguing with a professor, or snorkeling and conducting research, students are soon immersed in the topic of island management.

Although there are no typical days, students generally are up by 7:00 A.M., attend two lectures in the morning, have a lecture or field work in the afternoon, and then another lecture in the evening. The days are indeed filled—students have only a few hours free each day, as well as a few hours at night (there is a national midnight curfew).

"Through daily living experiences and the academics, the learning was amazing."

To our surprise, guest lecturers are common and of excellent quality—we had figured that on a small island lecturers are hard to find. But the entire nation of Palau seems excited by SFS's presence—lecturers may include high government officials, leading scientists (such as experts on giant clams), leaders of conservation efforts, farmers, and managers of resorts, just to name a few. One student said, "We probably could have had the president visit, Palau is so impressed with us."

Students attend class six days a week, except for the last four weeks, which are devoted to the Directed Research projects.

CASE STUDIES

Case Study #1: "Is tourism, in comparison with other economic development options, a viable alternative for the economic development of Ngaraard State?" In this segment, students investigate the integration of ecotourism and resort development in the island chain. The group travels to fully developed sites, as well as prospective ones. The students evaluate the best means for tourists to access the areas, and determine the possible impact on the environment.

Case Study #2: "How can the marine resources of Ngaraard State be managed in a sustainable manner?" This study assesses the status of the Palauan fishing industry, and determines its ability to maintain the strict sense of conservation that has preserved the ecosystem for generations. The students investigate methods of fish harvesting and the technology it uses, evaluating its effectiveness against its sustainability and its impact on the tourist trade.

Case Study #3: "How can farmers in the Ngaraard State increase productivity and profitability in harmony with the environment and society?" In this final segment, students investigate potential markets for exporting Palauan crops. Students evaluate

Palau as a farming environment, and determine alternate crops to taro production, which is too labor-intensive for its market value.

WORKLOAD

The case studies are the centerpiece of the academic program, and the general workload revolves around them with comprehensive tests at the end of each segment. As for day-to-day work, students have a good deal of reading—mainly photocopied articles, textbook selections, and journals. Students are also expected to. be able to recognize and name local plants, trees, coral, and fish species, often including the Latin classification in addition to both its English and Palauan name.

DIRECTED RESEARCH

The program's youth is especially evident in the Directed Research projects—students have little or no previous work on which to base their research. However, that has an advantage as well—students feel like they are creating the direction in which future SFS semesters will go. The Directed Research right now leans toward conservation, resource management, and ecology, as well as the role that Palau will play in tourism and how it will manage a yearly increase of visitors. Past projects include the role of seabirds in coastal ecology, studies of the population of giant clams (Palau is home to seven of the eight known species), and land-use rights of women who produce taro. Students also investigated the attitude of Palauans toward development.

FIELD TRIPS

The theme of the program is Island Management, so obviously students are taken all over the Palauan island chain. There are two to three trips a week, and one "big trip" at the end of each case study. The program visits possible tourist sites, resorts, fisheries, and farms. Favorite trips include a spectacular waterfall that is reached by hiking through jungle for an hour, and a beautiful atoll located north of the main island. Students should be prepared to do *a lot* of snorkeling (scuba is not an option on the field trips).

FACILITIES

The facilities in Ulimang are relatively untried, as the program is fairly new, and there isn't the same impressive file history from past participants' field work that other SFS programs have. The equipment available is standard for SFS centers, with a few computers, some reference textbooks, and a limited amount of lab equipment. Students did mention struggling to find more time to use the computers, but also conceded that they weren't needed all that much.

The fact that electricity is available only from six to six also cuts down on use time. An interesting side effect when the computers are used is that it interferes with Ulimang's TV reception!

The classroom the program uses is a room in the elementary school, and this room also holds the lab equipment, TV and VCR, computers, and library. There is a truck ("Grover") and a boat ("Gimpy") dedicated for use by the program, although students said Gimpy is in constant repair (hence its name).

COURSES (1995)

*Tropical Ecology and Sustainable
  Development*
*Principles of Resource
  Management*
*Environmental Policy and
  Socioeconomic Values*
Directed Research

Off the Track

Students have Sundays, many of the evenings, and a five-day break in the middle of the program for their own explorations. Here is what happened to some students of SFS' Island Management program:

Predating any intrusion by the European powers, Palau actually had a flourishing civilization. There is evidence of this in the ancient stone paths that wind through the jungle. The paths were so meticulously kept that they still connect the villages around Ulimang, although a few of them simply end abruptly. Students would walk along these and explore, or even jog on them for a bit of exercise in a completely surreal setting.

Most students mentioned the people of Ulimang when recalling memorable times in Palau. Students were welcomed into the village literally with open arms—the entire village showed up when SFS landed, and the children had made leis to put around the necks of the students. For their departure, there was a nighttime celebration of their new friendship, complete with dances that the children made up in their honor.

The waters of Palau are amazing for diving or snorkeling. Incredible visibility, warm temperatures, and an abundant, untouched environment make exploring the undersea world a must. Most students mentioned swimming with sea turtles, a few were close to black-tipped reef sharks, and nearly everyone saw manta rays.

One group of women camped on one of the Rock Islands, a group of small islands to the south of Koror, during their semester break. They were grilling some fish they had caught when they realized that their island had been overrun with rats, some of which attacked their dinner—even as it cooked. Their boat driver luckily stopped by with some fresh unicorn fish he had just caught, and they started to cook them. Much to his horror they filleted them—evidently in Palau the head and intestines are considered the best part.

The children of Palau taught students as much as they taught them. One youngster invited a student to go crabbing during a full moon, when the mangrove crabs come out. He taught her the proper way to catch a crab, without getting pinched. For those taking notes—push down on its shell to keep its legs pinned, then pick it up from behind.

Advice and Warnings from the Students

▶ "Bring good snorkeling equipment! It's great to have."

▶ "Bring Crazy Creek chairs, Tevas, and Umbro shorts (so you don't have to wash them as much)."

▶ "Bring a cookbook—you're cooking all the time."

▶ $600 to $800 is a good amount to bring for personal expenses ($300 more is recommended for those who want to scuba during their semester break).

▶ "Get certified for scuba before you go! This is the best place for diving."

▶ "Don't bring leather—it doesn't do so well in the sun, salt, and humidity."

▶ "Bring lots of sunscreen and film. It's almost double the price in Koror."

▶ "A thermarest, mosquito netting, and mosquito repellent are great to have."

▶ "Be patient—the attitude in Palau is 'Time is Meaningless.'"

▶ "Bring a good pair of running shoes if you like to run."

The Best + The Worst

👍 The kids

👎 It's a new program—so things are still being worked out.

👍 Snorkeling

👎 The mosquitoes

👍 The field trip to the waterfall

👎 Leaving

👍 The content of the academics

👎 Being stuck in a classroom when there's so much to see outside

👍 Palau

👍 The variety of life around the island

👍 The stars at night

St. Olaf College

General Description

> *"From peasants to government officials, St. Olaf introduced us to everybody."*

In the semester abroad world, the college of St. Olaf continues to impress us. Any organization that has students attending their school simply *because* of their abroad programs is worth a second, or even a third, look. St. Olaf has a reputation for offering first-class abroad programs, a reputation they live up to. They have been in the semester abroad business for about three decades now—and it shows. Not only are their fifty-plus programs some of the most organized we have seen, but the in-country contacts they have established over the years astound us—from Zen masters to members of the Thai royal family—encompassing some of the elite of the academic world.

The scope of programs Olaf has to offer is impressive, and it would seem that the only thing they have in common is the Olaf name, and with it an almost guaranteed well-run, interesting program. There's everything from studying biology in South India to traveling to nine countries around the globe studying sociocultural developments.

The three programs we have chosen to review—Global Semester, Term in the Middle East, and Term in Asia—do share many facets. To avoid repetition, we will discuss shared aspects of the St. Olaf programs. (Some information will be repeated, however.)

Orientation

There is an orientation weekend for all Olaf programs three months before the semesters even begin. Students get inundated with any information they may need to know for the five months of their program—health concerns, social mores, packing advice, and traveling tips are just a few of the many issues addressed at this forum. Past trip leaders relate their experiences and any wisdom they gained in hindsight. Students from the previous semester show up as well, full of stories and advice for the new participants.

The famous "Blue Book" is also handed out here. This book is an incredibly useful cache of information, and it is revised each year by participants who have just returned from overseas. In it are descriptions of the cities and towns students will be visiting, information on topics ranging from AIDS to jet lag, and advice from the students on everything from what to bring to great things to do and see once they're there.

Academics

The programs share a few things academically. Both the Global and Asia programs stay in Hong Kong and attend classes at the Chinese University at Hong Kong. Also, the Global and Middle East programs both stay in Cairo and attend classes at the American University in Cairo (although not at the same time). These will all be covered in the individual program reviews.

All of the programs, however, share the format of having their individual field supervisors teach one class. This is the only class that runs throughout the entire semester, from country to country, and therefore has the most unifying and comparative format of all the courses offered. We heard nothing but praise for these classes, and we attribute that to Olaf's screening process for the faculty. Class topics are usually broad, encompassing ideas that can be compared between many countries, like art and architecture, religion, philosophy, political science, etc.

The field supervisor's class is truly a class without boundaries, as it not only meets at scheduled times, but its discussions and lectures spill over into field trips, tours, or even over dinner. Journals, projects, and/or small tests are the norm for the workload. Although it's not written into the syllabus, this class usually becomes the place for comparing and contrasting the countries visited, as well as discussing and relating individual and group experiences.

FACULTY

Each group is accompanied by a St. Olaf faculty member who serves as the field supervisor, and one person who serves as assistant field supervisor. The two are selected eighteen months before the program departure, in order to allow ample time for orientation and preparation. From all student accounts, St. Olaf has an excellent screening process, and the field supervisors generally end up being enthusiastic, knowledgeable, and sensitive to group concerns.

COMMITTEES

One of the major factors that makes the group dynamics an integral part of the St. Olaf programs are the "committees" formed to make the program run smoothly. Each program creates its own committees, but there are some fairly common ones. For example, the travel committee's job is to ensure that luggage gets to where it is going, and that the transportation is in order. The health committee not only covers the health aspects of the Olaf students themselves (keeping the first-aid kit in order, for example), but also investigates the health issues of the countries with visits to health organizations and offices. Other include the communications committee, which not only supervises correspondence with the program office back at St. Olaf, but also creates group letters to the students' parents.

The group discusses their committee activities at least once per country, twice during longer stays. These meetings are often called "Story Time" by the students, as people generally just end up telling tales of their adventures. However, we see the committees as an excellent way for students to manage and share their experiences, as well as giving them all an added share in the responsibilities of the group.

GLOBAL SEMESTER

LOCATION: Global

HOST SCHOOL: St. Olaf College

DESCRIPTION: A five-month academic tour of nine countries examining the sociocultural developments in the nonwestern world

DURATION: Semester

COST: $13,450 (airfare from Chicago included)

FINANCIAL AID: Federal grants and scholarships may be used. Aid directly from St. Olaf is available to full-time St. Olaf students only.

PREREQUISITES: None

COURSE FULFILLMENT: History, Political Science, Art History, Religion

NO. OF STUDENTS: 28   M/F RATIO: 5/8

HOUSING: Hotels, hostels, and university dormitories

COMPUTERS: Not provided. Personal computers not suggested or needed.

CONTACT INFORMATION
Karen Jenkins
Director
St. Olaf College
1520 St. Olaf Avenue
Northfield, MN 55057
Phone: (507) 646-3069
Fax: (507) 646-3789
E-mail: Not available
WWW: http://www.stolaf.edu/stolaf/student/off-campus/global

244

Overview

"Nine countries, five months, and a thousand stories."

To travel around the world is a dream many people have, but one which few ever have the chance of realizing. St. Olaf College's Global Semester gives students this opportunity, and does it in style. Instead of taking students on a five-month whirlwind tourist trip, the program stops in four out of the nine countries it visits for an entire month. Here, solid academics, world-renowned professors, and incredible field trips combine to make the semester memorable in more ways than one.

Traveling once each year from late August until late January, the Global Semester takes twenty-five to thirty students around the world to study sociocultural developments in the nonwestern world. The itinerary starts off in Switzerland, and from there everyone travels to Greece, Israel, Egypt, India, Nepal, Hong Kong, China, South Korea, and Hawaii. The program stays for a month in Egypt, India, Hong Kong, and South Korea, while staying for six to ten days in the other countries.

Students take one course during each of the month-long country stays—Egyptian history in Egypt, Religion in India, Chinese Art in Hong Kong, and Sociology in South Korea. In addition, the field supervisor's course runs throughout the entire semester. Comments from the students on the lectures ranged from "fantastic" to simply "very good," and the professors throughout the program received unanimous praise.

"I'd recommend this program for every U.S. citizen."

However, this is not merely dry and dusty book learning. In most circumstances, the students go on field trips to see the very things they were studying just hours before. In general, it was the field trips that stood out in people's minds—visiting the Taj Mahal, the pyramids, the Gaza Strip, and Tiananmen Square, simply to name a few. As one student said, "We actually knew what we were looking at—its history, what it meant to the people who built it, etc. It wasn't just like, 'Oh, another temple.' "

Most of the days and nights can be jam-packed with group activities, but students have weekends off in a few of the countries, a week-long break in India, and the time in Nepal is basically free.

Environment

"You live what you learn."

Students on the Global Semester attempt the seemingly impossible—that is, not to be tourists. While traveling through countries, cities, and sites, the students try to remember that each place is a class in itself. It's not uncommon for students on Global to take extensive notes as a tour

> *"You were a student past the point of the average tourist."*

guide leads them—to the astonishment of the tour guides. (How many tourists do that?)

The program passes through an incredible array of environments, all of them rich and exciting, and deserving of the many travel books that have been written about them. The pace of the program *can* get a bit hectic, at times, and it can also be exhausting. As one student said, "We were going to see something nearly every day. Sometimes it felt much too rushed." Very briefly, we'll touch upon each place the program visits, just to give a general idea of what to expect:

Nestled in the Alps, **Geneva** is the first stop of the program, where the group stays for a week. With crooked streets and amazing architecture, it is perhaps one of the most pristine examples of European architecture—untouched by the ravages of the wars of this century. There are plenty of sights to see, such as visiting the Old Town with all its shops, parks, and even a carnival if it's in town. Students can take a day trip into France via gondola, or, of course, go hiking in the mountains. There are cafés on almost every street where you can spend the day people-watching over a cup of java or a beer, as well as tons of restaurants and clubs.

The schedule in **Greece** is at the field supervisor's discretion. Typically staying for about a week, the program visits sites that reflect the field supervisor's course. For example, one year's class that studied art—in particular, architecture—visited Mycenae, the Parthenon, and the temple of Poseidon. Since it really is the first "travel destination," it is a good starting point for the group to get to know one another and to test out their traveling legs.

The program then flies across the Aegean Sea to **Israel,** where students stay right in the middle of the Old City in Jerusalem. Students told us of how nearly every major sight in the city was within a short walk of their hostel. In Jerusalem, you will feel the ancient pulse of the three religions that continue to battle for control of this region. Muslim, Jewish, and Christian influences fill the city with domed centers of worship, remnants of holy architecture, and the vivid images of prophets, kings, and faith.

However, even the St. Olaf literature warns students that they won't have time to see everything. There are, of course, sites that students should not miss. The Western Wall (also known as the Wailing Wall), the Dome of the Rock, and the Church of the Holy Sepulchre are all highly recommended by past students. There are also excursions on the program schedules that are just as amazing, including a trip to a Palestinian refugee camp in the Gaza Strip—something ordinary tourists have no chance of seeing. Here, students can experience firsthand the political turmoil that has affected this region for the latter half of the century.

Egypt is the first "big stop," and the program stays in busy downtown Cairo (pop. 10,000,000) for about a month. Centered right in the middle of the city, students have the chance to get completely immersed in the culture and flavor of Cairo. Other than filling your head with images of Cleopatra, King Tut, and Nefertiti, you can fill your pockets and your stomach with exotic Egyptian offerings as well. There are street vendors and huge markets offering jewelry, perfumes, and food, although some cuisine is only for those with a *really* brave stomach. Prices are amazingly low for the treasures you find and haggling is the norm.

The field trips are some of the best offered—with visits to sites such as Luxor, the Valley of the Kings, and, most important on everyone's list, the pyramids. On the downside, however, attitudes toward women seemingly haven't changed since the 1700s. Women should keep a cool head when the comments and marriage proposals start flying, and traveling with a male friend is highly recommended. This remains true for the time in India as well.

India is a study in contrasts for the program. Students stay in Bombay for the first week, where the heat, human suffering, pollution, and simply the crush of the 12,500,000 people in the city will overwhelm even the most seasoned traveler. Bombay is also the Hollywood of India, although not as glitzy, and there are new movies to see practically every day.

"Now I feel like I can conquer anything that gets in my path."

The next three weeks, however, are spent thirty miles outside Bangalore, near the small town of Whitefield. It is a very rural setting, with green grass, banana trees, and dirt roads making it almost idyllic. The villagers you will meet know the program well, and invitations into homes are common. The students respond in kind, as most years they threw the locals a talent show, and/or a Halloween party. Most students loved this segment, as it's very relaxed and peaceful, and it provides the opportunity to reflect upon previous countries and experiences, not to mention India itself.

There are also a few days in New Delhi before going to Nepal, a city much like Bombay, except a bit smaller, calmer, and less polluted. Some past semesters have traveled to Agra for a day to visit the Taj Mahal as well.

Nepal is a breath of fresh air for the program, after being in the hot and humid climates of India and Egypt. Most students compared the weather to a cool autumn day at home. The program stays in Katmandu, a fascinating city filled with Westerners seeking spiritual enlightenment from the mountains, or just die-hard trekkers. The Nepalese people are very friendly and open to foreigners, and there are tons of interesting sites to see. However, as the week in Nepal is free time for students, most opt to go on treks.

Trekking in Nepal is a wonderful opportunity, as students can hike through impressive passes (16,000 to 18,000 feet high!), terraced farms, and rural villages. The scenery, we are told, is incredible, and a few students even boasted of finding Shangri-La. If it's a clear day, Mt. Everest can be seen in the distance. Students warn to go easy, however, as altitude sickness is a very real possibility.

Affectionately called the "City of Neon," **Hong Kong** is all hustle and bustle. Possessing one of the finest harbors in the world, it is also arguably the most Western non-Western site the program visits. Everyone here appears to own a cellular phone, and they talk on them while walking to the many restaurants, bars, jazz clubs, and electronics stores that dot the city. The lights of Nathan Road make Times Square look subdued, and there is a great public transportation system.

However, you will notice the Asian influence in the modern skyscrapers that are put up with bamboo scaffolding, the temples scattered throughout the city, and all the families that live on the houseboats in Aberdeen Harbor. The islands surrounding Hong Kong provide for a good day of escape from the city, with hikes through forests to monasteries, or old opium-smuggling sites. Of course, a day hike up Victoria Peak is a must.

The ten days in **China,** however, may seem like a visit to another world. Not only is it *much* more nonwestern than Hong Kong, but it is also a lot colder as well—time to break out the gloves and hats. Students should be prepared to be *constantly* stared at by the Chinese, as western visitors are still a novelty. Everything will seem more subdued and restrained, and students may find the fact that nearly all of their time is scheduled very frustrating.

> *"It was the best semester you could do without going to the moon."*

However, even the scheduled experiences that students have while here—like visiting the Great Wall, walking through Tiananmen Square, and visiting the Forbidden City—will be incredible. Students even have a chance to visit a Chinese university, although great strides are taken by the Chinese government to keep the program away from any unauthorized contact with the actual students there. The program visits Beijing and Shanghai.

Finally, the program stays a month in **South Korea.** The 1996 Global Semester will be the first Olaf trip to do so, as previous years had visited Japan during this segment. The primary reason for switching, St. Olaf tells us, is to base the program in a more solid academic setting, where they have stronger cultural and academic contacts. It's also, we feel, an incredible place to spend a month.

The program stays in Seoul, the capital of South Korea, with a population of about 16,000,000. The site of the summer Olympics in 1992, it is a fascinating place to study—a modern city that has roots dating back to 2333 B.C. Prepare to be *very* cold, as the average temperature in winter is 23°. Also prepare for the shock of being almost a complete minority—as there are only 30,000 resident foreigners in the country, it is almost a completely homogenous society. Finally, simply be ready to experience a culture that few American tourists venture near.

Housing

> *"I would go running in the morning, and feel like I was in the Jungle Book."*

While traveling around the world, you can stay in some really crummy places along the way. Fortunately, the St. Olaf programs have been running for years, and the students gain full benefit of the wisdom of those who have gone before them. The people of the countries also begin to know St. Olaf—you may see an Olaf banner hanging in a tailor's shop in India, or be welcomed wholeheartedly by a manager of a hostel in Nepal. The housing on Global Semester ranges from good to excellent—we only heard of one dump. Here is a lowdown on where you stay throughout:

Geneva: The program resides at the John Knox Center, a guest house within the U.N. compound itself. Students are housed in doubles (much like hotel doubles), and the center is close to all group activity sites.

Greece: Throughout the week of travel, the program stays in average hotels.

Israel: Once in Jerusalem, the program stays at the Ecce Homo convent, right in the downtown area of the Old City. The Global Semester has been coming to this location for years, and is also used by other Olaf programs. The accommodations are cozy and comfortable (shared rooms, shared bath—the usual hostel fare), and meals are served family style in the dining area. Most students find refuge in the lounge, where they can hang out and read, study, or decompress.

Egypt: Traveling to Egypt by bus, the program stops briefly at Mt. Sinai. The lodging is at St. Catherine's monastery, which got the worst reviews of the program. The only reason to stay here is for a sunrise hike up Mt. Sinai, a field trip the students felt was well worth the dingy accommodations.

When the program reaches Cairo, students stay at the Cosmopolitan Hotel, which is within walking distance of the American University of Cairo, the site for classes. Students share doubles, and there are breakfasts offered in the morning. The hotel was described as average, but with a lot more character than a Holiday Inn. It is done up in a 1920s art deco style, and it even has bellhops! Students enjoyed being so close to everything downtown and appreciated the fact that they were able to walk to the university.

> *"You will definitely form some 'Cry and Die' friendships."*

India: The first week is spent in Bombay, where the program is housed at the Methodist Home. This is basically a youth hostel connected with the church, and students stay in doubles. Here, students are provided with breakfast, afternoon tea, and dinner.

For the last three weeks, the program stays at the Ecumenical Christian Centre (ECC), a short stroll away from the rural town of Whitefield. Students each get a single (!), complete with their own bathroom. There is no hot water (although you can get a bucket of it if you really want), and the toilets are Asian-style. ("The cleanest squatters I've ever seen!") Students are fed perhaps a bit too much, as there are five meals a day—breakfast, tea, lunch, tea, and dinner. Almost everyone described the ECC as beautiful, green, and peaceful, and they got so used to the monkeys that roam everywhere that they began to think of them as being squirrels.

Two to five days are also spent in New Delhi, depending on the field supervisor's interest in the area. The group resides in hotels here, before flying off to Nepal.

Nepal: Although the time in Nepal is the students' own, the first and last nights are paid for by the program at a local hotel. This is usually an average hotel, and this is done simply to make sure the group is in one place. As for the rest of the time, extremely cheap and clean housing can be found almost anywhere. Prices for "communal living" hostels can be as low as 25 cents a night, but normal hotels can be found for $5 to $13.

Hong Kong: Get ready to feel pampered. Compared to the other accommodations, the housing in Hong Kong is a palace. Students are housed in the guest house of the Chinese University, with fabulous views of Hong Kong Harbor. Students are put in doubles, and each room has air-conditioning, a television, a bathroom (with hot water!), a small kitchenette, and daily maid service. There is a full kitchen with a microwave and water boiler on every floor. Although the guest house is locked at midnight, the reception desk next door is open twenty-four hours and can let all of the night owls in. A stipend is provided for meals in Hong Kong.

China: East China Normal University in Shanghai arranges the tours for the group, and also handles all of the accommodations. Foreigners are usually put up in special designated hotels, and these are also where the program stays. Rooms are typically doubles with their own bathroom, and also televisions, although you more than likely won't understand a word. However, central heating is still a mystery in China, so even nights in a good hotel can wind up being very cold.

In Shanghai, the group also has the opportunity to stay in the guest house of the East China Normal University (where student contact is still very limited). All meals are provided for by ECNU.

South Korea: Since this is the first time the program visits South Korea, all of the arrangements had not been finalized by the time this book went to press. However, a few details were available. The program will stay at Yonsei University, on the west side of Seoul, in visitor dormitories. Students share double rooms, with all amenities usually found in dormitories.

Academics

"This program combines depth and breadth—the perfect combination of the academic and the experiential."

It may appear at first that with all of the traveling, the academic portion of the program is lost in the wash. This is decidedly not so, as there are classes in each of the month-long country stays, and past students reported that they were some of the more interesting ones in their college career.

Remember that these are intensive classes for a month at a time, supplemented by field trips in the afternoons. There is also the field supervisor's course that runs throughout the length of the program. Take this into account with the fact that students have to catch up on reading for classes at night, and write a paper and/or take a test at the end of the month-stay, and the academics seem to become more and more of a factor. In fact, it can be said that the students are *never* away from the academics.

However, so as not to get the wrong impression, the academics are easier than at U.S. universities. With only one paper and test on average per class, it

"Everything about this program was spectacular."

can *seem* ridiculously easy. The academics are, though, usually more impressive as well. The professors are the top names in their fields, and students have the opportunity to go out and actually *see* what they are learning about. Anyone would leap at the opportunity to study Chinese art, and then go on a tour throughout China, viewing the actual masterpieces they had studied.

EGYPT

Everyone had something to say about the Egyptian History course in Egypt. John Swanson, the professor, is reportedly no less an Egyptian god than the ones he lectures about. According to the students, he is *the* expert on Egyptology in the country, and can lecture for hours on the subject. His packets of information on field sites will give students far more knowledge than any tour guide could ever dream of. Students didn't even mind attending his lectures for two to three hours every day, and, remarkably, they seemed to absorb a great deal of it.

Classes are held at the American University in Cairo, right down the street from where the students are living for the month. The workload consists of a few short papers, as well as two tests based on lectures and reading assignments. The group visits a sizable selection of sites around Cairo, and even makes a trip up the Nile to visit the city of Luxor, as well as to see the Valley of the Kings and the Temple of Karnak.

INDIA

The bulk of the time in India is spent, as was previously mentioned, at the Ecumenical Christian Centre, and this is also where daily lectures are held. Set up as a conference center, the program uses its facilities fully—it's not merely for Olaf students. The program receives a variety of lectures from both resident faculty of the Ecumenical Centre and guest lecturers. Students found that the topics were interesting, but they said it seemed unfocused on a central theme. They also mentioned that they were not graded on the lecture material directly, but were held more responsible for the information in the text readings and handouts they were given.

There are no excursions taken by the group while staying at the ECC. However, a two-day excursion to Mysore is followed by a four-day travel break. Past destinations included areas such as Goa, Sri Lanka, Kodaikanal, and Madras.

HONG KONG

The Chinese Art course is held at the Chinese University of Hong Kong. Class meets five days a week, for most of the mornings. Those afternoons not scheduled for trips to museums or galleries are free. There are comparatively few field trips here, as the sites in Hong Kong can hardly compare with the ten days in China.

The professors here were thought to be excellent and extremely knowledgeable. Topics ranged all over the spectrum of Chinese Art, although none of the students thought the course was unfocused. As one said, "Who would have thought I'd be able to recognize a Shang from a Tang dynasty vase just by looking at it?" Past students recommend taking especially good notes on all lectures and slide shows.

True to the spirit of the city, the university is very well-equipped. Students will appreciate its excellent library (there are actually books in English!), as well as the university's own impressive art gallery. The workload is average, with a few short exams, and one five-to-ten-page paper.

SOUTH KOREA

Although the Korean segment has not had its first semester yet, the subject matter is sociology and the intricacies of Korean society. Topics include, but are not limited to, urbanization in Korea, women's issues, and the effects of postwar democracy. The program plans to use the facilities of Yonsei University in Seoul, and will include various field trips throughout the South Korean peninsula.

> **COURSES (1995)**
>
> *Egyptian History*
> *Religions of India*
> *Art in China*
> *Korean Sociology*

Off the Track

Although the semester can seem jam-packed with activities, students actually have some weekends, and two weeks during the semester, for their own explorations. Here's what happened to some students on the St. Olaf Global Semester:

Goa, on the west coast of India, was the destination for a few students during their travel break. They were staying in a bungalow on the beach, and were watching a sunset when they heard the music of Bob Marley coming from somewhere. They went to investigate and soon befriended some fishermen who were playing the music. In the days that followed, the fishermen took them out to see dolphins, taught them how to haul in their nets, and showed them a different place to stay on the beach for only $5!

Some students spent their week break working at Ashra Daan, Mother Teresa's shelter for the sick and dying in Bombay. The best description someone gave us of this week was that it was the best and worst week of her life.

Lost in Cairo, one student came across a group of young men playing soccer. Since he was an avid player back home, he wandered over to see if he could get in the game. The young Egyptians welcomed him in and, after the game was over, related in broken English that they had pickup games here every afternoon. He returned often, sometimes bringing other people from the program as well.

Trying to get to Sri Lanka, two students were stuck at the airline terminal since they knew no Hindi or even if they could buy a ticket. The first person they approached looked at them oddly and said, "I will help you." At some point their newfound friend pulled out a picture. They recognized it as Sai Baba, a prominent religious figure in Whitefield, whom many consider to be God incarnate. As a result, he took them in a rickshaw, bought them tickets, brought them to the gate, and was even waiting for them when they returned.

Walking with an Egyptian friend in Cairo, one student saw a sight he couldn't believe. On a small motorcycle an entire family drove past—father, mother, daughter, and son. He pointed and exclaimed, "That's not possible!" His Egyptian friend smiled and said, "In Egypt, it's possible."

Advice and Warnings from the Students

► "Don't bring many clothes—you can buy what you need everywhere the program goes, and cheaply."

► "The noise and pollution of Egypt will get to you—tough it out."

► "This trip is not for those who need to be independent all the time."

► $2,000 to $2,500 is a good amount of money to bring for personal expenses.

► "Read the blue book—it has everything you need to know."

► "Get to know the staff of the places you are staying at in Israel and India."

► "The more involved you get in this program, the better it gets."

The Best + The Worst

👍 Going around the world in five months!

👎 Egyptian food

👍 Getting off the track, away from the group, and on your own

👎 Getting altitude sickness in Nepal!

👍 Hong Kong

👎 Too little time in Israel

👍 Going around with a great group

👎 Group tours

👍 The professors!

👎 Reverse culture shock

👍 The time in Egypt

👍 India—and how the language and culture change from town to town

TERM
IN
ASIA

LOCATION: Indonesia, Hong Kong, China, Thailand

HOST SCHOOL: St. Olaf College

DESCRIPTION: A five-month academic study of three Asian cultures. The itinerary includes a three-month stay in Thailand.

DURATION: Semester

COST: $10,525

FINANCIAL AID: Federal grants and scholarships may be used. Aid directly from St. Olaf is available to full-time St. Olaf students only.

PREREQUISITES: None

COURSE FULFILLMENT: History, Political Science, Art History, Religion

NO. OF STUDENTS: 25 to 30   M/F RATIO: 5/7

HOUSING: Hotels, hostels, and a homestay in Thailand

COMPUTERS: Not provided. Personal computers not suggested or needed.

CONTACT INFORMATION
Karen Jenkins
Director
St. Olaf College
1520 St. Olaf Avenue
Northfield, MN 55057
Phone: (507) 646-3069
Fax: (507) 646-3789
E-mail: Not available
WWW: Not available

Overview

"What was the best? It was all the best."

The continent of Asia, for the typical American, heralds a vision of languages, rituals, and customs that seem totally alien and inaccessible. Some still think in terms of rice paddies and pointy straw hats, while others cringe at the economic might of Hong Kong and Tokyo. Few, however, have an understanding of even one of the many cultures it holds. The St. Olaf Term in Asia program sets out to examine a few of these cultures, and offers students a semester complete with incredible field trips, excellent faculty, intensive language study, and a lengthy homestay.

From late August to January each year, St. Olaf takes twenty to twenty-five students through four Asian countries, combining cross-cultural experiences with in-depth academic study. Touching upon the cultures of Indonesia, Hong Kong, China, and Thailand, this program gives students the incredible opportunity for travel in the East, while also providing the time and background to experience each country beyond the "picture-in-front-of-national-monuments" mentality.

Beginning on the island of Sumatra in Indonesia, the program visits Medan, Siantar, and Tuk-Tuk for a week. This time is, really, an orientation period to the program structure, the culture of Indonesia, and the group itself. Students attend functions arranged through Nommensen University, take excursions to nearby areas, and attend the field supervisor's class.

> *"Traveling with twenty people through Asia—I made lifelong friends."*

The next stop is Hong Kong, where the program stays at the Chinese University of Hong Kong for a month. The arts of China is the academic focus, with mornings devoted to lectures, and afternoons scheduled for field trips or the field supervisor's course.

The program then travels to the People's Republic of China, allowing students to see some of the actual works of art they had been studying in Hong Kong. The two weeks here are some of the toughest, as the program visits up to five cities, and most of the tour guides feel compelled to create sunrise-to-after-sunset schedules. This time is also some of the most rewarding—St. Olaf students will be honored guests in most places they visit in China, and the college has enough pull to get them to sites often off-limits to tourists.

The last and longest stop is Thailand, where the program remains in the northern city of Chiang Mai for three months. The first two weeks are devoted to intensive Thai language study, while the remaining time is divided among the History of Southeast Asia, Thai Society, and a continuation of Thai language study.

> *"One-quarter of the time you're a tourist—the rest you're totally immersed."*

Students are placed in homestay families here for two and a half months, an aspect of the semester that got rave reviews. The program moves to Bangkok for four days at the end of the semester, where students hand in any work due and attend a few final meetings.

There is not much free time in the program until it reaches Thailand, where students have a few weekends off (others are devoted to field trips). Past students have traveled extensively at the end of the semester to places like Vietnam and Malaysia, taking advantage of being in a part of the world they may never have the chance to visit again.

Environment

> *"I was always thinking, 'I can't believe I'm actually here!' "*

Students will quickly realize that all Asian cities are not the same—not all of them are as modern as Hong Kong, nor are they as simple and untouched by the West as the Thai hill tribe villages the program typically visits. Although, sadly, the western influence can show up even in the nuclear family of Thailand, where one student's homestay brothers were named "Pepsi" and "Cola"!

Western influences aside, though, each country the program visits will be incredibly *unlike* the United States. Although each deserves their own book of description, we'll touch upon them briefly to give you an idea of what to expect:

Indonesia is perhaps the most stereotypical Asian country, at least in the students' views, that the program visits. Hot, humid, poor, and incredibly inexpensive, students were a little surprised at their first destination. Coming directly from air-conditioning, the Simpsons, and Dairy Queen, the "third worldness" of the country comes as a major culture shock. Although only in Sumatra for a week, students get an impression of the friendly and polite people of the region, as they are treated practically as ambassadors from the U.S. by local authorities and university heads.

Affectionately called the "City of Neon," **Hong Kong** is all hustle and bustle. With one of the finest harbors in the world, it is also arguably the most Western non-Western site the program visits. Everyone here appears to own a cellular phone, and they talk on them while walking to the many restaurants, bars, jazz clubs, and electronics stores that dot the city. The lights of Nathan Road make Times Square look subdued, and there is a wonderfully modern public transportation system.

However, you will notice the Asian influence in the way modern skyscrapers that are put up with bamboo scaffolding, the temples scattered throughout the city, and all the families that live on the houseboats in Aberdeen harbor. The islands surrounding Hong Kong provide for a good day of escape from the city, with hikes through forests to monasteries, or old opium-smuggling sites. Of course, a day hike up Victoria Peak is a must.

The two weeks in **China,** however, may seem like a visit to another world. Not only is it *much* more nonwestern than Hong Kong, but it is also a lot colder as well—time to break out the jackets. Students should be prepared to be *constantly* stared at by the Chinese, as western visitors are still a novelty. ("We were like a zoo attraction!") Everything will seem more subdued and restrained, and students may find the fact that nearly all of their time is scheduled very frustrating.

However, even the scheduled experiences that students can

> *"Nothing compares to the square (Tiananmen)!"*

have while here—like visiting the Great Wall, walking through Tiananmen Square, and visiting the Forbidden City—will be incredible. Students even have a chance to visit a Chinese university, although great strides are taken by the Chinese government to keep the program away from any unauthorized contact with the actual students there. Although the schedule of cities is subject to the field supervisor's discretion, probable visits include Guilin, Nanjing, Xian, Shanghai, and Beijing.

Of course, the main environment is **Thailand,** and, in particular, the city of Chiang Mai. Based on flat plains surrounded by mountains, it is the second largest city in Thailand, although compared to Bangkok it's minuscule (about 350,000 people). Chiang Mai has recently experienced a huge expansion growth, though, and is dealing with the many problems this has caused. Cars, motorcycles, and *siilaas* (public transportation—big pickup trucks with benches in them) fight for space down dangerous and polluted streets. The traffic cops need to wear gas masks.

On the flip side, however, there are Buddhist temples on practically every street, and the weather in the winter is extremely nice (85°, sunny, and dry). Although the city can have the charm of a more provincial town, with its small shops and popular night market, it is also a modern one, with Burger Kings, state-of-the-art medical centers, and universities. Favorite activities included playing soccer, doing aerobics ("Mostly men, and Thais don't seem to sweat!"), swimming, or just hanging out with new Thai friends met at the university.

Chiang Mai is also a lovely place to walk around, and, once off the streets, students described it as a remarkably tranquil place. The city was best described by one student who said, "The people had the friendly quality of a small town, but it had all the hustle and bustle of a big city."

Housing

"They accepted me into their family from Day One."

The housing throughout the program is excellent. St. Olaf has been doing the program so long that it has almost all of the wrinkles ironed out. Ranging from hotels to homestays, throughout the entire five months we heard of only one hotel that received bad reviews.

Sumatra: The hotel that the program stays at in Medan for the first days got the worst reviews of the entire trip. Students compared it to a bad Motel 6 in the U.S., but admitted that it was actually pretty good by Indonesian standards. The big plus of the housing here is that the hotel is right across from Nommensen University, where students attend lectures. Students share double rooms, and all meals are provided by the university.

Hong Kong: Get ready to feel pampered. Compared to the other accommodations, the housing in Hong Kong is a palace. Students are housed in the guest house of the Chinese University, with fabulous views of Hong Kong Harbor. Students are put in doubles, and each room has air-conditioning, a television, a bathroom (with hot water!), a small kitchenette, and daily maid service. There is a full kitchen with a microwave and water boiler on every floor. Although the guest house is locked at midnight, the

"Everything was fantastic. I couldn't recommend this program more."

reception desk next door is open twenty-four hours and can let all of the night owls in. A stipend is provided for two meals a day in Hong Kong, while breakfast is served at the guest house.

China: East China Normal University in Shanghai arranges the tours for the group and also handles all of the accommodations. Foreigners are usually put up in special, designated hotels, and these are also where the program stays. Rooms are typically doubles with their own bathroom, and also televisions, although you more than likely won't understand a word. However, central heating is still a mystery in China, so even nights in a good hotel can wind up being very cold.

In Shanghai, the group also has the opportunity to stay in the guest house of the East China Normal University (where student contact is still very limited). All meals are provided for by ECNU.

Thailand: For the first two weeks, students stay at a guest house near Chiang Mai University. This is primarily intended as decompression time after the hectic traveling in China, as well as affording a "no distractions" time for intensive language classes. The staff at the guest house is friendly and quite helpful and encourage students to use their Thai language skills as they gain them.

The students are then placed in homestays. Everyone we talked to said that this was one of the best parts of the program for them. Students are placed separately with families around the city—some are located right downtown, while others are up to a half-hour ride away by *siilaa* (no one seemed to mind this in the past). The families are all either middle- or upper-class families, although interpretations of these social strata can be a little misleading. Some students stayed with families that choose not to have hot water (in a place where the winters can be 85° and sunny, why bother?), although that seems to be where the limits on creature comforts end. "They have everything we have—electricity, running water, bathrooms, TV."

The homestays are important to the experience in Thailand. As one student said, "My family really integrated me into their life. We went on little family outings together all the time when I wasn't doing things with Olaf." Students were also grateful for the amount of cultural insight and fine-tuning of their Thai language skills they receive while at home (although one student said her "family activity" at night was to watch TV). Students agreed that Chiang Mai University does a commendable job finding good families and matching them with students. Breakfast and dinner are provided by the homestay family, and lunch is taken at the university.

> *"This program let me find out what it was like to be Thai."*

Academics

"The lecturers ruined my life—I was constantly thinking about everything they said."

As with all the St. Olaf programs, students are actively learning outside of the classroom as well as in it. Field trips emphasize and illustrate what students had been studying only weeks, sometimes only hours, before. There are, however, only two countries where students attend structured classes—Hong Kong and Thailand.

The month in Hong Kong is filled with program activities. Mornings are devoted to lectures for the Arts of China course, while the afternoons are reserved for the field supervisor's class and field trips to museums and art galleries. There may be an occasional weekend off, but don't count on it. Field trips are usually scheduled on the weekends, to the outer islands and the New Territories.

The time in Thailand, however, is structured more like a regular university semester back in the States. Students take four classes—Southeast Asian History, Thai Language, Thai Society, and the Field Supervisor's course. Each class meets two or three times a week, while the weekends are

> *"There's not a thing I would change about the program."*

mostly free. The field trips are no longer daily; rather, they are scheduled as weekend trips throughout the three-month stay.

The workload is comparable to universities in the States, albeit a little easier. However, students insist that they came back knowing far more than they ever retained from a college course, and the entire trip *can* get very intense academic-wise. When in college did anyone ever have the knowledge or confidence to debate the origins and exact nature of museum pieces? The language proficiency that students come back with *alone* is impressive.

HONG KONG

The Chinese Art course is held at the Chinese University of Hong Kong. Class meets five days a week, for most of the mornings. Those afternoons not scheduled for the field supervisor's course, or for trips to museums and galleries are free. Although there are field trips here, there are comparatively few, as the sites in Hong Kong can hardly compare with the ten days in China. Trips to see the Great Wall, the Forbidden City, the famous terra-cotta warriors, numerous state museums, hidden Catholic churches, and Tiananmen Square are just a few of the sites past semesters have visited while in China.

The professors in Hong Kong were thought to be excellent and extremely knowledgeable. Topics ranged all over the spectrum of Chinese Art, although none of the students thought the course was unfocused. As one said, "Who would have thought I'd be able to recognize a Shang from a Tang dynasty vase just by looking at it?" Past students recommend taking especially good notes on all lectures and slide shows.

True to the spirit of the city, the university is very well-equipped. Students will appreciate its excellent library (there are actually books in English!), as well as the university's own impressive art gallery. The workload is average, with a few short exams, and one five-to-ten-page paper.

THAILAND

Though the academics in Chiang Mai are the most "scholastic" of the program, they run at a much more relaxed pace. The program starts out with language-intensive classes every afternoon for five hours during the first two weeks, but slows down after this to only meeting twice a week, for an hour each day. The other courses during these three months are all held either two or three times a week.

Students are at the university all day—with classes in the mornings and afternoons. The professors all got good to excellent reviews, and all seem to have a very knowledgeable grasp of their subject. One is even related to the royal family of Thailand! Students are expected to be respectful of their professors, and the dress code is dark pants for men, dark colored skirts for women, and white shirts.

Students said that the workload was average, with readings, papers, and tests typical of university classes. However, most mentioned that their professors tried to make their classes more demanding than they had time for. Consequently, many students end up being behind in the required reading for the semester that St. Olaf assigns. The facilities of Chiang Mai University are excellent, and students have access to a very good library, a post office, bookstore, and bank—all on campus (the campus is *very* large). There is very limited computer and E-mail access.

The most successful segment of the time in Thailand is the language study. Students felt that the rigorous pace of the course at the beginning, combined with the requirements of a homestay environment, made for great leaps in fluency. "I met up with my parents in Bangkok," recalled one student, "and I stopped a woman on the street and asked directions. My mother looked at me astonished, and I only then realized that I had carried the whole conversation in Thai without knowing it."

While there are not as many field trips in Thailand compared with China, they are perhaps a little more involving. Two field trips in particular stand out in students' minds as extraordinary. One is a weekend stay at a hill tribe village near Chiang Mai. Students are placed with families who truly have no modern conveniences—electricity, running water, etc. While there, students help with whatever the family does—working (farming, growing coffee, etc.), cooking, and truly experiencing Thai rural life. The other is a weekend spent at a Buddhist temple, where students live the life of Buddhist monks. They get up at 5:00 A.M., meditate, chant, and help the members beg for alms around the city (they themselves aren't allowed to beg as they haven't taken any vows).

> COURSES (1995)
>
> *The Arts of China*
> *Southeast Asian History*
> *Thai Language*
> *Thai Society*
> *Field Supervisor's Course*

Off the Track

Students have weekends off in Thailand and occasionally in Hong Kong, and most participants travel at the end of the semester. Here is what happened to some students on their own:

Most students we talked to volunteered at something called the New Life Center in Chiang Mai. This is a center for prostitutes who want to escape from the brothels and need a place to go where people can help them. Students all called it an incredible experience to have—while it was only a few days a week for them, it was a lifetime for the people they were helping.

The Toast Man was a popular personality during the students' stay in Hong Kong. During breakfast there was one waiter whose sole responsibility was to serve toast—two slices per person only. The students on the trip were amused by the fact that he was easily offended if they asked for more, or, heaven forbid, served themselves. The Toast Man lives forever.

Traveling at the end of the semester is common, as students take advantage of their location to get to some places they may never have the chance to go again. One pair of students went to Vietnam, and made their way from Hanoi to Saigon. Still other students traveled to Malaysia, while a few managed to get into Burma. Many also opted to decompress with a few days on the beautiful beaches of southern Thailand.

Gift-giving is highly symbolic in Thailand. One student became friends with his neighbor, who lived in a house on bamboo stilts and had practically nothing. He said goodbye and gave her some T-shirts to remember him by, and was astonished when she seemed reluctant to take them. His Thai mother explained that by accepting them, the woman felt as if she had to give something in return. The woman stopped by soon after that and gave the student an old, worn ring—probably the only piece of jewelry she owned.

In Changzhou, China, the group took a ferry ride six hours upriver to a small town. Once there, some students rented bicycles and biked far into the country. They were amazed at the geology of the region—the land is flat as a tabletop with rice paddies dotting it, interrupted every now and then by mountains jutting straight up. They were even more amazed to realize that this was the landscape they had seen in some of the Chinese paintings they had studied while in Hong Kong.

Advice and Warnings from the Students

▶ "Watch out for pickpockets in Thailand!"

▶ "Don't just hang out with people from Olaf, mix with the Thais."

▶ "Thai is tonal—it's easy to confuse the word 'mother' with 'horse'—so be careful."

▶ $1,500 to $2,000 is a good amount of money to bring for personal expenses.

▶ "Bring a Walkman with a recorder—both for music and correspondence."

▶ "If it tastes good, don't ask what it is."

▶ "Hang with your Thai families—it can make the trip so great!"

The Best + The Worst

👍 The homestays

👎 Pollution in Chiang Mai

👍 The hill tribe visits

👎 No real contact with students in Hong Kong

👍 The field trips in general

👎 The culture shock in Indonesia

👍 Learning Thai

👎 Trying to learn Thai

👍 China

👍 The art class in China

TERM
IN THE
MIDDLE
EAST

LOCATION: Morocco, Turkey, Israel, Egypt

HOST SCHOOL: St. Olaf College

DESCRIPTION: A five-month examination of the cultural and political achievements and problems of four Middle Eastern nations

DURATION: Semester

COST: $11,975

FINANCIAL AID: Federal grants and scholarships may be used. Aid directly from St. Olaf is available to full-time St. Olaf students only.

PREREQUISITES: None

COURSE FULFILLMENT: History, Political Science, Art History, Religion

NO. OF STUDENTS: 25 to 30   M/F RATIO: 5/8

HOUSING: Hotels, hostels, and university dormitories

COMPUTERS: Not provided. Personal computers not suggested or needed.

CONTACT INFORMATION
Karen Jenkins
Director
St. Olaf College
1520 St. Olaf Avenue
Northfield, MN 55057
Phone: (507) 646-3069
Fax: (507) 646-3789
E-mail: Not available
WWW: http://www.stolaf.edu/stolaf/student/off-
    campus/mideast

Overview

*"Every day you wake up, and it's one of the most
exciting days of your life."*

"I would walk down the street and have tea with an Egyptian store owner that I knew. Or sit down with a Palestinian and ask what he thought about the Israel/Palestine conflict, and then ask my Israeli friends the same thing. Or I'd talk with a Moroccan student in a café. I learned by experiencing."

Every September through January, St. Olaf's Term in the Middle East program exposes twenty-five to thirty students to the cultural achievements, diverse peoples, and incredible problems of four countries in the Middle East—Turkey, Morocco, Egypt, and Israel. Staying for five weeks in each country, entailing a month of intensive study and a week of touring, St. Olaf gives students an excellent introduction to perhaps the most complicated region on earth. Impressive field trips, solid academics, and excellent professors combine to make this an extraordinary semester.

Beginning in Turkey, in the city of Istanbul, students work out of Bogazici University. Here, they study the complex problems and goals of the political institutions of the Middle East. An ancient city with architecture and influences from the Romans, Greeks, and Turks, Istanbul is a joy to explore.

Traveling next to the opposite end of the Mediterranean, the program moves to the city of Marrakech, in Morocco. Based out of Cadi Ayyad University, students examine the sociology of the region, attending class in the morning and then marching off to sites in and around the city for field trips in the afternoons. "This is a culture very far removed from ours," one student said, while describing the circuslike streets of Marrakech, complete with snake charmers and monkeys.

The city of Cairo, Egypt, is the next stop for the program. Students have the chance to learn from one of the world's top Egyptologists here, as they attend class and study Egyptian history at the American University in Cairo. The field trips in Egypt are some of the more impressive, as the pyramids, Luxor, and the Valley of the Kings are all just bus rides away.

The last stop of the program is Jerusalem, Israel. Students spend what is perhaps the most intense time of the trip right in the middle of the Old City. Examining Judaism, Christianity, and Islam, students are as immersed as they could be in the topic—a leisurely walk brings them to sites like the Western (Wailing) Wall, the Church of the Holy Sepulchre, and the Dome of the Rock.

Although there is not a tremendous amount of free time, the program *does* tour through each country for a week—allowing students the opportunity to concentrate simply on seeing some of the sites they had been studying only weeks before.

Environment

"If you're a poli-sci or philosophy major, this is the place to go."

Although technically in the same region (the Middle East), the four countries the program visits are extremely different cultures. They may share certain aspects, but their differences far outweigh their similarities. Because students are in each country for five weeks, they can actually start to *know* a country, rather than just take pictures from tour bus windows.

The countries deserve far more description than a few paragraphs, but, very briefly, we'll touch upon a few aspects of each to give you an idea of what to expect:

Turkey for many will be a pleasant surprise. Wipe away visions from the movie *Midnight Express*—Istanbul is a pleasantly modern city with an Arabic flavor to it. Domed mosques and minarets loom over the city, while the Aegean Sea sparkles right off the coast. With a population of 6,750,000, it's a crowded city, and traffic clogs the streets. "They have a game over there," one student told us, "where they see how many people they can fit on a city bus." Because of the traffic, the city is also fairly polluted. The city dates as far back as 660 B.C., and it has since been occupied or under siege by the Greeks, Romans, Turks, British, Arabs, French, and Bulgarians.

Because of its rich history, students will delight in exploring the many sites around Istanbul, including Hagia Sophia and the Blue Mosque. Many of our interviewees mentioned the pleasant, easygoing attitude of the people in the city, who always seemed willing to lend a hand if they were lost. Being a large, modern city, it also has plenty of attractions at night—from small cafés to glitzy nightclubs. The field trips and week of touring are impressive, as the program visits sites on the Aegean, Mediterranean, and Black seas. Students see too many fantastic Roman and Greek ruins to count. As a few said, "The best part of Greece is in Turkey."

Morocco will be the first major culture shock for participants. It is the most "non-Western" of the countries the program visits. Beautifully situated at the foot of the Atlas Mountains, Marrakech has twisting streets, extensive gardens, a sultan's palace (now a museum), and the famous Koutoubya mosque. A walk through the dusty streets of Marrakech will lead students past snake charmers, magicians, small vendors, dentists' booths, antiques dealers, and men with trained monkeys. One student called the city "a carnival that starts at dusk."

However, almost all the students mentioned that they ran out of things to do by the second week, as it's a small city compared to the others, (pop. 1,500,000), and stores and cafés

> *"It can get very tiring emotionally, physically, spiritually."*

close early. Many found the city to be a little *too* conservative, and could only truly relax when they could change into shorts and sit by the hotel pool. Women in particular mentioned having a difficult time here, and strongly recommended never going out alone. This remains true for Cairo as well, and to a lesser extent Israel and Istanbul.

Field trips and the week of touring include visits to Berber villages, Fez, Casablanca (where they look at the famed waters), and the Atlas Mountains.

Egypt is the next stop, and the program stays in busy downtown Cairo (pop. 10,000,000) for about a month. Living right in the middle of the city, students have the chance to get completely immersed in the culture and flavor of Cairo. Other than filling your head with images of Cleopatra, King Tut, and Nefertiti, you can fill your pockets and your stomach with exotic Egyptian offerings as well. There are street vendors and huge markets offering jewelry, perfumes, and food, although some cuisine is only for those with a *really* brave stomach. Prices are amazingly low for the treasures you find and haggling is the norm. Cairo is also fairly polluted, and students may encounter sinus problems associated with smog until they get used to it.

The field trips are some of the best offered—with visits to sites such as Luxor, the Valley of the Kings, and, most important on everyone's list, the pyramids at Giza.

The program then travels across the desert to **Israel,** where students stay in the middle of the Old City, in Jerusalem. Students told us of how nearly every major sight in the city was within a short walk of their hostel. In Jerusalem, you will feel the ancient pulse of the three religions that continue to battle for control of this region. Muslim, Jewish, and Christian influences fill the city with domed centers of worship, remnants of holy architecture, and the vivid images of prophets, kings, and faith.

There are also excursions the program schedules that are just as amazing, including a trip to a Palestinian refugee camp in the Gaza Strip, something ordinary tourists have no chance of seeing. Here, students can experience firsthand the political turmoil that has affected this region for the latter half of the century.

Housing

"The hostel really felt like a home."

Although the idea of living in the Middle East can conjure up visions of tents in a raging sandstorm, the accommodations throughout the Term in the Middle East are actually quite nice. With years of experience under its belt, St. Olaf has been able to avoid any of the horror stories of housing one can hear. For all of the places it stays in five months, only one received relatively bad reviews.

Turkey: The program stays at Bogazici University, and, as school is not in session at the time, students are housed in dorms. This is a good beginning for the program, as students are in a familiar school setting in which to get to know each other. The dorm rooms are triples, which reportedly are quite comfortable, and have their own kitchenettes. Stipends are provided for meals, and if you don't want to cook there is a wide range of cuisine available downtown. More than one student recommended going as "native" as possible and feasting on northern Mediterranean dishes.

Students also can take full advantage of their "residency" at BU, which has all the amenities of a U.S. university. It even has barber shops, its own phone center for overseas calls, and a stretch of private beach reserved exclusively for BU students on the Black Sea. Students can also use their BU identification cards to get discounts at tourist sites! Students complained a bit about the fact that they were fairly far from the Golden Horn section of the city, the main part of Istanbul. However, everyone conceded that it was very easy to hop a bus to get there.

Morocco: Students stay at Oudaya Hotel in Marrakech, and share doubles. It is a rather nice hotel, complete with courtyard and a pool that students can relax around and not worry about "the madness of the streets." Typically, the program takes over two floors of the hotel, allowing students to live in their own protective environment. Students mentioned that the only downside to the accommodations was that, because they were seen living in a hotel, they were *constantly* hassled for money. Breakfast is served at the hotel, and stipends are provided for lunch and dinner.

Egypt: In Cairo, students stay at the Cosmopolitan Hotel, which is within walking distance of the American University of Cairo, the site for classes. Students share doubles, and there are breakfasts offered in the morning. The hotel was described as average, but with a lot more character than a Holiday Inn. It is done up in a 1920s art deco style, and it even has bellhops! Students enjoyed being in the heart of downtown Cairo, as well as two blocks from the Nile, and appreciated the fact that they were able to walk to the university.

Israel: Traveling to Israel by bus, the program stops briefly at Mt. Sinai. The lodging is at St. Catherine's monastery, which got the worst reviews of the program. The only reason to stay here is for a sunrise hike up Mt. Sinai, a field trip the students loved. Students also liked the fact that their route to Israel basically followed the path that the Israelites took when they fled Egypt.

Once in Jerusalem, the program stays at the Lutheran Hostel, right in the downtown area of the Old City. The Middle East Semester has been coming here for years. The hostel is filled with items donated by people from the programs or by the college itself, including a piano! The accommodations are cozy and comfortable (shared rooms, shared bath—the usual hostel fare), and meals are served family-style in the dining area. Most students find refuge in the lounge, where they can hang out and read, study, or decompress. The housing here was a favorite of students, as it is comfortable, centrally located, and the proprietors treat them like family.

Academics

> *"We learned from the world's experts on the topics."*

Because there is not a tremendous amount of traveling, and the program stays in basically one region, the Term in the Middle East is perhaps the most academically stable of the three Olaf programs.

Examining one topic for a month in each of the four countries, students have the typical Olaf advantage of actually going on field trips to see what they had just been studying, sometimes only hours before. They also have the advantage of a more structured

> *"You don't go abroad to read."*

travel schedule, as they tour for a week through the country they had just studied, and then move on to a new country and topic together.

The courses all received excellent marks, as did the professors. The workload is comparatively lighter than what students may be used to—readings, a test, and perhaps a few short papers are the norm for each class. However, students are also going out on field trips, trying to deal with a new culture, and comprehensively assembling what they are seeing with what they are learning.

Classes are usually held a few hours each weekday, either in the mornings or the afternoons. There are also one or two days of basic language training in each location, to help students get around town, order food, etc. Students should expect to have some free time, but not complete freedom, as field trips and special events are scheduled frequently.

TURKEY

Based at Bogazici University, the topic of study is *Political Institutions of the Middle East*. The course examines social changes and political developments in the Middle East, and their impact on emerging political institutions. Classes here are more lecture-oriented than they are at other locations, and students also thought that they were the hardest academically. The content of what they learned, most agreed, was excellent.

There are two to five hours of lectures during the mornings, and some afternoons are reserved for field trips. The workload is average, with three exams that cover both the lecture content and reading assignments. As far as the facilities at the university are concerned, students are considered enrolled in BU and have access to a great deal of the campus. This includes a decent library, and limited E-mail access. However, the university is out of session while the program is here, and this limits what is available.

Students in the past were a bit disappointed by the fact that the places they visited during their week-long tour were much older than the period the curriculum here covers. Much of the time is spent examining Greek and Roman ruins, which were hardly covered in class.

MOROCCO

Although the title of the course is *Social Change in the Middle East and North Africa*, the class here really examines the sociology of Morocco, and in particular, Marrakech. Classes are held every day, but the time here is more experiential than lecture-oriented. The mornings are slated for lectures, while short

> *"The lectures were a tool to help us with what we were experiencing."*

field trips are scheduled in the afternoons to examine what the lecture had covered. Students visit sites such as bazaars and cattle markets, where they can mingle with the buyers and sellers and examine the process firsthand. The class also takes walking tours of the city to examine the local architecture, and why the houses and even the city itself are built the way they are. The professor received enthusiastic reviews.

Classes are also occasionally held at the English Language Institute, which the students loved, as they were able to meet and interact with Moroccan students who were learning English. As for the workload, there are two papers and two exams. The field trips and week of touring takes the group to places like Fez, Casablanca, Rabat, the fringes of the Sahara Desert, Essaouira, and the Atlas Mountains.

EGYPT

Everyone had something positive to say about the Egyptian History course in Egypt. John Swanson, the professor, is reportedly no less an Egyptian god than the ones he lectures about. According to the students, he is *the* expert on Egyptology in the country and can lecture for hours on the subject. His packets of information on field sites will give students far more knowledge than any tour guide. Students didn't even mind attending his lectures for two to three hours every day, and, remarkably, they seemed to absorb a great deal of it.

Classes are held at the American University of Cairo, right down the street from where the students are living. The workload consists of a few short papers, as well as two tests based on lectures and reading assignments. The group visits a sizable selection of sites around Cairo, and even makes a trip up the Nile to visit the city of Luxor, as well as see the Valley of the Kings, the pyramids at Giza, and the Temple of Karnak.

ISRAEL

In Jerusalem, the program switches focus from History to Comparative Religion Studies. This is a prime spot for this topic, as the city is a holy site for three of the world's largest religions: Judaism, Christianity, and Islam. Classes are held in the afternoons at Hebrew University, not

"The emphasis is on learning by experiencing."

far from the Ecce Homo Hostel where students stay. The workload is average for the semester, with a couple of handwritten papers, and a few tests on the reading and lecture contents. The professors and lectures all received solid marks.

The highlight for most students, however, are the field trips that the program takes here. Traveling to refugee camps, the Gaza Strip, the Golan Heights, *kibbutzim* (Jewish working co-ops), and even Jordan, students are exposed to the intricacies and many faces of a highly controversial land. Field trips are organized in conjunction with the Palestine University Organization and Hebrew University, which also gives students on the Middle East program the opportunity to meet and talk with students from both places.

Off the Track

Although there are tons of activities and trips planned through St. Olaf, the students actually do have some nights, afternoons, and weekends off. Here's what happened to some students while on the Middle East program:

One night, a few students decided they wanted to see the pyramids at Giza by moonlight. They rented a van to get there from Cairo, and then took a horseback tour of the monuments at midnight.

> **COURSES (1995)**
>
> *Egypt in the Ancient and Modern World*
>
> *Social Change in the Middle East and North Africa*
>
> *Political Institutions in the Middle East*
>
> *Judaism, Christianity, and Islam*

For a little extra money, one students was allowed to take her horse on a dead-run across the desert, with nothing around but the stars, the sand, and the moon.

A few students were camping on Bogazici University's beach on the Black Sea. It was a warm night, and they all decided to go for a swim *au naturel*. This soon became a tradition for them, and they managed to skinny-dip in the Mediterranean, Aegean, and Red seas, as well as the Sea of Galilee and the Atlantic Ocean during the course of the semester.

Climbing up Mt. Sinai was a highlight for a few students. The mountain on which Moses was supposed to have talked to the burning bush and brought down the Ten Commandments from is actually a fairly good hike as well. To get to the top by sunrise, you have to leave in the middle of the night. Students loved this, as there are no artificial lights for miles around, and they could see every star in the sky.

Some students made lifelong friends while abroad. In Morocco, there was a group of young men from Cadi Ayyad University who would hang out on a particular street corner every night, and talk until late at night. A small group from St. Olaf made it a point to join in with them in these street-corner discussions. It was a terrific way to learn about the culture, the language, and the opinions of the youth of the nation that they were visiting.

Advice and Warnings from the Students

► "Don't wear revealing things, and don't show affection in public."

► "It's perfectly safe—I feel more in danger at home in Chicago."

► "Don't be put off by the images of violence in the Mideast."

► A good amount of money to bring for personal expenses is $1,500 to $2,000.

► "Don't trust anyone, and keep your eyes open all the time."

► "It's hard traveling as a woman, but it doesn't take away from the experience."

► "If you're looking for the West, go to Europe!"

► "Throw yourself into the culture, or you'll regret it later."

The Best + The Worst

👍 Traveling with a great group

👎 Dealing with harassment

👍 Seeing all of the different cultures

👎 No homestay

👍 The field trip to Petra in Jordan (an optional trip)

👎 Not a lot of time to yourself

👍 Climbing the pyramids

👎 The time in Morocco is a little too long

👍 Being in Bethlehem on Christmas Eve

👎 Touring *all* day

👍 Jerusalem

👍 The week of touring in Turkey

**THE
2nd
25**

American University in Buenos Aires

LOCATION: Buenos Aires, Argentina
PROGRAM DURATION: Fall semester
AFFILIATION: American University
COST: $11,945
NOTE: Airfare not included
PREREQUISITES: Sophomore, two years college-level Spanish, 2.75/4.0 GPA
NO. OF STUDENTS: 25
PHONE: (202) 895-4900
E-MAIL: Not available

THE AMERICAN UNIVERSITY IN BUENOS AIRES

The most remarkable aspect of this American University program is the fact that it is one of very few Argentine programs that is open to all students in the US. The largest Spanish-speaking nation in the world and eighth largest overall, one-third of its population lives in the capital of Buenos Aires. It is a very modern city, reminiscent of Washington, D.C., with broad streets and monuments. It is also home to one of the most efficient subway systems in the Western Hemisphere.

There are only two required courses—*Argentine Politics, Economy, and Society* and *History and Culture of Argentina*—but there is no lack of academic intensity on this program. Lectures are given by not only the American University faculty, but also by notable figures from the Argentine government, leaders in local and national business, labor organizers, and church leaders. The program uses facilities at Universidad Argentina de la Empresa, one of the most prestigious higher-learning institutions in the country, and boasts an alumni of many of the nation's leaders. There is also an internship available to those students proficient in Spanish. For two days a week, students work for U.S. and Argentine companies and governmental agencies. Past internships have included students involved in the U.S. Embassy in Buenos Aires, research institutions, and multinational corporations operating in Argentina. For those not fluent enough in Spanish for internship placement, intensive Spanish language study is offered instead. Students are taught at all levels of proficiency by local professors from the university.

Students live with Argentine host families during their stay in Buenos Aires. All students are placed in residences well within the framework of the local mass transit system, and so are able to commute to the university easily. Students' host families provide them with two meals a day. Field trips are also planned, including visits to some of the most impressive natural regions of the continent.

The group travels to Cordoba, Mendoza, and the natural wonders of Iguaçu Falls on the Brazilian border.

The Czech Program

LOCATION: Olomouc, Czech Republic
PROGRAM DURATION: Fall and spring semesters or year program
AFFILIATION: Associated Colleges of the Midwest
COST: Not available, depends on home university tuition
NOTE: Airfare not included
PREREQUISITES: Sophomore, 2.0/4.0 GPA
NO. OF STUDENTS: 25
PHONE: (312) 263-5000
E-MAIL: acm@midwest.netwave.net

ACM—THE CZECH PROGRAM

After over forty years of Communist control, the Czech Republic has found itself challenged with the task of restructuring both its political framework and its economy. As a result, it is one of the front-runners of Democratic restoration in Eastern Europe. It is this legacy of history and politics that the Associated Colleges of the Midwest/Great Lakes College Association Czech program undertakes as its focus. Centered in the city of Olomouc, the capital of Moravia in medieval times, students will soon discover its historic charm. The streets are mostly paved with cobblestones, and the architecture dates back to the 1700s, yet it's a lively city with nightclubs and bars, philharmonics and sports teams. As a hub city to the nation's railway system, most of the region's main cities, such as Vienna and Prague, are easily accessible.

As for the academic program, the semester is broken up into three segments, each roughly a month long, the scholastic intensity increasing with each successive block. All classes are held at Palacky University and are taught by Czech professors in English, except, obviously, for the language course. The director's history course is taught by a professor from an Associated Colleges of the Midwest or Great Lakes College Association college. In the first month, the students are introduced to the Czech language with intensive language study, along with a history course that runs for the duration of the semester. The next segment examines the Czech Republic's Politics and its Social Structures, and also continues with the Czech History, while the language study is taught at a lesser pace. In the final month, students take the History and Language courses alongside an elective course in either Environmental Studies or Czech Literature. During the semester, students take field trips to sites of interest throughout the Republic, as well as trips to nearby Austria, Hungary, Poland, and Slovakia.

While in Olomouc, students are living in Palacky University dormitory suites with Czech students. Participants are given stipends for meals, and there are kitchen facilities available.

The Russia Program

LOCATION: **Krasnodar, Russia**
PROGRAM DURATION: **Fall semester**
AFFILIATION: **Associated Colleges of the Midwest**
COST: **Not available, depends on home university tuition**
NOTE: **Airfare not included**
PREREQUISITES: **Sophomore, two years college-level Russian**
NO. OF STUDENTS: **25**
PHONE: **(312) 263-5000**
E-MAIL: **acm@midwest.netwave.net**

ACM—THE RUSSIA PROGRAM

A vast nation undergoing an incredible transformation, Russia is a country struggling to regain its culture and its identity. No longer bound together by the all-encompassing Soviet, the Russian peoples must reforge their ethnic image from their own memories. In southern Russia, down by the Black Sea, this is true as well. The Associated Colleges of the Midwest/Great Lakes College Association Russia program is focused in this area, based in the city of Krasnodar, an agricultural center in the shadow of the Caucasus Mountains. Here the contact with the West is extremely limited, and the culture is close at hand. With strong ethnic ties to the Kuban Cossacks of the nineteenth century, the regional flavor remains alive in the folklore and history of the people.

This program is intended for those with previous Russian language training. Students are immersed in the language, as daily life requires a decent working knowledge of Russian, and the program strives to improve students' usage of conversational and written language skills. The language program also includes cultural investigation, and explores the local customs and the history and arts of the region. The second part of the program is dedicated to the introduction of Russian Society. Taught by the resident director, this course strives to integrate the students into the Russian culture. Students keep an academic journal and are expected to complete a project tied into the curriculum. Often students' projects are concerned with their extracurricular activities, as many students become involved with local issues and activities, such as churches and community services. This program also leads students on field trips to Moscow and St. Petersburg, where they can tour the remnants of the Soviet Union and the palaces of the czars.

But perhaps the best cultural interaction that the students are exposed to are the homestays. This is an optional part of the program that most choose as their living arrangement, as it places each student with a local family. Students are also offered the chance to stay in student dormitories, which allows participants the opportunity to be integrated with the student population in Krasnodar. In both settings, the lifestyle is very Spartan, and students must overcome hardships such as overcrowding and limits to things that they would normally take for granted, such as hot water. Despite these limitations, students would be hard pressed to find such an intensive exploration into the culture of southern Russia, its people, and its history.

Parliamentary Internship Program

LOCATION: Dublin, Ireland
PROGRAM DURATION: Fall and spring semesters
AFFILIATION: Beaver College, Institute of Public Administration
COST: $7,500
NOTE: Airfare included
PREREQUISITES: 3.0/4.0 GPA
NO. OF STUDENTS: 5 +
PHONE: (800) 755-5607
E-MAIL: cea@beaver.edu

BEAVER—PARLIAMENTARY INTERNSHIP PROGRAM

Based at the Dail, the Lower House of the Irish Parliament, students spend the semester in Dublin, working as unpaid aides to members of the Irish government. Concurrently, participants on this full semester program are enrolled in courses at the Institute of Public Administration (IPA). The IPA was formed nearly forty years ago as a training ground/think tank for some of Ireland's sharpest civic leaders, and it is the source of many national research projects.

This program is a unique collaboration between Beaver College and the IPA, allowing an intensive investigation of the inner workings of the Irish government. Students are required to take three courses involving Irish issues, including Irish Society and Politics and Modern Irish History. In addition to the course work, students are engaged as interns in the Parliament and fill a wide variety of roles, from conducting surveys, to preparing briefings, to doing research papers on regional and national topics.

Students are housed in flats with other Beaver College students in the heart of the city of Dublin (pop. 1,000,000). In their free time, students can explore Ireland's capital city, and all its charms. Dublin is home to hundreds of pubs, the famed Guinness Brewery, and the renowned Abbey Theater. The city is also a fine jumping-off spot for students who wish to take quick weekend trips to nearby locales by ferry, or off to more distant destinations via the international airport.

Semester Programs in Peace Studies

LOCATION: Stadtschlaining, Austria
PROGRAM DURATION: Fall or year program
AFFILIATION: Beaver College, European University Center for Peace Studies
COST: $6,900
NOTE: Airfare not included
PREREQUISITES: Junior, 3.0 GPA
NO. OF STUDENTS: 5+
PHONE: (800) 755-5607
E-MAIL: cea@beaver.edu

BEAVER—SEMESTER IN PEACE STUDIES

As the world rapidly leaves the cold war and the East/West rivalry behind, the nations of the world must face the prospect of actually keeping the newfound peace. Beaver College, in conjuction with the European University Center for Peace Studies (EPU), sends students to Stadtschlaining, Austria, twice a year to gain an understanding of peace, development as it relates to peace, and conflict resolution. The center is not linked to any government or national agency, yet it is affiliated with the United Nations Educational, Scientific, and Cultural Organization (UNESCO).

Based on the site of a medieval castle, the modernized facility offers its students a well-equipped environment, with an extensive library on the subject of Peace Studies, brand-new student housing, conference centers, and modern classrooms. The academic program consists of a selection of EPU's overall course list, and covers such areas as Theory, Peace and Development, Security and Conflict, and Global Transformation. The program's faculty is made up of professors and qualified professionals, who represent many of the nations in UNESCO, as well as colleges and universities in the U.S.

Students are also offered optional pre-session German language study in Vienna for three weeks before the program begins. This instruction not only offers the advantage of improving one's *Hochdeutsch* ("high German"), but provides an opportunity for students to see different sides of the country while in Austria. Starting off in the small mountain village of Dorfgastein in the Austrian Alps for a week, students spend the remaining two weeks of language study in Vienna, where they participate in a homestay in the city. The regular term is held in Stadtschlaining for its entirety.

Students are housed in modern dormitory-style residences, which offer private rooms in suites, with a shared bathroom per suite. Meals are not provided, although there are kitchenette facilities available (*not* full kitchens). Stadtschlaining is nestled in the rolling hills of central Austria, and is a picturesque setting to study the architecture of peace on the international level.

Niamey, Niger Program

LOCATION: Niamey, Niger
PROGRAM DURATION: Fall semester
AFFILIATION: Boston University
COST: $8,295 (Round-trip airfare included)
NOTE: Airfare included
PREREQUISITES: Good academic standing at home university
NO. OF STUDENTS: 20
PHONE: (617) 353-9888
E-MAIL: abroad@bu.edu

BOSTON UNIVERSITY—NIAMEY, NIGER

As the capital of the West African country of Niger, Niamey holds the promise of a variety of experiences for students—the streets are lined with vendors, food stands, and open-air markets, while the city is host to numerous foreign agencies and consulates, plus the Nigerian research and resource facilities. Niamey is one of the few cities still relatively untouched by western influences. The road from the airport still gets blocked by overloaded camels on the way to the markets.

Boston University, in association with the Université de Niamey's Faculté de Pedagogie and Faculté des Lettres et Sciences Humains, offers a program that enables students to examine and participate in Sahelian life and development efforts in Niger. During the first few weeks, students have an intensive orientation, begin their language classes in both French and Hausa, and attend the required course in the culture and society of Niger. Students may take the Hausa language course noncredit, or take a course that focuses on Nigerian life, such as the problems of educational reform, or a workshop in cultural awareness. Students must enroll in sixteen to eighteen semester credits, and all courses meet at the Centre de Formation des Cadres d'Alphabetisation (CFCA), a regional literacy training center, and are taught by Nigerian educators.

Focusing on development issues, students also participate in a fieldwork course, which can be taken for up to six semester credits. This course involves students in some aspect of Nigerian development, such as development in museums, community projects, development organizations, or an independent project. Students decide upon their fieldwork content with academic advisors during the orientation. Students are housed at the CFCA, in communal apartments with participants and scholars from other West African countries and Europe. One meal is provided, and students must manage a household budget that is provided for the rest of their meals, as well as the purchase of any household items.

University of Otago

LOCATION: Dunedin, New Zealand
PROGRAM DURATION: Semester or year
AFFILIATION: Butler University
COST: $6,650/semester, $11,350/year
NOTE: Airfare not included
PREREQUISITES: None
NO. OF STUDENTS: 20+
PHONE: (800) 858-0229
E-MAIL: Not available

BUTLER UNIVERSITY—DUNEDIN, NEW ZEALAND

Dunedin is just about as far south as you can go on a semester abroad program. However, probably few people have even *heard* of the second-largest city on the South Island of New Zealand. A picturesque Victorian town by the sea, Dunedin is located on steep hills overlooking Otago Harbor and the Otago Peninsula. The city has well-planned streets, long beaches, spacious parks, beautiful gardens, and nature preserves. It's also fairly cultural, with excellent art galleries, museums, theaters, and concert halls. A few hours' drive brings you to great skiing, dense rain forest, waterfalls, and stunning lakes.

Butler University has created a minimally structured program, which simply allows students to be fully immersed in the culture and education system of New Zealand without dealing with an armful of paperwork. The University of Otago dates back to 1871, making it New Zealand's oldest university. Today, it has an enrollment of 11,500 and is internationally known as an excellent university. It has a 1.1-million-volume library, theater, concert hall, gymnasium, audiovisual center, computing center, post office, book shop, radio station, coffee shops, dining hall, and even a Bank of New Zealand branch office. The school is in its own quarter adjacent to the city, making it New Zealand's only "university town." Just like large schools back in the U.S., the course offerings are diverse, and students may study anything from anatomy to art, Hebrew to history. Students must take at least fifteen credit hours a semester.

All students are guaranteed housing, in the form of furnished flats (apartments). Students cook for themselves, or go out to eat. Students are fully integrated into the university and are strongly urged by both Butler and the university administration to participate in a student society or club for an athletic, academic, cultural, or political interest. Butler also organizes a field trip to see a working New Zealand farm, at no additional cost.

Hanoi University Program

LOCATION: Hanoi, Vietnam
PROGRAM DURATION: Fall and spring semesters
AFFILIATION: Council on International Educational Exchange
COST: $6,750
NOTE: Airfare from Bangkok included
PREREQUISITES: One Asian Studies Course, 2.75/4.0 GPA
NO. OF STUDENTS: 20
PHONE: (212) 661-1414
E-MAIL: univprogs@ciee.org

CIEE—HANOI UNIVERSITY

The "reopening" of Vietnam affords students the opportunity to study in a truly fascinating place. Ravaged by years of war, Vietnam has nevertheless retained its own customs and culture. A predominantly Buddhist state, Vietnamese society also reflects Confucian influences and beliefs in animism. Hanoi (pop. 3,000,000) is a modern city that still has the feeling of a French colony—complete with tree-lined streets, numerous squares, and villas of former colonial administrators. Hanoi also holds thirty-four libraries, three major museums, and numerous parks, lakes, and gardens. While there is a system of buses, most people opt to walk or bike.

Venturing into this relatively new semester abroad location is CIEE's Council Study Center at Hanoi National University. Attending Hanoi National University, students must take three mandatory classes: *Vietnamese Language, Vietnamese Culture and Society,* and *Vietnamese History.* Students also may elect to take either *Vietnamese Literature* or *Vietnamese Culture and the Arts* as a fourth course. All classes are taught by faculty from Hanoi National University, except the history course, which is taught by the resident director. All courses are taught in English.

In addition to the course work, students in the past have taught English to students and faculty of Hanoi University, and even to government officials! Past resident directors have been able to place students in internships, such as at an English language newspaper. CIEE also provides students with a one- to two-week tour through central and southern Vietnam, affording students the opportunity to experience Vietnamese life other than in Hanoi. There are also small day or weekend cultural trips to places such as Ha Long Bay, Mount Hung, Lang Son, and local villages and factories.

Students are housed in foreign student guest houses at the university. A full meal stipend is included in the program fee.

IKIP Malang Program

LOCATION: Malang, Indonesia
PROGRAM DURATION: Fall and spring semesters
AFFILIATION: Council on International Educational Exchange
COST: $6,450
NOTE: Airfare to Indonesia not included
PREREQUISITES: One Asian Studies Course, 2.75/4.0 GPA
NO. OF STUDENTS: 25
PHONE: (212) 661-1414
E-MAIL: univprogs@ciee.org

CIEE—IKIP, MALANG

Indonesia is a country seldom visited by students, despite the fact that it's the world's fifth most populous nation in the world, and the world's largest Islamic state. With a tropical climate, everything from beaches to volcanoes, and a fascinating and rich culture (including 360 ethnic groups), it's a puzzle why there aren't more study abroad programs here. Luckily, CIEE's Council Study Center at IKIP Malang program is extremely well structured and offers students an impressive amount for their money, including language study and homestays.

Based out of the Institut Kerguruan Dan Ilmu Pendidikan in Malang (fifty-six miles south of Surabaya), students are immersed in the culture of Indonesia for fifteen weeks. There are two mandatory courses: *Indonesian Language* and *Contemporary Indonesian History and Society*. Students must also take an area studies course, although they can choose a concentration either of anthropology, development studies, business, or Indonesian culture and the arts. The area studies courses have a marvelous attribute to them—as a field component, students are placed in homestays in a rural village for three to four weeks, during which time they complete a final paper or project for their course. This stay not only allows students to sharpen their language skills, but also gives them a feeling for life in an East Javanese village.

Students may also take elective courses for credit in batik, gamelan, woodcarving, and dance, depending on the availability of professors. Not stopping at impressive academics, the IKIP program also gives students field trips to such sites as Mount Kawi, Bromo volcano, ancient temples, factories, historical sites, and various cultural activities. All meals are included in the program fee—students eat with their homestay families in Malang, and are provided with a stipend for meals during the field component. There is a three-day orientation in east Java for students, a trip to Bali as part of the Indonesian History course, and a one-week break for independent travel in the middle of each semester.

DiS

LOCATION: Copenhagen
PROGRAM DURATION: Fall and spring semesters, or year
AFFILIATION: Denmark's International Study Program
COST: $5,200/semester, $9,150/year
NOTE: Airfare to Denmark not included
PREREQUISITES: Junior, 3.0/4.0 GPA
NO. OF STUDENTS: 500
PHONE: (800) 247-3477
E-MAIL: windi001@gold.tc.umn.edu

DIS—DENMARK'S INTERNATIONAL STUDY PROGRAM

Although most people would say the world is influenced more by Spain, Italy, England, and France, Denmark's culture is quietly prevalent around the globe. Denmark's International Study program (DiS) brings students to the land of Lego, Tivoli, and the original Little Mermaid each year to participate in a wide range of academic opportunities. Despite its proximity to the Arctic Circle, Copenhagen, DiS's host city, is a (culturally) warm and comfortable locale in which students will feel welcome. Denmark's standard of living is relatively high, and it is an easy, safe, and clean environment in which to enhance one's college experience. The city of Copenhagen is rather old, dating back to the eleventh century, yet its architecture is a mix of richly ornate spires, cobblestone streets, boldly engineered steel bridges, and the clean lines of modern design.

This is all the backdrop to the DiS experience. Based out of their own headquarters and the University of Copenhagen, students are able to select a wide variety of courses. Areas of study include, but are not limited to, Humanities and Social Sciences, Environmental Studies, Marine Biology and Ecology, International Business, Architecture, and Landscape Architecture and Design. Also, Danish language instruction is offered at different levels of proficiency. One of the highlights of the DiS courses is the fact that field trips play a significant role in the curriculum. Not only are there weekly trips throughout Denmark for a majority of curricular studies, but many of the courses offered involve weeklong (or longer) study tours in Scandinavia, Western, Eastern, and Central Europe, and Russia and the Baltic States as part of the course requirements.

Despite the broad range of courses, students are somewhat detached from the main student body, and all courses are taught in English, as Danish can be somewhat prohibitive to the novice. This is not to say that there are no interactions between DiS students and Danish students at the university, as most students in Copenhagen (which boasts a student population from all corners of Europe) speak English rather well.

Students should also gain considerable cultural immersion from their housing situations. Students have the choice of two different arrangements; either in the Kollegium, which is comparable to dorms, or with a Danish family. In the Kollegium, students live in assigned dormitory facilities—generally with their own room, sharing a kitchen with a handful of others. In DiS's family placement, students are placed with families living in the suburbs outside Copenhagen. In either housing arrangement, students must commute to and from the university daily. Fortunately, DIS covers the tab for student's transportation, and Denmark has some of the best mass transit in Europe. In either situation, students should become familiar with the concept of *Hygge*, the Danish value of being together and having a good time.

ACM/GLCA Japan Program

LOCATION: Tokyo
PROGRAM DURATION: Year
AFFILIATION: Great Lakes College Association and ACM
COST: $23,150/year
NOTE: Airfare to Japan not included
PREREQUISITES: Sophomore, one year of college-level Japanese, 3.0/4.0 GPA
NO. OF STUDENTS: 30
PHONE: (317) 983-1224
E-MAIL: japanstu@earlham.edu

ACM/GLCA JAPAN STUDY

Perhaps one of the world's most complex societies, the Japanese culture will be a key ingredient in the world's business and technological future. Clearly, those who have insight into its workings and structure will have an upper hand as this island nation grows and develops its economic might. For nine months, Great Lakes College Association/Associated Colleges of the Midwest Japan program brings American students to Tokyo to experience firsthand the Japanese culture and history, and to approach mastery of its language.

Beginning in late August, students have a ten-day orientation in Tokyo emphasizing intensive language study and culture. During the academic year, students take language study for one-third of their daily workload at Waseda University. This intensive instruction is crucial to their time on the program, as they are placed in Japanese homes for the duration of the program. The other classes, however, are taught in English and cover a broad range—the politics, history, culture, and economics of Japan. Courses are taught by local professors and four visiting instructors from American colleges and universities. Students are also offered field trips at an additional small expense, allowing them to visit some of the beautiful destinations that the country has to offer. The program includes a three-week break in late December, and a two-week break in late March.

Perhaps the most unique facet of this program is the Rural Stay, which takes place in the spring. After several months of language training, students travel to Shimane Prefecture, a rural region of Japan on the west coast of the main island of Honshu, roughly 500 miles from Tokyo. For about a month they live with local families, get involved with the community, and experience a side of Japanese culture much different from that of the big cities.

IAS Beijing Program

LOCATION: Beijing, People's Republic of China
PROGRAM DURATION: Fall and spring semesters
AFFILIATION: Institute of European/Asian Studies
COST: $7,000/semester, $12,500/year
NOTE: Airfare not included
PREREQUISITES: One year of college-level Mandarin Chinese (spring option)
NO. OF STUDENTS: 20
PHONE: (800) 995-2300
E-MAIL: iesrecrt@mcs.net

IAS—BEIJING

China, for overseas study, poses a few problems—many programs must put their students in schools and dormitories designed just for foreigners, with little contact with Chinese students or locals. Strict control by the government insures that interaction is kept at a minimum. This is indeed a pity, as China is a dynamic and culturally rich land, and its people extremely interesting. Beijing, the capital of imperial and modern communist China, is itself an immense and fascinating place to study.

However, the IAS program places students with homestay families—an almost unheard-of privilege in China. The program begins in northwest China, where students receive an orientation on the current political and social conditions while staying in an active Buddhist monastery. Field trips to cultural and natural attractions in the region are also taken. Students then move to Beijing, where they stay in university dormitories until homestays can be arranged. However, students may also choose to live in dormitories and may be assigned Chinese roommates. There is a one-week field trip during the semester, and past sites visited have included Xi'an, Shandong, Shanghai, and Inner Mongolia. Meals are not included in the program fee.

The academics are impressive as well. Students are required to enroll in a ten-semester-credit Chinese language class and two area studies courses taught in English. For the language study, students also have private instruction with a tutor. During the summer, fall semester students with little or no background in Chinese may opt to take an intensive language course for an additional fee ($2,500, with a $1,000 rebate on the fall or year-long program fee).

Area study courses cover Chinese culture, society, economics, philosophy, literature, and religion. Additionally, students can take classes in minority languages such as Tibetan, Mongolian, and Uighur, or take noncredit courses in ethnic dance, Chinese calligraphy, and martial arts.

IAS Singapore Program

LOCATION: Singapore
PROGRAM DURATION: Fall and spring semesters
AFFILIATION: Institute of European/Asian Studies
COST: $7,800/semester, $13,600/year
NOTE: Airfare not included
PREREQUISITES: Junior or senior standing
NO. OF STUDENTS: 10
PHONE: (800) 995-2300
E-MAIL: iesrecrt@mcs.net

IAS—SINGAPORE

Despite Singapore's recent image of a bamboo-cane-wielding, American-hating country, it actually is a fairly nice and peaceful place to visit. One of the few city-states in the world, Singapore has long since risen as a powerful economic force. Today, it is a major center of banking and finance, as well as manufacturing and trade, and has the highest standard of living in East Asia after Japan. It's an attractive and clean city, with modern buildings standing next to picturesque shop-houses dating back to Singapore's colonial times. With a tropical climate year-round, outdoor activities are popular. As English is the language of Singapore business and government, students have the chance to study and live in an East Asian country without prior knowledge of an Asian language.

Students have two choices on the Singapore program. They may either take courses in arts and humanities, science, and business at the National University of Singapore (NUS), or take courses in business, accounting, communications, computer technology, and engineering at Nanyang Technological University (NTU). Both schools are highly regarded international schools, offer a full range of classes, and have excellent facilities. All classes are taught in English. In addition to this course work, students have the opportunity to take intensive Mandarin Chinese at NUS, either at the beginner or intermediate level. Students taking Chinese may take only one other course.

Students are housed in university dorms, and may be assigned a Singaporean roommate. Most meals are included at NUS, but students must pay for their own meals at NTU. One extended field trip is included in the program fee, and students visit either Indonesia or Vietnam during their week-long break.

Undergraduate Study in Kenya

LOCATION: Nairobi, Kenya
PROGRAM DURATION: Year
AFFILIATION: Kalamazoo College
COST: $19,113/year
NOTE: Airfare included
PREREQUISITES: 2.75/4.0 GPA
NO. OF STUDENTS: 20
PHONE: (616) 337-7133
E-MAIL: Not available

KALAMAZOO COLLEGE—KENYA

Kenya is often unfairly thought of as just a large wildlife preserve. While Kenya's game parks *are* its most important economic asset, there is so much more to experience in the country than just lions and impala. There are more than forty ethnic groups in Kenya, who all have a rich history that is distinctive for trading with India, Persia, Arabia, and even China. The Swahili (a generic term encompassing a number of these ethnic groups) at the peak of their civilization were known as devout Muslims, impressive poets, and affluent traders. Swahili civilization and Kiswahili language remain a fascinating subject of study.

The Kalamazoo Kenya program offers students an academic and immersive view into Kenyan life. The program begins even before students arrive in Kenya. A four-day intensive orientation is held on Kalamazoo campus, where students receive predeparture information, advice, warnings, and even a few introductory Kiswahili lessons! Once in Nairobi, students continue the orientation with intensive Kiswahili classes, and a Special Topics Course, *Kenya Culture and Society*. This course covers such issues as Islam, the role of women in Kenyan society, and public health issues, and even offers homestays with urban and rural families, wildlife and Indian Ocean dhow safaris, and overnight camping.

Students are also enrolled in a few courses specifically designed for this program. During the first semester, students receive credit for 120 hours of instruction in Kiswahili, a Fieldwork Methods and Practice course, an Individualized Cultural Research Project, and an elective course. Past elective courses have covered the history, political economy, environmental issues, archaeology, and literature of Kenya or East Africa. During the second semester, students take two elective courses, continue with their Individualized Cultural Research Projects, and participate in an unpaid internship with the help and guidance of the resident director. Past internships have included work with famine relief organizations, social welfare agencies, and small businesses. Students live in two houses in a semirural area of Nairobi, and all meals are provided.

Undergraduate Study in Senegal

LOCATION: Dakar, Senegal
PROGRAM DURATION: Year
AFFILIATION: Kalamazoo College
COST: $19,113/year
NOTE: Airfare included
PREREQUISITES: 2.75/4.0 GPA
NO. OF STUDENTS: 10
PHONE: (616) 337-7133
E-MAIL: Not available

KALAMAZOO COLLEGE—SENEGAL

Senegal is the westernmost country in Africa, and its capital, Dakar, is the westernmost city. Senegal was the birthplace of *Negritude*, a movement that encouraged Africans to examine and celebrate the richness of their own cultural heritage, and to value their own traditions. The Wolof, a people that still dominate rural and urban culture in Senegal, were among the first to come in contact with European traders. Wolof is also the most common language heard on the streets of Dakar.

The Kalamazoo Senegal program starts even before the group arrives in Senegal. There is a four-day intensive orientation at the Kalamazoo campus, where students are given predeparture tips, advice, warnings, and even a few introductory Wolof language lessons. Once in Senegal, the program continues its orientation at the Africa Consultants International's Baobab Center, where students begin intensive study of Wolof and Senegalese culture. After the orientation, students are enrolled directly at L'Université Cheikh Anta Diop, and take classes with Senegalese students. Students may choose their classes from the full selection offered by the university. All courses are taught in French.

Students also continue their study of French at the Institut Français pour les Etudiants Etrangers with students from other African countries, and their study of Wolof at the Baobab Center. Additionally, students attend a Special Topics class at the center that focuses on aspects of Senegalese culture. Topics may include *The Sociocultural Impact of Aids* and *Women and Issues of Development*, among others. After a few months, students begin an Individualized Cultural Research Project or unpaid internship, organized with the help and guidance of the resident director. Students live in a rented house in the city, and most meals are prepared for them. A small number of homestays may also be available.

Luxembourg Program

LOCATION: Luxembourg
PROGRAM DURATION: Fall and spring semesters
AFFILIATION: Miami University
COST: $9,894/semester, $19,009/year
NOTE: Airfare included
PREREQUISITES: 2.5/4.0 GPA
NO. OF STUDENTS: 100/semester
PHONE: (513) 529-5050
E-MAIL: mudec_oxford.acsmail@msmail.muohio.edu

MIAMI UNIVERSITY—LUXEMBOURG PROGRAM

Usually passed over for its bigger neighbors of Germany and France, Luxembourg is nevertheless an interesting nation to study in. Despite the fact that some people may wonder aloud, "Which country is Luxembourg in again?," it has its own culture, people, and beauty. Its history goes back a thousand years, and it is the current home for several European Common Market Institutions, such as the Court of Justice of the European Community. Reflecting its historical place in the world, Luxembourg is on the "language-line" that separates the Germanic tongues of the East and North from the Romance languages of the West and South. Both German and French are spoken in Luxembourg (as well as English, usually).

The Miami University Luxembourg program at the Dolibois European Center (MUDEC) allows students an intensive look at *all* of Europe, not just the small nation they're staying in. Students must take a core course in either the Social Sciences or the Humanities. This class accounts for six of the required sixteen credits, and is part of two themes students choose from to study—*Culture and Society—Discovering the European Heritage* and *The Uniting of Modern Europe—The Economic and Political Challenge*. Other courses in the themes include history, geography, art history, music, literature, economics, and political science. There is a field study component to the core course that takes students on a week-long visit to such sites as Paris, Berlin, Prague, and London (this aspect has an extra fee).

Students must also take a language course, either in French or German. Language is not a prerequisite for students in the fall semester, as the beginning-level classes are offered then. Classes meet four and a half days a week and, except for the language component, are taught in English. Students are housed with homestays, which Miami University considers an integral and important part of the program. There is usually a one- or two-week-long break midsemester.

Salzburg College

LOCATION: Salzburg, Austria
PROGRAM DURATION: Semester or year
AFFILIATION: Northern Illinois University
COST: $7,295/semester
NOTE: Airfare not included
PREREQUISITES: 2.74/4.0 GPA
NO. OF STUDENTS: 150
PHONE: (815) 753-0420
E-MAIL: Not available

NORTHERN ILLINOIS UNIVERSITY—SALZBURG COLLEGE

The city of Salzburg is considered by some to be one of the most beautiful cities in Europe. Situated on the northern edge of the eastern Alps, the city is surrounded by picturesque mountains and is near a famous lake district. Salzburg has a rich musical heritage, and its frequent concerts and other musical events reflect this (the town was also the setting for *The Sound of Music*). An overnight train ride takes travelers to Paris, Venice, Florence, and Rome. Hungary and the Czech Republic are also close by.

Northern Illinois University's Salzburg College program begins with a one-week field trip through Germany that serves as an introduction to Europe. Sites include Bonn, Cologne, Heidelberg, Nuremberg, and Trier, among others. The program then settles in Salzburg, at Salzburg College. The college is located in the Meierhof, an eighteenth-century building on the estate of Lepoldskron Palace, and within walking distance of downtown Salzburg. Students choose from a wide array of courses in language, literature, communications, international relations, political science, business, economics, history, music, art history, and studio art. There are also one-hour courses offered in skiing, cooking, rafting, and folk dancing. Students must register for fifteen semester hours.

Salzburg also offers a "Special Lecture" series on global events as seen from a non-American perspective. These are a series of lectures and panel discussions by people from different European nations, followed by a reception and dinner. Additionally, at the end of the semester, students may participate in a four-week unpaid internship program. As for housing, students are placed with Austrian families, an important part of the experience. Most families do speak some English, although not a lot (which is all the better for your German language practice!). The homestay family provides all meals except lunch during weekdays, which is provided by Salzburg College. Additional field trips offered are a five-day trip to Vienna, a one day trip to Munich, a one-day trip to Salzkammergut (the lake district), and small trips to places like museums, schools, and businesses. Students also have a two-week midsemester break each term for their own explorations and course-related research.

Australia

LOCATION: Sydney, Australia
PROGRAM DURATION: Fall semester
AFFILIATION: Rollins College
COST: $7,850
NOTE: Airfare not included
PREREQUISITES: Good academic and social standing at home university
NO. OF STUDENTS: 30
PHONE: (407) 646-2466
E-MAIL: intprog@rollins.edu

ROLLINS COLLEGE—SYDNEY, AUSTRALIA

Australia is rarely a student's first choice for studying overseas. After all, if you're going to a country that speaks English, why not go to England? We imagine most fail to consider the better weather, friendly people, far better food, rain forests, spectacular beaches, clean and safe cities, and interesting culture as adequate reasons.

Operating in Sydney since 1972, the Rollins College Australian Studies program is a well-established, excellent semester for its price. Hosted by the University of Sydney, Rollins College offers students an introduction into Australian studies. Students choose all of their courses, but the pickings are rather slim. There are usually eight courses offered, from *Australian Art* to *Australian History* to *Flora and Fauna of Australia*. All courses are taught by resident faculty. Students have the advantage of being centrally located in a terrific city, as well as on a major university campus. Unfortunately, the program's courses are for the program's students only.

But students aren't completely isolated—they are housed with homestay families. Naturally, this is a very important part of the program, as students have the opportunity for more cultural immersion than they would get in dorms or apartments, as well as the chance to make lifelong friendships. Students are also encouraged to join University of Sydney clubs and sports teams, and are able to meet Australian students in this manner. Field trips are also an added bonus, visiting such sites as museums, state parks, zoos, plays, and opera performances at no extra cost. All meals are included in the program fee. Students have a two-week break mid-semester.

Junior Year Abroad in Israel

LOCATION: Haifa, Israel
PROGRAM DURATION: Fall and spring semesters
AFFILIATION: Rutgers University, The State University of New Jersey
COST: $7,530/semester, $13,560/year
NOTE: Airfare not included
PREREQUISITES: Junior, 2.5/4.0 GPA
NO. OF STUDENTS: 35
PHONE: (908) 932-7787
E-MAIL: ru_abroad@email.rutgers.edu

RUTGERS UNIVERSITY—HAIFA, ISRAEL

Haifa, "the Israeli capital of the north," is a pleasant city located next to some interesting cultural and historical sites—the towns of Safed, Tiberias, Acre, and Caesarea, as well as the Galilee and the Jordan Valley, are all short trips away. It's also got some of the best Mediterranean beaches you'll ever find, making it, as a whole, one of Israel's premier vacation areas. The University of Haifa is situated high on Mount Carmel, with stunning views of the Mediterranean on one side, and the rest of northern Israel on the other.

However, Rutgers' Junior Year Abroad in Israel program is not a vacation. It's simply a well-rounded, established, and excellent semester overseas. It also has something that other programs in Haifa don't—eight weeks in Jerusalem. Starting in early August, students study Hebrew at Ben Gurion University at either the beginner, intermediate, or advanced level, six days a week. Students live in dorms at the university, and also have the opportunity to spend two weeks on a kibbutz. At the end of the eight weeks, the program moves to Haifa, where it stays for the remainder of the time.

In Haifa, students are enrolled directly in the University of Haifa. Choosing from a full range of university courses, students can either take regular courses or "Challenge Courses." In a Challenge Course, students enroll in regular university courses, but take tests, write papers, and receive a bibliography in English. Additionally, each Challenge Course student is assigned an Israeli partner who helps them fully understand the lectures. Haifa also has a Department of Overseas Studies that offers a full range of courses in the humanities and social sciences in English. Students may also sign up for internships (for an additional fee). Internships are based on student interest and proficiency in Hebrew, and ones in the past have included law firms, archaeological teams, hospital administration, and working for the *Jerusalem Post*.

Students are housed in apartments, with six other students. These are not American-only dorms—roommates can be Jewish, Arab, and other overseas students as well. Students share double rooms, and each apartment has a kitchen and bathroom. Additionally, the program offers field trips to places such as the Negev Desert, Masada, the Galilee, Tiberias, Elat, and parts of southern Israel. Meals are not included in the program fee.

Coastal Rain Forests and Marine Resources

LOCATION: Vancouver Island, Canada
PROGRAM DURATION: Fall and spring semesters
AFFILIATION: The School for Field Studies
COST: $10,970/semester
NOTE: Airfare not included
PREREQUISITES: One college-level ecology or biology course
NO. OF STUDENTS: 30
PHONE: (508) 927-7777
E-MAIL: sfshome@igc.apc.org

SFS—VANCOUVER ISLAND, CANADA

Canada is hardly high up on students' wish lists for study abroad locations. After all, isn't Canada the place that simply has Toronto, legal drinking when you're eighteen, and nothing else except vast tracts of land? However, just off the border from the United States lie the Barkley and Clayoquot Sound regions of Vancouver Island, in British Columbia. Here, there is much of the world's remaining temperate rain forest, and it's home to some of the largest and oldest trees in the world. The region has coastal rain forests and marine ecosystems that are considered to be among the richest and rarest in the world—and they are being increasingly threatened by excessive logging. The region is also home to several thousand First Nation peoples, including the Nuu-chah-nulth, Tla-oqui-aht, Ucluelet, and Hequiaht tribes.

The School for Field Studies (SFS) Coastal Rain Forests and Marine Resources program examines the issues surrounding the restoration of degraded timberlands, wetlands, and fisheries. SFS generates recommendations each semester that could in the future lead to creating a sustainable timber industry, the development of a local ecotourism industry, building a sustainable fisheries system, and promoting the conservation of threatened species. Students are enrolled in three courses, *Coastal Ecology, Principles of Resource Management, Economic and Ethical Issues in Sustainable Development,* and also complete a Directed Research project. The courses are taught together under three themes, or, as SFS calls them, Case Studies—"Can ecosystem management of forests maintain a healthy ecosystem as well as support the local, regional, national, and international logging economy?", "How can the coastal watershed be managed to support a healthy marine ecosystem as well as viable fisheries?", and "What alternative resource management and development strategies are sustainable for Barkley and Clayoquot Sounds?"

SFS centers are usually rustic and beautiful, and this program is no exception. The Center for Coastal Studies is located in the west coast fishing village of Bamfield on South Barkley Sound, with satellite facilities in Ucluelet, North Barkley Sound, and Tofino on Clayoquot Sound. Each student is housed with two to three others in a room with bathroom at the Bamfield Inn. This is not a resort stay, however—students do all of their own cooking and also help clean. Classes, dining, library, and computer facilities are housed in the main lodge of the inn, which looks out to the inlet and beyond to the islands of the Deer and Broken Groups in Barkley Sound. Students also have access to the Bamfield Marine Station Library. The faculty are all highly respected in their fields of study, and the semester is enhanced by interacting with them nearly twenty-four hours a day. Students also participate in community and environmental cleanup activities.

Florence Program

LOCATION: Florence, Italy
PROGRAM DURATION: Fall and spring semesters or year
AFFILIATION: Studio Art Centers International
COST: $9,525/semester (includes accommodations)
NOTE: Airfare not included
PREREQUISITES: 2.5/4.0 GPA
NO. OF STUDENTS: N/A
PHONE: (800) 344-9186
E-MAIL: Not available

FLORENCE PROGRAM (SACI)

For the last twenty years, Studio Art Centers International (SACI) has been bringing students to Florence to seek excellence in art instruction at the university level. Located in the heart of Florence and surrounded by Renaissance art, architecture, and the rich culture of Italy, the SACI Florence program is an exceptional opportunity for American students to take advantage of on-site resources in the study of Fine Arts.

The curriculum revolves mainly around studio work, however the program augments the learning environment with a steady stream of scholars and artists to provide an engaging atmosphere in which to study art. Although SACI covers a wide range of studio art courses, all of the programs take advantage of the city of Florence itself. Field trips to museums, artists' studios, craft centers, and trips to other Italian cities are all part of the program. SACI leads field trips to Naples, Pompeii, and Venice, and offers students organized trips to Paris, Amsterdam, and London.

Students are housed during their stay in Florence in student apartments located throughout the city, which offers a sense of individual independence while living in Florence. Food is not included in the program cost for either housing situation, so students should include the cost of meals in their budget and bring a good cookbook, as most students opt to prepare their own meals. All apartment kitchens are supplied with cooking utensils.

Junior Year in France

LOCATION: Tours and Paris, France
PROGRAM DURATION: Year
AFFILIATION: Sweet Briar College
COST: $18,900 (New York–Paris roundtrip airfare included)
NOTE: Airfare included
PREREQUISITES: Two years college-level French
NO. OF STUDENTS: 100
PHONE: (804) 381-6109
E-MAIL: jyf@sbf.edu

SWEET BRIAR COLLEGE—JUNIOR YEAR IN FRANCE

Usually regarded as the first junior year abroad program offered for U.S. students, Sweet Briar's Junior Year in France program began in 1923. It is a year-long, immersive program in France, with a history of exceptionally high quality.

Beginning in Tours, the program offers students a solid month of orientation and intensive language study. This is a helpful acclimation period, as students get used to being in a different culture and speaking a foreign language, and the program can figure out what level of proficiency they are at. During the time in Tours, students are housed with French families, and all meals are provided.

In October, the program moves to Paris, where students have the chance to study directly with French students in French universities, as opposed to just studying "at the Sorbonne." Sweet Briar has associations with three Paris universities, Paris III (literature, theater, and cinema), Paris IV (history, languages, geography, and philosophy), and Paris VII (science, psychology, sociology, and anthropology). Sweet Briar will also help students apply to take classes at any of the other ten universities in Paris; acceptance is based upon ability.

Through Sweet Briar, hundreds of courses are offered in Paris, ranging throughout the full academic spectrum. Sweet Briar also provides tutorial services and discussion groups for those students who need extra help. Sweet Briar offers its own classes as well, mainly for French majors who need specific classes for their major. While in Paris, students are placed with French families, who also provide breakfast and dinner.

The program also offers students several weekend excursions (included in the program fee) to places such as a Loire Valley château, Mont Saint-Michel, Giverny, and Vaux-le-Vicomte, as well as social events.

Florence Program

LOCATION: Florence, Italy
PROGRAM DURATION: Semester or year
AFFILIATION: Syracuse University
Cost: $12,250/semester
NOTE: Airfare included
PREREQUISITES: Good academic standing at home university
NO. OF STUDENTS: 300
PHONE: (800) 235-3472
E-MAIL: DIPA@suadmin.syr.edu

SYRACUSE UNIVERSITY—FLORENCE PROGRAM

The home of Leonardo da Vinci, Michelangelo, Botticelli, and Donatello, Florence has retained its passion for the arts throughout the centuries and preserved its history with strong devotion. Called the "Jewel of the Renaissance," Florence offers students historical and cultural resources almost unparalleled on earth.

One of the first American programs established in Italy, Syracuse University offers not one program but four for students to choose from. All programs offer a broad range of art history courses, and are designed for both students with proficiency in Italian, and those without. All students are required to take Italian, as Syracuse tries to get students as immersed as possible in Italian culture.

1) Arts and Sciences: Courses offered include Italian language and literature, political science, history, art history, architectural history, and women's studies. At least two courses per semester focus on women's studies. Students are required to take six credits of Italian language or literature.

2) School of Art: This combines studio work with Arts and Science courses. Students study in Florentine workshops, as well as in the art studios of the Syracuse Center. Students can study metalsmithing, etching, jewelry casting, restoration, batik, fibers, silkscreen, sculpture, drawing, painting, art photography, as well as on-and-off weaving. The balance of the workload consists of courses from the College of Arts and Sciences. Students are required to take at least three credits of Italian language.

3) School of Architecture: Pre-architecture is for the student who is interested in architecture, but doesn't really know a protractor from a contractor. The program focuses more on the history of architecture, while giving students a foundation of visual and graphic training. Students also take courses from the College of Arts and Sciences, and at least three credits of Italian.

4) School of Architecture: Professional program. Students must have completed a third-year architectural design course before being admitted. The program is structured around fourth-year design studios and architectural history. Students are required to take at least three credits of Italian.

All programs are based out of the Villa Rossa, Syracuse's Center in Florence. The center is located close to the heart of the city, and offers an impressive amount of facilities for students. It houses the largest English library in Florence, a small coffee bar and lounge, classrooms, studios, faculty offices, and reading rooms. Students have the advantage of a resident director, staff members, personal and academic counselors, a housing director, weekly access to a visiting doctor, and a certified counselor for students with learning disabilities.

Most students are placed in pairs in Italian homes. Breakfast is provided by the homestay family seven days a week, and dinner five times. For the rest of the meals, students receive a stipend from

Syracuse. Some students are placed in apartments and must prepare their own meals (again, with a stipend from Syracuse). There are a number of field trips included in the program fee to such sites as Rome, Venice, Assisi, Siena, Pisa, and Milan.

Literature and Theater in London

LOCATION: London, England
PROGRAM DURATION: Spring quarter
AFFILIATION: University of Minnesota
COST: $3,650
NOTE: Airfare not included
PREREQUISITES: 2.5/4.0 GPA
NO. OF STUDENTS: 35
PHONE: (612) 625-3379
E-MAIL: globalc@maroon.tc.umn.edu

UNIVERSITY OF MINNESOTA—LITERATURE AND THEATER IN LONDON

Set in the center of the British capital, students live out the quintessential lifestyle of London, while at the same time they are immersed in the richness of British theater, the London experience, and the literature of our neighbors across the Atlantic. This ten-week program is hosted in part by the Centres for Academic Programs Abroad (CAPA), which has played host to study abroad programs for over two decades. The program implements CAPA's facilities as both classrooms and living space, located in the very heart of the city, just south of Hyde Park.

Students choose two courses from a rather assiduous coverage of British theater and literature during their stay in London. The course offerings cover literary theory, investigating the representations of literary methods by British authors, and Topics in Anglophone (Queen's English) Literature, ranging from Colonial, Modern, and Feminist topics. Of course, the program looks intensively at British theater, including Shakespeare, traditional works, as well as plays currently in production. The final option course, the Fringe Theater Internship, is open to twelve to fifteen students per quarter. Praised by many past participants as being a "don't miss" aspect of the program, those involved with the internship are placed in a variety of positions in an active theater company in London.

In addition to these course offerings, the students are involved with the London Experience, a mandatory class designed to immerse them into the British culture. Students spend class time visiting the traditional tourist sites as well as some that are a bit off the track. Students share their experiences in journal entries as well as in classroom discussion. All courses except the London Experience may change from year to year.

Students are housed within the CAPA Field Court House Student Center, which offers housing options ranging from singles to quads. Students enjoy easy access to their classes as well as study areas and resources—the Field Court House is a short walk away from the Tube. It also provides its residents with a television lounge complete with a VCR, as well as communal dining and kitchen facilities.

International Program in Toledo, Spain

LOCATION: Toledo, Spain
PROGRAM DURATION: Fall and spring semesters
AFFILIATION: University of Minnesota
COST: $7,480/semester
NOTE: Airfare not included
PREREQUISITES: Two years of college-level Spanish, 2.5/4.0 GPA
NO. OF STUDENTS: 60
PHONE: (612) 625-9008
E-MAIL: globalc@maroon.tc.umn.edu

UNIVERSITY OF MINNESOTA—INTERNATIONAL PROGRAM IN TOLEDO, SPAIN

Located on a high island created by the Tajo River and approximately forty-five miles south of Madrid, some would say Toledo is one of Spain's most beautiful cities. It's a wonderful place to visit, let alone have a chance to study in. The city in its entirety was declared a national monument nearly fifty years ago, and as a result has become a living museum. Predating Rome (which conquered it in 193 B.C.), Toledo was the capital of the Visigothic kingdom, a center for Moorish, Christian, and Jewish culture, and even the seat for the Spanish Inquisition. Cobblestone streets, shaded plazas, cathedrals, mosques, and artisans' shops all add to the charm of Toledo.

Sponsored by the University of Minnesota and the Ortega y Gasset Foundation, the Toledo program gives students with an already solid background in Spanish the opportunity to expand their language skills and learn more about the history and culture of Spain. Other topics of study may include anthropology, archaeology, art history, culture, economics, geography, literature, and political science. It's a bit of a grab bag for classes—students register for twelve to eighteen semester credits per semester, and whatever classes that have at least eleven participants are then taught. All classes are held Monday through Thursday, and are taught in Spanish. Graduate and individual research credit is available through special arrangement.

One of the impressive aspects of the University of Minnesota's Toledo program is that participants are not just from the U.S. Students from Latin America, Japan, and other places give the program the opportunity to touch upon cultures other than that of Spain. Another unique aspect is that the program is based in a renovated sixteenth-century convent, in the heart of downtown Toledo. The convent has dining, classroom, library, recreational, and housing facilities. Student may live in single, double, or triple rooms. For an additional fee, students can choose to live in a homestay with a Spanish family. Additionally, four one-day excursions are included with the cost of the program to places such as Madrid, El Escorial, Aranjuez, Cuenca, or the Route of Don Quixote. There is a four-day trip to Galicia during the fall and Andalucia in the spring for an additional fee.

Appendix

Argentina

LOCATION: Buenos Aires
SPONSOR: CIEE
PROGRAM NAME: Council Study Center:
  Argentina
ACADEMIC FOCUS: Art History, History,
  Economics, Education, International
  Relations, Literature, Philosophy,
  Political Science, Sociology
DURATION: Semester or year
COST: (S)$6,975 (Y)$12,875 (some meals
  not incl.)
PHONE NUMBER: (212) 661-1414

LOCATION: Buenos Aires
SPONSOR: Lexia Exchange International
PROGRAM NAME: Semester in Buenos
  Aires
ACADEMIC FOCUS: Anthropology,
  Business, History, Humanities,
  International Relations, Linguistics,
  Literature, Political Science, Spanish,
  Economics, Political Science
DURATION: Semester or summer (eight
  weeks)
COST: (S)$7,495 (Summer) $4,495
PHONE NUMBER: (415) 327-9191

LOCATION: Buenos Aires
SPONSOR: SUNY Plattsburgh
PROGRAM NAME: Latin American
  Southern Core Programs; Buenos Aires
ACADEMIC FOCUS: Biology, Chemistry,
  Communications, Culture Studies, Fine
  Arts, Literature, Psychology, Spanish,
  Business, Public Administration
  (internships available)

DURATION: Semester or year
COST: (S)$10,170 (Y)$15,070
PHONE NUMBER: (518) 564-2086

LOCATION: Buenos Aires
SPONSOR: University of Illinois/Urbana-
  Champaign
PROGRAM NAME: Argentine University
  Programs
ACADEMIC FOCUS: Full curriculum
DURATION: Semester or year
COST: (S)$4,570 (Y)$8,570 (R/B not incl.)
PHONE NUMBER: (217) 333-6322

LOCATION: Buenos Aires
SPONSOR: University of Miami
PROGRAM NAME: Universidad del
  Salvador
ACADEMIC FOCUS: Spanish, Spanish
  Literature, Business, Communications,
  Law, Liberal Arts
DURATION: Semester or year
COST: (S)$11,670 (Y)$23,340
PHONE NUMBER: (800) 557-5421

LOCATION: Buenos Aires
SPONSOR: University of North Carolina/
  Chapel Hill
PROGRAM NAME: University of North
  Carolina/University of Illinois Program
  in Buenos Aires, Argentina
ACADEMIC FOCUS: Economics, The Arts,
  History, Latin American Studies,
  Psychology, International Studies
DURATION: Semester or year
COST: (S)$2,250 (Y)$4,500 (tuition only)
PHONE NUMBER: (919) 962-7001

LOCATION: Córdoba
SPONSOR: Universidad Blas Pascal
PROGRAM NAME: Argentum
ACADEMIC FOCUS: Business,
   Communication Services, Computer
   Science, Education, Economics,
   International Relations, Engineering,
   Latin American Studies, Liberal Arts,
   Spanish Language, and Literature
DURATION: Semester or year
COST: (S)$6,100 (Y)$10,100
PHONE NUMBER: (617) 448-3552

LOCATION: Gobernarador Virasoro
SPONSOR: SUNY Plattsburgh
PROGRAM NAME: Latin American
   Southern Core Programs;
   Gobernarador Virasoro
ACADEMIC FOCUS: Argentine Culture,
   History, Science, Spanish, Guarani
DURATION: Semester or year
COST: (S)$10,170 (Y)$15,070
PHONE NUMBER: (518) 564-2086

Australia

LOCATION: Hobart, Tasmania
SPONSOR: Butler University
PROGRAM NAME: University of Tasmania
ACADEMIC FOCUS: Economics, Fine Arts,
   Humanities, Science, Business,
   Education, Languages, Political Science
DURATION: Semester or year
COST: (S)$7,825 (Y)$12,725
PHONE NUMBER: (317) 283-9336

LOCATION: Melbourne
SPONSOR: Australearn
PROGRAM NAME: LaTrobe University
ACADEMIC FOCUS: Applied Science,
   Australian Studies, Business, Film
   Studies, Health Studies, Women's
   Studies
DURATION: Semester or year
COST: (S)$6,450 (Y)$11,800 (board not
   incl.)
PHONE NUMBER: (303) 491-0228

LOCATION: Melbourne
SPONSOR: Bentley College
PROGRAM NAME: Business Program in
   Australia
ACADEMIC FOCUS: Business, Accounting,
   Cultural Studies, Environmental
   Science, Finance, Literature,
   Management, Marketing, Economics
DURATION: Semester or year
COST: (S)$9,875 (Y)$19,750
PHONE NUMBER: (617) 891-3141

LOCATION: Melbourne
SPONSOR: University of Miami
PROGRAM NAME: University of
   Melbourne
ACADEMIC FOCUS: Australian Studies,
   Biology, Business, History, Chemistry,
   Education, Engineering, English,
   Political Studies
DURATION: Semester or year
COST: (S)$10,850 (Y)$21,700
PHONE NUMBER: (800) 557-5421

LOCATION: Perth
SPONSOR: University of Western
   Australia
PROGRAM NAME: Study Abroad Program
ACADEMIC FOCUS: Agriculture,
   Architecture, Arts, Commerce,
   Economics, Engineering, Fine Arts,
   Education, Law, Science
DURATION: Semester or year
COST: (S)$5,000 (Y)$10,000
PHONE NUMBER: (619) 380-3537

LOCATION: Sydney
SPONSOR: Boston University
PROGRAM NAME: Sydney Internship
   Program
ACADEMIC FOCUS: Communications,
   Economics, Law, Psychology, Arts,
   Business, International Relations,
   Liberal Arts, Political Science
DURATION: Semester
COST: $8,900 (board not incl.)
PHONE NUMBER: (617) 353-9888

LOCATION: Sydney
SPONSOR: Marymount College
PROGRAM NAME: Maquarie University
ACADEMIC FOCUS: Full curriculum
DURATION: Semester or year
COST: (S)$7,850 (Y)$15,700
PHONE NUMBER: (914) 332-8343

LOCATION: Sydney
SPONSOR: University of New South Wales

PROGRAM NAME: Study Abroad Program
ACADEMIC FOCUS: Business, Economics, Engineering, Fine Arts, Law, Liberal Arts, Science
DURATION: Semester or year
COST: (S)$6,200 (Y)$11,900
PHONE NUMBER: (612) 385-3175

LOCATION: Wagga Wagga
SPONSOR: Australearn
PROGRAM NAME: Charles Stuart University
ACADEMIC FOCUS: Agriculture, Education, Psychology, Social Work, Television, Wine Science
DURATION: Semester or year
COST: (S)$5,350 (Y)$11,900 (meals not incl.)
PHONE NUMBER: (303) 491-0228

LOCATION: Wollongong
SPONSOR: University of North Carolina
PROGRAM NAME: University of Wollongong
ACADEMIC FOCUS: Business, Australian Studies, Biological Sciences, Chemical Sciences, Ecology, Economics, Education, History, Pacific Rim Studies, Physical Education, Engineering, Humanities
DURATION: Semester or year
COST: (S)$4,400 (Y)$8,500 (R/B not incl.)
PHONE NUMBER: (919) 962-7001

Austria

LOCATION: Graz
SPONSOR: Binghamton University
PROGRAM NAME: Graz Program
ACADEMIC FOCUS: Austrian Studies and German Studies
DURATION: Semester or year
COST: (S)$6,200 (Y)$11,600
PHONE NUMBER: (607) 777-2656

LOCATION: Graz
SPONSOR: Rider College
PROGRAM NAME: Study Abroad in Austria
ACADEMIC FOCUS: Austrian Studies, German, Literature
DURATION: Semester or year

COST: (S)$6,347 (Y)$12,750
PHONE NUMBER: (609) 896-5125

LOCATION: Innsbruck
SPONSOR: University of Notre Dame
PROGRAM NAME: Innsbruck Program
ACADEMIC FOCUS: European Studies, Austrian Studies, German
DURATION: Year
COST: $21,000 (RT air incl.)
PHONE NUMBER: (219) 631-5882

LOCATION: Salzburg
SPONSOR: AIFS
PROGRAM NAME: University of Salzburg
ACADEMIC FOCUS: Business, Economics, Humanities, German, History, German Literature
DURATION: Semester or year
COST: (S)$8,125 (Y)$16,000
PHONE NUMBER: (800) 727-2437

LOCATION: Salzburg
SPONSOR: Bowling Green State University
PROGRAM NAME: Academic Year Abroad in Austria
ACADEMIC FOCUS: Austrian Studies, European Studies, Music, German, German Literature, International Relations
DURATION: Year
COST: $11,441
PHONE NUMBER: (419) 372-2268

LOCATION: Salzburg
SPONSOR: Ouachita Baptist University
PROGRAM NAME: Austrian Study Program
ACADEMIC FOCUS: Austrian Studies, German
DURATION: Semester
COST: $6,500 (RT air incl.)
PHONE NUMBER: (501) 245-5197

LOCATION: Salzburg
SPONSOR: University of Maine
PROGRAM NAME: New England Universities in Salzburg
ACADEMIC FOCUS: Full curriculum
DURATION: Semester or year
COST: (S)$2,400 (Y)$3,650 (tuition only)
PHONE NUMBER: (207) 581-1947

LOCATION: Vienna
SPONSOR: American University
PROGRAM NAME: Semester in Vienna
ACADEMIC FOCUS: Foreign Policy,
German, International Relations,
International Studies, German Studies,
History, Political Science
DURATION: Semester
COST: $12,145 (board not incl.)
PHONE NUMBER: (202) 895-4960

LOCATION: Vienna
SPONSOR: Beaver College
PROGRAM NAME: Study in Austria
ACADEMIC FOCUS: Art History,
Economics, German History, Political
Science
DURATION: Semester or year
COST: (S)$10,850 (Y)$21,500
PHONE NUMBER: (800) 755-5607

LOCATION: Vienna
SPONSOR: University of North Carolina
PROGRAM NAME: Exchange Program at
Wirtschaftuniversität Wien
ACADEMIC FOCUS: Economics,
International Business, International
Relations
DURATION: Semester or year
COST: (S)$5,100 (Y)$9,700 (R/B not incl.)
PHONE NUMBER: (919) 962-7001

Brazil

LOCATION: Belem
SPONSOR: School For International
Training
PROGRAM NAME: Amazon Studies and
Ecology
ACADEMIC FOCUS: Amazonian Studies,
Land Use, Tropical Ecology, Field
Methods
DURATION: Semester
COST: (S)$9,600
PHONE NUMBER: (800) 336-1616

LOCATION: Campinas
SPONSOR: SUNY Albany
PROGRAM NAME: University of Albany
Exchange

ACADEMIC FOCUS: Linguistics,
Literature, Portuguese, Social Sciences
DURATION: Semester or year
COST: (S)$7,309 (Y)$13,565
PHONE NUMBER: (518) 442-3525

LOCATION: Fortaleza
SPONSOR: School For International
Training
PROGRAM NAME: Brazil Program
(Culture)
ACADEMIC FOCUS: Brazilian Studies,
Ecology, Economics, Field Methods,
Health Studies, Political Science,
Popular Culture, Religion, Social
Science
DURATION: Semester
COST: $9,300
PHONE NUMBER: (800) 336-1616

LOCATION: Fortaleza
SPONSOR: University of Arizona
PROGRAM NAME: Semester in Brazil
ACADEMIC FOCUS: Portuguese
DURATION: Semester (Fall only) or
Summer
COST: (S)$4,359 (Summer)$1,000
PHONE NUMBER: (602) 621-4819

LOCATION: Rio de Janeiro
SPONSOR: Brown University
PROGRAM NAME: Brown in Brazil
ACADEMIC FOCUS: Full curriculum
DURATION: Semester
COST: $10,304
PHONE NUMBER: (401) 863-2489

LOCATION: São Paulo
SPONSOR: CIEE
PROGRAM NAME: Council Study Center
at the University of São Paulo
ACADEMIC FOCUS: Brazilian Studies,
Portuguese, Humanities, Natural
Sciences, Social Sciences
DURATION: Semester or year
COST: (S)$5,350 (Y)$7,550
PHONE NUMBER: (212) 661-1414

Chile

LOCATION: Concepción
SPONSOR: SUNY Plattsburgh

PROGRAM NAME: Latin American
  Southern Cone Program
ACADEMIC FOCUS: Biology, Fine Arts,
  Literature, Marine Sciences,
  Psychology, Social Sciences, Social
  Services, Spanish Studies
DURATION: Semester or year
COST: (S)$6,835 (Y)$13,670
PHONE NUMBER: (518) 564-2112

LOCATION: Santiago
SPONSOR: American University
PROGRAM NAME: Semester in Santiago
ACADEMIC FOCUS: Foreign Policy,
  History, Political Science, Spanish
DURATION: Semester
COST: $11,945
PHONE NUMBER: (202) 895-4900

LOCATION: Santiago
SPONSOR: University of Miami
PROGRAM NAME: Pontifica Universidad
  Catolica de Chile Program
ACADEMIC FOCUS: History, Literature,
  Architecture, Engineering, Latin
  American Studies, Mathematics,
  Political Science, Spanish
DURATION: Semester or year
COST: (S)$11,670 (Y)$23,340
PHONE NUMBER: (800) 557-5421

LOCATION: Santiago
SPONSOR: Worldstudy
PROGRAM NAME: Study in Santiago,
  Chile
ACADEMIC FOCUS: Economics,
  Humanities, Natural Sciences, Physical
  Sciences, Social Sciences, Spanish,
  Spanish Literature
DURATION: Semester or year
COST: (S)$4,450 (Y)$8,900
PHONE NUMBER: (800) 780-1095

LOCATION: Santiago
SPONSOR: University of Michigan
PROGRAM NAME: University of Michigan/
  University of Wisconsin Study Abroad
  in Santiago, Chile
ACADEMIC FOCUS: Science, Humanities,
  Social Sciences
DURATION: Semester or year

COST: (S)$3,550 (Y)$7,100 (some meals
  not incl.)
PHONE NUMBER: (313) 764-4311

China

LOCATION: Nationwide
SPONSOR: Duke University
PROGRAM NAME: Duke Study in China
  Program
ACADEMIC FOCUS: Chinese, History,
  Literature
DURATION: Six months
COST: $13,200
PHONE NUMBER: (919) 684-2174

LOCATION: Nationwide
SPONSOR: University of Massachusetts,
  Amherst
PROGRAM NAME: University of
  Massachusetts in China
ACADEMIC FOCUS: Chinese
DURATION: Semester or year
COST: (S)$4,400 (Y)$7,750
PHONE NUMBER: (413) 545-4350

LOCATION: Beijing
SPONSOR: American University
PROGRAM NAME: Semester in Beijing/
  Hong Kong
ACADEMIC FOCUS: Business, Chinese,
  Economics, Chinese Studies
DURATION: Semester
COST: $11,445
PHONE NUMBER: (202) 985-4900

LOCATION: Beijing
SPONSOR: Center for Study Abroad
PROGRAM NAME: Chinese Language and
  Culture
ACADEMIC FOCUS: Chinese, Chinese
  Studies, Economics, History, Literature
DURATION: Semester or year
COST: (S)$5,895 (Y)$9,895
PHONE NUMBER: (206) 726-1498

LOCATION: Beijing
SPONSOR: CIEE
PROGRAM NAME: Council Study Center
  at Peking University
ACADEMIC FOCUS: Chinese

DURATION: Semester
COST: $6,750
PHONE NUMBER: (212) 661-1414

———

LOCATION: Beijing
SPONSOR: SUNY Oswego
PROGRAM NAME: Beijing Exchange
  Program
ACADEMIC FOCUS: Chinese, Chinese Art,
  Chinese Studies
DURATION: Semester or year
COST: (S)$6,275 (Y)$12,550
PHONE NUMBER: (315) 341-2118

———

LOCATION: Dalian
SPONSOR: Brethren Colleges Abroad
PROGRAM NAME: BCA Program in Dalian
ACADEMIC FOCUS: Chinese, Japanese,
  Russian, Chinese Culture, Chinese
  Studies, Comparative Religion
DURATION: Semester or year
COST: (S)$7,875 (Y)$13,795
PHONE NUMBER: (219) 982-5238

———

LOCATION: Hangzhou
SPONSOR: Long Island University
PROGRAM NAME: Friends World
  Programs–China
ACADEMIC FOCUS: Anthropology, Peace
  Studies, Religious Studies, Rural
  Development, Comparative Religions,
  Ecology, Women's Studies
DURATION: Semester or year
COST: (S)$9,835 (Y)$19,670
PHONE NUMBER: (516) 287-1273

———

LOCATION: Nanjing
SPONSOR: CCIS
PROGRAM NAME: CCIS Semester in
  China
ACADEMIC FOCUS: Culture and Society,
  Geography, History, Chinese
DURATION: Semester
COST: $2,766 (board not incl.)
PHONE NUMBER: (800) 453-6956

———

LOCATION: Shanghai
SPONSOR: Beloit College
PROGRAM NAME: Fudan Exchange
  Program
ACADEMIC FOCUS: Chinese, Chinese
  Culture, Chinese Studies, Chinese
  Literature

DURATION: Semester or year
COST: (S)$10,592 (Y)$21,184
PHONE NUMBER: (608) 363-2269

———

Costa Rica

LOCATION: Alajuela
SPONSOR: University of Miami
PROGRAM NAME: Instituto
  Centroamericano de Administration de
  Empreses Program
ACADEMIC FOCUS: Business
DURATION: Semester or year
COST: (S)$11,370 (Y)$22,740
PHONE NUMBER: (800) 557-5421

———

LOCATION: Heredia
SPONSOR: Lock Haven University
PROGRAM NAME: Semester in Costa Rica
ACADEMIC FOCUS: Economics, History,
  Latin American Studies, Pollution
  Studies, Sociology, Environmental
  Studies
DURATION: Semester
COST: $6,241
PHONE NUMBER: (717) 893-2140

———

LOCATION: San José
SPONSOR: ACM
PROGRAM NAME: Tropical Field Research
ACADEMIC FOCUS: Archaeology, Biology,
  Geology, and Spanish
DURATION: Semester
COST: $6,825
PHONE NUMBER: (312) 263-5000

———

LOCATION: San José
SPONSOR: Long Island University
PROGRAM NAME: Friends World
  Program–Costa Rica
ACADEMIC FOCUS: Anthropology, Peace
  Studies, Rural Development, Religion,
  Ecology, Women's Studies
DURATION: Semester or year
COST: (S)$9,660 (Y)$19,320
PHONE NUMBER: (516) 287-1273

———

LOCATION: San José
SPONSOR: University of Kansas
PROGRAM NAME: Study Abroad in Costa
  Rica

ACADEMIC FOCUS: Business, Education, Economics, Latin American Studies, Social Work, Liberal Arts, Natural Sciences
DURATION: Semester or year
COST: (S)$4,400 (Y)$6,800
PHONE NUMBER: (913) 864-3742

Czech Republic

LOCATION: Prague
SPONSOR: American University
PROGRAM NAME: Semester in Prague
ACADEMIC FOCUS: Communications, Czech, Economics, Media Studies, History, Literature, Photography, Political Science, Screenwriting, Film
DURATION: Semester
COST: $11,445
PHONE NUMBER: (202) 895-4900

LOCATION: Prague
SPONSOR: Lexia Exchange International
PROGRAM NAME: Semester in Prague
ACADEMIC FOCUS: Czech Studies, Anthropology, Business, Czech, Fine Arts, Sociology, Economics, History, Humanities, Political Science
DURATION: Semester or year
COST: (S)$5,995 (Y)$11,495
PHONE NUMBER: (415) 327-9191

LOCATION: Prague
SPONSOR: School for International Training
PROGRAM NAME: Czech Republic
ACADEMIC FOCUS: Anthropology, Environmental Studies, Arts, Economics, History, Humanities, Geography, Political Science
DURATION: Semester
COST: $9,600
PHONE NUMBER: (800) 336-1616

LOCATION: Prague
SPONSOR: University of Pennsylvania
PROGRAM NAME: Central European Studies Semester in Prague
ACADEMIC FOCUS: Sociology, Czech, Eastern European Studies, Economics, History, Jewish Studies, Literature, Political Science
DURATION: Semester
COST: $9,824 (R/B not incl.)
PHONE NUMBER: (215) 898-9073

Ecuador

LOCATION: Cuenca
SPONSOR: University of Massachusetts, Amherst
PROGRAM NAME: Ecuador Exchange
ACADEMIC FOCUS: Art, Education, Latin American Studies, Spanish
DURATION: Semester or year
COST: (S)$4,900 (Y)$8,800
PHONE NUMBER: (413) 545-2710

LOCATION: Guayaquil
SPONSOR: Partnership for Service-Learning
PROGRAM NAME: Ecuador Service-Learning
ACADEMIC FOCUS: Education, Social Sciences, Humanities, International Studies, Liberal Arts
DURATION: Semester or year
COST: (S)$5,200 (Y)$9,800
PHONE NUMBER: (212) 986-0989

LOCATION: Quito
SPONSOR: Beloit College
PROGRAM NAME: Ecuador Seminar
ACADEMIC FOCUS: Ecuadorian Studies, Spanish, Ecuadorian Culture
DURATION: Semester or year
COST: (S)$10,592 (Y)$21,184
PHONE NUMBER: (608) 363-2269

LOCATION: Quito
SPONSOR: Brethren Colleges Abroad
PROGRAM NAME: BCA Program in Quito
ACADEMIC FOCUS: Full curriculum
DURATION: Semester or year
COST: (S)$9,345 (Y)$16,745
PHONE NUMBER: (219) 982-5238

LOCATION: Quito
SPONSOR: Center for Study Abroad
PROGRAM NAME: Spanish Language Program, Quito
ACADEMIC FOCUS: Spanish
DURATION: Semester

COST: $2,695
PHONE NUMBER: (206) 726-1498

LOCATION: Quito
SPONSOR: Kalamazoo College
PROGRAM NAME: Environmental Studies
in Ecuador
ACADEMIC FOCUS: Anthropology,
Sociology, Ecology, Environmental
Studies, Political Science
DURATION: Semester or year
COST: (S)$11,788 (Y)$19,113 (RT air incl.)
PHONE NUMBER: (616) 337-7133

LOCATION: Quito
SPONSOR: Oregon State University
PROGRAM NAME: Ecuador Exchange
Program
ACADEMIC FOCUS: Anthropology,
Literature, Art History, Economics,
Latin American History, Spanish
DURATION: Semester or year
COST: (S)$3,400 (Y)$7,500
PHONE NUMBER: (503) 737-6481

LOCATION: Quito
SPONSOR: Scripps College
PROGRAM NAME: Scripps College in
Ecuador
ACADEMIC FOCUS: Fine Arts, Sciences,
Social Sciences, Spanish
DURATION: Semester or year
COST: (S)$12,884 (Y)$25,668 (RT air incl.)
PHONE NUMBER: (909) 621-8306

England

LOCATION: Arundel
SPONSOR: New England College
PROGRAM NAME: Arundel Campus
Program
ACADEMIC FOCUS: Business, English,
Humanities, International Relations
DURATION: Semester or year
COST: (S)$9,645 (Y)$19,270
PHONE NUMBER: (44) 903 882 259

LOCATION: Brighton
SPONSOR: University of North Carolina/
Chapel Hill

PROGRAM NAME: Exchange Program at
University of Sussex, England
ACADEMIC FOCUS: Environmental
Sciences, History, Premedicine,
Humanities, Psychology, Social
Sciences
DURATION: Semester or year
COST: (S)$5,100 (Y)$9,700
PHONE NUMBER: (919) 962-7001

LOCATION: Canterbury
SPONSOR: University of Arizona
PROGRAM NAME: Academic Year at the
University of Kent
ACADEMIC FOCUS: Fine Arts, English
Literature, Religious Studies, History
DURATION: Year
COST: $12,000
PHONE NUMBER: (602) 621-4819

LOCATION: Colchester
SPONSOR: Worldstudy
PROGRAM NAME: Study in Colchester,
England
ACADEMIC FOCUS: Business, Art History,
Humanities, Law, Mathematics, Social
Sciences, Natural Sciences
DURATION: Semester or year
COST: (Fall)$6,520 (Spring)$8,900
(Year)$14,975 (RT air incl. Board not
incl.)
PHONE NUMBER: (800) 780-1095

LOCATION: Exeter
SPONSOR: University of Kansas
PROGRAM NAME: Academic Year in
Exeter
ACADEMIC FOCUS: Earth Sciences,
Education, Classical Studies,
Humanities, Music, Natural Sciences,
Social Sciences
DURATION: Year
COST: $12,300
PHONE NUMBER: (913) 864-3742

LOCATION: Leeds
SPONSOR: University of Leeds
PROGRAM NAME: Junior Year Abroad
ACADEMIC FOCUS: Chemistry, Biological
Sciences, Engineering, Fine Arts,
English, Geography, History, Political
Studies, Psychology, Sociology
DURATION: Semester or year

COST: (S)$5,900 (Y)$11,200
PHONE NUMBER: 532-333-977

LOCATION: Liverpool
SPONSOR: Lock Haven University of
 Pennsylvania
PROGRAM NAME: Semester in Liverpool
ACADEMIC FOCUS: Biological Studies,
 American Studies, Drama, English,
 Education, Environmental Studies,
 Geography, History, Mathematics,
 Information Studies
DURATION: Semester
COST: $6,000
PHONE NUMBER: (717) 893-2140

LOCATION: London
SPONSOR: American Association of
 Overseas Studies
PROGRAM NAME: Acting in London
ACADEMIC FOCUS: Theater, Film Studies,
 Television
DURATION: Semester or year
COST: (S)$3,500 to $8,500 (Y)$10,000 to
 $20,000
PHONE NUMBER: (212) 724-0804

LOCATION: London
SPONSOR: Drew University
PROGRAM NAME: London Semester
ACADEMIC FOCUS: Literature, Political
 Science, Theater
DURATION: Semester
COST: $12,123
PHONE NUMBER: (201) 408-3438

LOCATION: London
SPONSOR: Ithaca College
PROGRAM NAME: London Center
ACADEMIC FOCUS: Communications, Art
 History, History, Literature, Political
 Studies, Sociology
DURATION: Semester or year
COST: (S)$13,112 (Y)$21,000 (RT air incl.)
PHONE NUMBER: (607) 274-3306

LOCATION: London
SPONSOR: University of Pittsburgh
PROGRAM NAME: London Semester
 Program
ACADEMIC FOCUS: Art History, British

Studies, English Literature, History,
 Political Science, Theater
DURATION: Semester
COST: $5,000
PHONE NUMBER: (412) 648-7390

LOCATION: London
SPONSOR: The American College in
 London
PROGRAM NAME: London Program
ACADEMIC FOCUS: Advertising and Public
 Relations, Commercial Arts,
 Communications, Marketing, Graphic
 Arts, International Business, Interior
 Design, Photography, Studio Arts,
 Video Production, Fashion Design
DURATION: Quarter or year
COST: (Q)$5,200 (Y)$15,600 (no board)
PHONE NUMBER: (800) 255-6839

LOCATION: London
SPONSOR: Butler College
PROGRAM NAME: King's College London
ACADEMIC FOCUS: Classics, English,
 Health Studies, History, Mathematics,
 Engineering, Humanities, Languages,
 Premedical Sciences, Physical Sciences
DURATION: Semester or year
COST: (S)$9,550 (Y)$16,575
PHONE NUMBER: (317) 283-9336

LOCATION: London
SPONSOR: Sarah Lawrence College
PROGRAM NAME: London Theater
 Program
ACADEMIC FOCUS: Theater
DURATION: Semester or year
COST: (S)$12,515 (Y)$27,930
PHONE NUMBER: (914) 395-2305

LOCATION: London
SPONSOR: Tufts University
PROGRAM NAME: Tufts in London
ACADEMIC FOCUS: Economics, English,
 History, Political Science, Psychology,
 Science
DURATION: Year
COST: $26,515
PHONE NUMBER: (617) 627-3152

LOCATION: Manchester
SPONSOR: Beaver College

PROGRAM NAME: University of
Manchester
ACADEMIC FOCUS: Engineering, Public
Policy, Humanities, Social Sciences,
Technology
DURATION: Year
COST: $12,500
PHONE NUMBER: (800) 755-5607

LOCATION: Norwich
SPONSOR: Dickinson College
PROGRAM NAME: Dickinson Program In
England
ACADEMIC FOCUS: Humanities,
Mathematics, Natural Sciences, Social
Sciences
DURATION: Year
COST: $23,400
PHONE NUMBER: (717) 245-1341

LOCATION: Oxford
SPONSOR: Boston University
PROGRAM NAME: Modern British Studies
Program at Oxford University
ACADEMIC FOCUS: History, Literature,
Political Science
DURATION: Semester or year
COST: (S)$13,260 (Y)$26,520 (RT air incl.)
PHONE NUMBER: (617) 353-9888

LOCATION: Reading
SPONSOR: Beaver College
PROGRAM NAME: University of Reading
Program
ACADEMIC FOCUS: Economics,
Engineering, International Relations,
Liberal Arts, Nutrition, Science
DURATION: Semester or year
COST: (S)$10,570 (Y)14,500
PHONE NUMBER: (800) 755-5607

LOCATION: Stratford
SPONSOR: Accent International
Consortium for Academic Programs
Abroad
PROGRAM NAME: Stratford Program
ACADEMIC FOCUS: British History,
International Business, International
Relations, Theater, English Literature,
Liberal Arts, Shakespeare
DURATION: Fall semester
COST: $4,600
PHONE NUMBER: (415) 904-7756

France

LOCATION: Aix-en-Provence
SPONSOR: American University Center
PROGRAM NAME: American University
Center of Provence Program
ACADEMIC FOCUS: Art, Film Studies,
Business, French, Literature, Political
Science, Theater
DURATION: Semester or year
COST: (S)$7,900 (Y)$14,500
PHONE NUMBER: (33) (42) 38 42 38

LOCATION: Bordeaux
SPONSOR: University of Colorado/
Boulder
PROGRAM NAME: Bordeaux Program
ACADEMIC FOCUS: Art History, Business,
French, French Literature, History,
International Relations, Political
Science
DURATION: Year
COST: $16,345
PHONE NUMBER: (303) 492-7741

LOCATION: Cannes
SPONSOR: Center for Study Abroad
PROGRAM NAME: French Language and
Culture, Cannes
ACADEMIC FOCUS: Art History, French,
French History, International Business
DURATION: Semester
COST: $6,295
PHONE NUMBER: (206) 726-1498

LOCATION: Grenoble
SPONSOR: Boston University
PROGRAM NAME: Program In Grenoble
ACADEMIC FOCUS: French, Civilization
Studies, French Literature, Humanities,
Social Sciences
DURATION: Semester or year
COST: (S)$13,260 (Y)$26,520 (RT air inc.)
PHONE NUMBER: (617) 353-9888

LOCATION: Montpellier
SPONSOR: Northern Arizona University
PROGRAM NAME: Study Abroad in France
ACADEMIC FOCUS: French Studies,
General Studies
DURATION: Year
COST: $3,500 (R/B not incl.)
PHONE NUMBER: (602) 523-2409

LOCATION: Montpellier
SPONSOR: University of Miami
PROGRAM NAME: Université des Sciences et Techniques du Languedoc
ACADEMIC FOCUS: Biochemistry, Biology, Chemistry, Geology, Marine Biology, Zoology
DURATION: Semester or year
COST: (S)$9,350 (Y)$19,980
PHONE NUMBER: (305) 284-6629

LOCATION: Nice
SPONSOR: University of Maryland College Park
PROGRAM NAME: Maryland in Nice
ACADEMIC FOCUS: French, French Studies, French Literature
DURATION: Semester or year
COST: (S)$3,350 (Y)$6,250 (tuition only)
PHONE NUMBER: (301) 314-7746

LOCATION: Paris
SPONSOR: Brown University
PROGRAM NAME: Brown in France
ACADEMIC FOCUS: Full curriculum
DURATION: Semester or year
COST: (S)$10,304 (Y)$20,608
PHONE NUMBER: (401) 863-2489

LOCATION: Paris
SPONSOR: Columbia University
PROGRAM NAME: Reid Hall Programs in Paris
ACADEMIC FOCUS: Art History, Film Studies, Literature, Women's Studies, French, French Studies, History, Philosophy, Political Science
DURATION: Semester or year
COST: (S)$9,312 (Y)$18,624
PHONE NUMBER: (212) 854-2559

LOCATION: Paris
SPONSOR: Middlebury College
PROGRAM NAME: Program in France
ACADEMIC FOCUS: French, American Studies, Art History, Economics, English, Film and Media Studies, French Literature, History, International Affairs, Humanities
DURATION: Year

COST: $10,300 (tuition only)
PHONE NUMBER: (802) 388-3711

LOCATION: Paris
SPONSOR: Ohio Wesleyan University
PROGRAM NAME: Semester in Paris
ACADEMIC FOCUS: French, French Culture, French Economics
DURATION: Semester
COST: $11,200
PHONE NUMBER: (614) 368-3672

LOCATION: Paris
SPONSOR: American University
PROGRAM NAME: Semester in Paris
ACADEMIC FOCUS: Economics, European Union, French Studies, French Art, French Literature
DURATION: Semester
COST: $12,767
PHONE NUMBER: (800) 424-2600

LOCATION: Paris
SPONSOR: New York University
PROGRAM NAME: Academic Year Abroad
ACADEMIC FOCUS: Art History, French, French Studies, French Literature, International Relations, Political Science
DURATION: Semester or year
COST: (S)$5,825 (Y)$11,650 (R/B not incl.)
PHONE NUMBER: (212) 998-8720

LOCATION: Paris
SPONSOR: Wells College
PROGRAM NAME: Program for the Arts in Paris
ACADEMIC FOCUS: Art History, Studio Art, French, French Culture, Performing Arts
DURATION: Semester or year
COST: (S)$10,800 (Y)$21,000
PHONE NUMBER: (315) 364-3308

LOCATION: Pau
SPONSOR: University of Minnesota, Duluth
PROGRAM NAME: Study in France
ACADEMIC FOCUS: French, French Culture
DURATION: Semester

COST: $4,750
PHONE NUMBER: (218) 726-8229

LOCATION: Rennes
SPONSOR: Beloit College
PROGRAM NAME: Seminar in France
ACADEMIC FOCUS: Architecture, Art,
 Breton History, European Community,
 French, French History, French
 Literature
DURATION: Semester
COST: $9,990
PHONE NUMBER: (608) 363-2269

LOCATION: Rouen
SPONSOR: University of Masachusetts,
 Amherst
PROGRAM NAME: French Studies in
 Rouen and Paris
ACADEMIC FOCUS: French, French Art
 History, French Culture, French
 Literature, History
DURATION: Year
COST: $10,900
PHONE NUMBER: (413) 545-4778

LOCATION: Strasbourg
SPONSOR: Brethren Colleges Abroad
PROGRAM NAME: BCA Program in
 Strasbourg
ACADEMIC FOCUS: Full curriculum
DURATION: Semester or year
COST: (S)$8,745 (Y)$15,545
PHONE NUMBER: (219) 982-5238

LOCATION: Toulouse
SPONSOR: Dickinson College
PROGRAM NAME: Dickinson Study Center
 in Toulouse
ACADEMIC FOCUS: French Studies,
 International Relations, Political
 Science, Humanities
DURATION: Year
COST: $24,550
PHONE NUMBER: (717) 245-1341

LOCATION: Tours
SPONSOR: International Studies Abroad
PROGRAM NAME: Tours, France
ACADEMIC FOCUS: Culture Studies,
 French, French Literature, Specialized
 Option Courses, Translation
DURATION: Semester

COST: $5,350
PHONE NUMBER: (800) 580-8826

Germany

LOCATION: Nationwide
SPONSOR: University of Connecticut
PROGRAM NAME: Baden-Wurttemberg
 Exchange Program
ACADEMIC FOCUS: Computer Science,
 Business Administration, Economics,
 German, Humanities, Mathematics,
 Philosophy, Sciences, Social Sciences
DURATION: Semester or year
COST: (S)$7,000 (Y)$14,000 (RT air incl.)
PHONE NUMBER: (203) 486-5022

LOCATION: Aachen
SPONSOR: Michigan State University
PROGRAM NAME: Mechanical
 Engineering in Aachen
ACADEMIC FOCUS: Mechanical
 Engineering
DURATION: Semester
COST: $2,500 (meals not incl.)
PHONE NUMBER: (517) 355-3338

LOCATION: Berlin
SPONSOR: AIFS
PROGRAM NAME: Richmond College in
 Berlin
ACADEMIC FOCUS: Business
 Administration, Economics, German,
 German Literature, History
DURATION: Semester or year
COST: (S)$8,995 (Y)$16,185 (OW air incl.)
PHONE NUMBER: (800) 727-2437

LOCATION: Berlin
SPONSOR: Institute for European Studies
PROGRAM NAME: Berlin
ACADEMIC FOCUS: Art History, Business,
 Economics, Film Studies, German
 Studies, History, Jewish Studies,
 Political Science, Theater, Women's
 Studies
DURATION: Semester or year
COST: (S)$8,000 (Y)$13,800
PHONE NUMBER: (312) 944-1750

LOCATION: Berlin
SPONSOR: Duke University

PROGRAM NAME: Duke in Berlin
ACADEMIC FOCUS: German Language, Economics, Environmental Studies, German Literature, Literature, Politics Science
DURATION: Semester
COST: $10,100
PHONE NUMBER: (919) 684-2174

___

LOCATION: Berlin
SPONSOR: Lexia Exchange International
PROGRAM NAME: Lexia-in-Berlin
ACADEMIC FOCUS: The Arts, Eastern European Studies, European Studies, German, German Studies, Independent Study, International Business, International Relations, Political Science, Social Sciences
DURATION: Semester
COST: $8,395
PHONE NUMBER: (415) 327-9191

___

LOCATION: Bonn
SPONSOR: DePaul University
PROGRAM NAME: Study in Germany
ACADEMIC FOCUS: German, German Studies, Literature, History, and International Studies
DURATION: Quarter
COST: $9,040 (RT air incl.)
PHONE NUMBER: (312) 365-7450

___

LOCATION: Bonn
SPONSOR: Ripon College
PROGRAM NAME: International Study Center at Bonn
ACADEMIC FOCUS: German Studies
DURATION: Semester or year
COST: (S)$10,645 (Y)$16,390 (RT air incl.)
PHONE NUMBER: (414) 748-8127

___

LOCATION: Bremen
SPONSOR: Dickinson College
PROGRAM NAME: Dickinson in Bremen
ACADEMIC FOCUS: Mathematics, Humanities, Natural Sciences, Social Sciences
DURATION: Year
COST: $21,200
PHONE NUMBER: (717) 245-1341

___

LOCATION: Constance
SPONSOR: Rutgers, The State University of New Jersey

PROGRAM NAME: Study Abroad in Germany
ACADEMIC FOCUS: Economics, Communications, German, History, Linguistics, Political Science
DURATION: Year
COST: $12,530 (no board)
PHONE NUMBER: (908) 932-7787

___

LOCATION: Frankfurt
SPONSOR: University of Wisconsin–Madison
PROGRAM NAME: Frankfurt, Germany
ACADEMIC FOCUS: Natural Sciences, Humanities, Physical Sciences, Social Sciences
DURATION: Year
COST: $9,582 (R/B not incl.)
PHONE NUMBER: (608) 262-2851

___

LOCATION: Freiburg
SPONSOR: Institute of European and Asian Studies
PROGRAM NAME: Freiburg EC Program
ACADEMIC FOCUS: European Community Studies, Economics, European Studies, Political Science
DURATION: Semester
COST: $7,500 (board not incl.)
PHONE NUMBER: (800) 995-2300

___

LOCATION: Freiburg
SPONSOR: Institute of European and Asian Studies
PROGRAM NAME: Freiburg EC Program
ACADEMIC FOCUS: Economics, European Community Studies, European Studies, Political Science
DURATION: Semester or year
COST: (S)$7,500 (Y)$13,000
PHONE NUMBER: (312) 944-1750

___

LOCATION: Hamburg
SPONSOR: Beloit College
PROGRAM NAME: Hamburg Seminar
ACADEMIC FOCUS: Focus on Economics, German, German History and Literature
DURATION: Semester
COST: $10,595
PHONE NUMBER: (608) 363-2269

___

LOCATION: Hamburg
SPONSOR: Cornell University

PROGRAM NAME: Cornell Abroad in Germany
ACADEMIC FOCUS: Literature, History, Political Science, Science, Social Science.
DURATION: Semester or year
COST: (S)$11,200 (Y)$22,400 (meals not incl.)
PHONE NUMBER: (607) 255-6224

LOCATION: Heidelberg
SPONSOR: Wells College
PROGRAM NAME: Program in Germany
ACADEMIC FOCUS: Economics, German, German Literature, International Business, European History, International Relations
DURATION: Semester or year
COST: (S)$10,425 (Y)$20,850 (RT air incl.)
PHONE NUMBER: (315) $364-3304

LOCATION: Heidelberg
SPONSOR: Heidelberg College
PROGRAM NAME: The American Junior Year at Heidelberg University
ACADEMIC FOCUS: German Studies, Economics, International Relations, Liberal Arts, Political Science
DURATION: Semester or year
COST: (S)$6,740 (Y)$13,830 (meals not incl.)
PHONE NUMBER: (419) 448-2090

LOCATION: Marburg
SPONSOR: Brethren Colleges Abroad
PROGRAM NAME: BCA Program in Marburg
ACADEMIC FOCUS: Full curriculum
DURATION: Semester or year
COST: (S)$8,745 (Y)$15,545 (RT air incl.)
PHONE NUMBER: (219) 982-5238

LOCATION: Munich
SPONSOR: University of Wisconsin/ Stevens Pt.
PROGRAM NAME: Semester in Germany
ACADEMIC FOCUS: Focuses on German literature, language and culture
DURATION: Semester
COST: $4,195 (RT air incl.)
PHONE NUMBER: (715) 346-2717

LOCATION: Munich
SPONSOR: Wayne State University
PROGRAM NAME: Junior Year in Munich
ACADEMIC FOCUS: Full curriculum
DURATION: Year
COST: $12,000 (RT air incl., some meals not incl.)
PHONE NUMBER: (313) 577-4605

Greece

LOCATION: Athens
SPONSOR: Beaver College
PROGRAM NAME: Study in Greece
ACADEMIC FOCUS: Archaeology, Greek Studies, Art, Byzantine Studies, Classical Studies, Greek
DURATION: Semester or year
COST: (S)$7,700 (Y)$13,750
PHONE NUMBER: (800) 755-5607

LOCATION: Athens
SPONSOR: Brethren Colleges Abroad
PROGRAM NAME: BCA Program in Athens
ACADEMIC FOCUS: Art, Computer Studies, Business, English, Greek Culture, Liberal Arts, Psychology
DURATION: Semester or year
COST: (S)$9,395 (Y)$16,795 (RT air incl.)
PHONE NUMBER: (219) 982-5238

LOCATION: Athens
SPONSOR: DePaul University
PROGRAM NAME: Study in Greece
ACADEMIC FOCUS: International Studies, History, Philosophy, Sociology, Political Science
DURATION: Semester
COST: $12,804 (RT air incl.)
PHONE NUMBER: (312) 362-6226

LOCATION: Athens
SPONSOR: College Year in Athens
PROGRAM NAME: Program in Athens
ACADEMIC FOCUS: Anthropology, Art History, Classical Language, Literature, Philosophy, Political Science, Religious Studies, Archaeology, Classics, History, Modern Greek Studies
DURATION: Semester or year

COST: (S)$9,600 (Y)$17,900
PHONE NUMBER: (617) 547-6141

LOCATION: Hania
SPONSOR: Ithaka Cultural Study
 Programs
PROGRAM NAME: Semester in Greece
ACADEMIC FOCUS: Anthropology,
 Writing, Archaeology, Classics, History,
 Literature, Modern Greek
DURATION: Semester
COST: $9,500
PHONE NUMBER: (617) 868-4547

India

LOCATION: Nationwide
SPONSOR: SUNY/Oneonta
PROGRAM NAME: India Program
ACADEMIC FOCUS: Art, Cultural Studies,
 History, Indian Studies,
 Interdisciplinary Studies, Philosophy,
 Hindi
DURATION: Semester
COST: Unavailable
PHONE NUMBER: (607) 436-3369

LOCATION: Calcutta
SPONSOR: Partnership for Service-
 Learning
PROGRAM NAME: India Service-Learning
ACADEMIC FOCUS: Asian Studies, Liberal
 Arts, Humanities, International
 Studies, Social Sciences
DURATION: Semester
COST: $7,300
PHONE NUMBER: (212) 986-0989

LOCATION: Delhi
SPONSOR: University of Massachusetts,
 Amherst
PROGRAM NAME: IIT Exchange
ACADEMIC FOCUS: Biology, Chemistry,
 Computer Science, Engineering,
 Mathematics, Physics
DURATION: Year
COST: $9,400
PHONE NUMBER: (413) 545-2710

LOCATION: Hyderabad
SPONSOR: University of Wisconsin–
 Madison

PROGRAM NAME: Year in India-
 Hyderabad
ACADEMIC FOCUS: Language, Performing
 Arts, Religious Studies, Social Sciences
DURATION: Year
COST: $10,500 (OW air incl.)
PHONE NUMBER: (608) 262-2851

LOCATION: Madras
SPONSOR: Davidson College
PROGRAM NAME: Semester in India
 Program
ACADEMIC FOCUS: Art History, Sociology,
 Contemporary Issues, History, Religion,
 Independent Study
DURATION: Semester
COST: $11,250 (RT air incl.)
PHONE NUMBER: (704) 892-2250

Ireland

LOCATION: Nationwide
SPONSOR: Northeastern University
PROGRAM NAME: Ireland: North and
 South
ACADEMIC FOCUS: Economics, History,
 Government, Political Science,
 Sociology
DURATION: Two quarters
COST: (Q)$7,950
PHONE NUMBER: (617) 373-5162

LOCATION: Cork
SPONSOR: Butler University
PROGRAM NAME: University College Cork
ACADEMIC FOCUS: The Arts, Archaeology,
 Folklore, Music, Social Work, Business,
 European Studies, Gaelic, Irish Studies,
 Science
DURATION: Semester or year
COST: (S)$7,975 (Y)$12,995
PHONE NUMBER: (317) 283-9336

LOCATION: Cork
SPONSOR: Colby College
PROGRAM NAME: Colby in Cork
ACADEMIC FOCUS: Art, Biology, English,
 History, International Studies, Irish
 Studies
DURATION: Semester or year
COST: (S)$13,200 (Y)$24,000 (RT air incl.)
PHONE NUMBER: (207) 872-3648

LOCATION: Dublin
SPONSOR: Beaver College
PROGRAM NAME: Trinity College Dublin
ACADEMIC FOCUS: Education, English,
    History, Languages, Literature, Science
DURATION: Year
COST: $14,000
PHONE NUMBER: (800) 755-5607

LOCATION: Dublin
SPONSOR: Iona College
PROGRAM NAME: Irish Studies Program
ACADEMIC FOCUS: Irish Culture,
    International Business, Peace and
    Justice in Ireland, Irish History, Irish
    Literature
DURATION: Semester
COST: $7,500 (some meals not incl.)
PHONE NUMBER: (914) 633-2695

LOCATION: Dublin
SPONSOR: Lynn University
PROGRAM NAME: Program in Ireland
ACADEMIC FOCUS: Business, Hospitality
    Services, Liberal Arts
DURATION: Semester
COST: $6,625 (meals not incl.)
PHONE NUMBER: (407) 994-0770

LOCATION: Galway
SPONSOR: Beaver College
PROGRAM NAME: University College
    Galway
ACADEMIC FOCUS: Business, Science,
    English, Law, Liberal Arts, Political
    Science
DURATION: Semester or year
COST: (S)$6,800 (Y)$11,500
PHONE NUMBER: (800) 755-5607

LOCATION: Limerick
SPONSOR: Butler University
PROGRAM NAME: University of Limerick
ACADEMIC FOCUS: Business, Education,
    Science, Computer Science,
    Engineering, European Studies, Irish
    Studies
DURATION: Semester or year
COST: (S)$6,775 (Y)$11,550
PHONE NUMBER: (317) 283-9336

LOCATION: Limerick
SPONSOR: University of Limerick
PROGRAM NAME: Study Abroad/Irish
    Studies
ACADEMIC FOCUS: Business, Equine
    Science, Science, Sport Science,
    Education, Engineering, Humanities,
    Irish Studies
DURATION: Semester or year
COST: Unavailable
PHONE NUMBER: (353) (61) 333 644

LOCATION: Maynooth
SPONSOR: Beaver College
PROGRAM NAME: St. Patrick's College
ACADEMIC FOCUS: English, History,
    Languages, Music, Philosophy, Science
DURATION: Year
COST: $12,250
PHONE NUMBER: (800) 755-5607

Israel

LOCATION: Nationwide
SPONSOR: Israel University Center
PROGRAM NAME: Program in Israel
ACADEMIC FOCUS: Arabic, Archaeology,
    International Relations, Jewish Studies,
    Hebrew, History, Israeli Studies,
    Hebrew Studies, Middle Eastern
    Studies
DURATION: Semester or year
COST: (S)$5,000 (Y)$10,000 (meals not
    incl.)
PHONE NUMBER: (212) 339-6941

LOCATION: Beersheba
SPONSOR: Partnership for Service-
    Learning
PROGRAM NAME: Israel Service-Learning
ACADEMIC FOCUS: Education, Religious
    Studies, Social Sciences, Humanities,
    International Studies, Liberal Arts
DURATION: Semester or year
COST: (S)$6,000 (Y)$11,000 (meals not
    incl.)
PHONE NUMBER: (212) 986-0989

LOCATION: Haifa
SPONSOR: College Consortium for
    International Studies

PROGRAM NAME: Program at Haifa
  University
ACADEMIC FOCUS: Environmental
  Studies, Archaeology, Intercultural
  Studies, International Studies, Israeli
  Studies, Jewish Studies, Literature,
  Middle Eastern Studies, Philosophy and
  Religious Thought, Psychology
DURATION: Semester
COST: $4,030 (tuition only)
PHONE NUMBER: (800) 453-6956

LOCATION: Haifa
SPONSOR: Rider University
PROGRAM NAME: Study Abroad in Israel
ACADEMIC FOCUS: Cultural Studies,
  Hebrew, History, Literature, Social
  Sciences
DURATION: Semester or year
COST: (S)$6,625 (Y)$13,250 (tuition only)
PHONE NUMBER: (609) 896-5125

LOCATION: Jerusalem
SPONSOR: Earlham College
PROGRAM NAME: Great Lakes Jerusalem
  Program in Peace Studies
ACADEMIC FOCUS: Liberal Arts, Peace
  Studies
DURATION: Semester
COST: $9,548
PHONE NUMBER: (317) 983-1424

LOCATION: Jerusalem
SPONSOR: Hebrew University
PROGRAM NAME: One Year Program
ACADEMIC FOCUS: Archaeology,
  Comparative Religion, Hebrew, Israeli
  Studies, Jewish Culture, Jewish Studies,
  Middle Eastern and Islamic Studies,
  Political Science, Art History,
  International Relations
DURATION: Semester or year
COST: (S)$7,700 (Y)$13,000 (RT air incl.)
PHONE NUMBER: (212) 472-2288

LOCATION: Jerusalem
SPONSOR: Institute of Holy Land Studies
PROGRAM NAME: Study Abroad
ACADEMIC FOCUS: Biblical Studies,
  Political Science, Biblical translation,
  Hebrew, Middle Eastern Studies
DURATION: Semester or year
COST: (S)$6,000 (Y)$12,000
PHONE NUMBER: (815) 229-5900

LOCATION: Jerusalem
SPONSOR: University of Arizona
PROGRAM NAME: Rothberg School for
  Overseas Students
ACADEMIC FOCUS: Economics, History,
  Area Study
DURATION: Semester or year
COST: (S)$6,100 (Y)$12,200 (meals not
  incl.)
PHONE NUMBER: (602) 621-4819

LOCATION: Jerusalem
SPONSOR: Wesleyan University
PROGRAM NAME: Wesleyan Program in
  Israel
ACADEMIC FOCUS: Focuses on
  Anthropology, Political Science, and
  Regional Studies
DURATION: Spring semester
COST: $14,200
PHONE NUMBER: (203) 685-2550

LOCATION: Ramat Gan
SPONSOR: Bar-Ilan University
PROGRAM NAME: One year/one semester
  Program
ACADEMIC FOCUS: Humanities, Middle
  Eastern Studies, Israeli Studies, Jewish
  Studies, Natural and Social Sciences
DURATION: Semester or year
COST: (S)$7,500 (Y)$14,000
PHONE NUMBER: (212) 337-1286

Italy

LOCATION: Nationwide
SPONSOR: CCIS
PROGRAM NAME: Rome Program
ACADEMIC FOCUS: Art History,
  International Relations, Italian Studies,
  International Business, Italian, Studio
  Art
DURATION: Semester or year
COST: (S)$4,095 (Y)$8,190 (tuition only)
PHONE NUMBER: (800) 453-6956

LOCATION: Bologna
SPONSOR: Dickinson College
PROGRAM NAME: The Dickenson Center
  for European Studies
ACADEMIC FOCUS: Economics, Fine Arts,

History, International Studies, Italian, Political Science
DURATION: Year
COST: $24,570
PHONE NUMBER: (717) 245-1341

———

LOCATION: Florence
SPONSOR: AIFS
PROGRAM NAME: Richmond College Program in Florence
ACADEMIC FOCUS: Art History, Economics, Fine Arts, History, Literature, Music, Social Sciences, Business, Italian, Studio Art
DURATION: Semester or year
COST: (S)$9,195 (Y)$16,385 (OW air incl.)
PHONE NUMBER: (800) 727-2437

———

LOCATION: Florence
SPONSOR: Institute of International Education
PROGRAM NAME: International Florence Program
ACADEMIC FOCUS: Art History, Museology, Italian, Studio Art
DURATION: Semester or year
COST: (S)$9,575 (Y)$19,150 (meals not incl.)
PHONE NUMBER: (212) 984-5548

———

LOCATION: Florence
SPONSOR: Sarah Lawrence College
PROGRAM NAME: Sarah Lawrence College in Florence
ACADEMIC FOCUS: Anthropology, Music, Art History, History, Italian, Literature, Studio Art
DURATION: Tri-semesters
COST: (S)$9,310 (Y)$27,930
PHONE NUMBER: (914) 395-2305

———

LOCATION: Florence
SPONSOR: University of Connecticut
PROGRAM NAME: Florence Study Program
ACADEMIC FOCUS: Full curriculum
DURATION: Year
COST: $14,781 (RT air incl.)
PHONE NUMBER: (203) 486-5022

———

LOCATION: Rome
SPONSOR: American University
PROGRAM NAME: Semester in Rome

ACADEMIC FOCUS: Art, Architectural Studies, Film and Media Studies, History, Italian, Sociology, Theater, Liberal Arts, Literature, Music, Political Science
DURATION: Semester
COST: $11,945 (meals not incl.)
PHONE NUMBER: (202) 895-4900

———

LOCATION: Rome
SPONSOR: Temple University
PROGRAM NAME: Rome Program
ACADEMIC FOCUS: Architectural Studies, Liberal Arts, Art History, International Business, Italian, Visual Arts
DURATION: Semester or year
COST: (S)$9,351 (Y)$18,702
PHONE NUMBER: (215) 204-4684

———

LOCATION: Siena
SPONSOR: School for International Training
PROGRAM NAME: Semester Abroad in Italy
ACADEMIC FOCUS: Arts and Humanities, Economics, Geography, Social Anthropology, History, Italian, Political Science
DURATION: Semester
COST: $10,300 (RT air incl.)
PHONE NUMBER: (800) 336-1616

———

LOCATION: Venice
SPONSOR: Lexia Exchange International
PROGRAM NAME: Semester in Venice
ACADEMIC FOCUS: Economics, Business, Fine Arts, International Relations, Literature, Sociology, History, Humanities, Italian, Political Science
DURATION: Semester or year
COST: (S)$7,495 (Y)$14,990
PHONE NUMBER: (415) 327-9191

———

Japan

LOCATION: Nationwide
SPONSOR: University of Massachusetts, Amherst
PROGRAM NAME: Japan Exchanges
ACADEMIC FOCUS: Art, Social Sciences, Business Economics, Humanities, Japanese, Japanese Studies

DURATION: Year
COST: $10,000 (room not incl.)
PHONE NUMBER: (413) 545-2710

———

LOCATION: Kyoto
SPONSOR: Long Island University
PROGRAM NAME: Friends World Program Japan
ACADEMIC FOCUS: Anthropology, Peace Studies, Rural Development, Comparative Religions, Ecology, Global Women's Studies
DURATION: Semester or year
COST: (S)$11,525 (Y)$22,050
PHONE NUMBER: (516) 287-1273

———

LOCATION: Nagoya
SPONSOR: IEAS
PROGRAM NAME: Program in Nagoya
ACADEMIC FOCUS: Japanese, Studio Art, Economics, History, Business, Literature, Political Science, Sociology, Religious Studies, Japanese Studies
DURATION: Semester or year
COST: (S)$10,360 (Y)$18,700
PHONE NUMBER: (312) 944-1750

———

LOCATION: Osaka
SPONSOR: SUNY Albany
PROGRAM NAME: Kansai Gaiadai Exchange
ACADEMIC FOCUS: Asian Studies, Business Administration, Japanese, Japanese Culture
DURATION: Semester or year
COST: (S)$7,465 (Y)$14,485
PHONE NUMBER: (518) 442-3525

———

LOCATION: Sapporo
SPONSOR: Earlham College
PROGRAM NAME: Hokkaido Intensive Program
ACADEMIC FOCUS: Japanese Culture and Society, Japanese
DURATION: Two terms
COST: $13,242
PHONE NUMBER: (317) 983-1224

———

LOCATION: Tokyo
SPONSOR: CIEE
PROGRAM NAME: Council Study Center: Tokyo, Japanese Studies Program

ACADEMIC FOCUS: Japanese, Japanese Studies, Political Science
DURATION: Semester or year
COST: (S)$9,150 (Y)$17,750
PHONE NUMBER: (212) 661-1414

———

LOCATION: Tokyo
SPONSOR: IEAS
PROGRAM NAME: Tokyo-Sophia Program
ACADEMIC FOCUS: Japanese, Business Administration, Humanities, Social Sciences, Japanese Studies
DURATION: Semester or year
COST: (S)$14,500 (Y)$26,500
PHONE NUMBER: (312) 944-1750

———

LOCATION: Tokyo (Mitaka)
SPONSOR: IEAS
PROGRAM NAME: Tokyo-ICU Program
ACADEMIC FOCUS: Japanese, Humanities, Japanese Studies, Liberal Arts, Natural Sciences, Social Sciences
DURATION: Year
COST: $18,000
PHONE NUMBER: (312) 944-1750

———

LOCATION: Tokyo
SPONSOR: Oregon State
PROGRAM NAME: Waseda Exchange Program
ACADEMIC FOCUS: Art History, Economics, History, Japanese, Linguistics, Political Science
DURATION: Year
COST: $17,300
PHONE NUMBER: (503) 737-3006

———

LOCATION: Tokyo
SPONSOR: Temple University
PROGRAM NAME: Temple University Semester in Japan
ACADEMIC FOCUS: Asian Studies, Art History, Economics, History, Political Science, Religion, Japanese
DURATION: Semester or year
COST: (S)$8,290 (Y)$16,580
PHONE NUMBER: (215) 204-4684

Mexico

LOCATION: Cuernavaca
SPONSOR: Colby College

PROGRAM NAME: Colby in Cuernavaca
ACADEMIC FOCUS: Mexican Studies,
  Spanish
DURATION: Semester
COST: $13,320
PHONE NUMBER: (207) 872-3648

LOCATION: Guadalajara
SPONSOR: Beaver College
PROGRAM NAME: Study in Mexico
ACADEMIC FOCUS: The Arts, Social
  Sciences, Cultural Studies, Literature,
  Political Science, Spanish
DURATION: Semester or year
COST: (S)$6,150 (Y)$9,500
PHONE NUMBER: (800) 755-5607

LOCATION: Guadalajara
SPONSOR: Partnership for Service-
  Learning
PROGRAM NAME: Mexico Service-
  Learning
ACADEMIC FOCUS: Education, Liberal
  Arts, Sociology, Humanities,
  International Studies, Spanish
DURATION: Semester or year
COST: (S)$5,200 (Y)$9,900
PHONE NUMBER: (212) 986-0989

LOCATION: Guadalajara
SPONSOR: University of Colorado/
  Boulder
PROGRAM NAME: Study Spanish in
  Mexico
ACADEMIC FOCUS: Anthropology,
  International Relations, History,
  Literature, Spanish
DURATION: Semester
COST: $4,361
PHONE NUMBER: (303) 492-7741

LOCATION: Guanajuato
SPONSOR: International Studies Abroad
PROGRAM NAME: Program in Mexico
ACADEMIC FOCUS: Economics, Art,
  History, Law, Literature, International
  Business, Spanish
DURATION: Semester
COST: $4,975
PHONE NUMBER: (512) 480-8522

LOCATION: Merida
SPONSOR: AIFS
PROGRAM NAME: University of Yucatan
  Program
ACADEMIC FOCUS: Anthropology,
  Ecology, Archaeology, History,
  Linguistics, Spanish, Mayan Culture
DURATION: Semester or year
COST: (S)$4,985 (Y)$9,600
PHONE NUMBER: (800) 727-2437

LOCATION: Merida
SPONSOR: Rollins College
PROGRAM NAME: Rollins in Mexico
ACADEMIC FOCUS: Anthropology,
  Environmental Studies, Spanish, Latin
  America Studies
DURATION: Semester
COST: $6,250
PHONE NUMBER: (407) 646-2466

LOCATION: Mexico City
SPONSOR: Universidad Iberoamericana
PROGRAM NAME: Junior Year Abroad
ACADEMIC FOCUS: Anthropology,
  Sociology, History, Literature, Political
  Science, Spanish
DURATION: Semester or year
COST: (S)$3,353 (Y)$6,506
PHONE NUMBER: (525) 292-1883

LOCATION: Mexico City
SPONSOR: University of North Carolina
PROGRAM NAME: Mexico City
ACADEMIC FOCUS: Anthropology, Art,
  Culture, Political Science, Spanish
DURATION: Year
COST: $6,741
PHONE NUMBER: (919) 962-7001

LOCATION: Monterrey
SPONSOR: University of Wisconsin,
  Madison
PROGRAM NAME: Monterrey, Mexico
  Exchange
ACADEMIC FOCUS: Mexican Studies,
  Spanish
DURATION: Semester or year
COST: (S)$6,000 (Y)$12,000
PHONE NUMBER: (715) 836-4411

Netherlands

LOCATION: Nationwide
SPONSOR: SUNY Albany
PROGRAM NAME: Program in The
   Netherlands
ACADEMIC FOCUS: Business, Law,
   Literature, Economics, Education,
   International Studies, Languages
DURATION: Semester or year
COST: (S)$3,895 (Y)$8,139
PHONE NUMBER: (518) 442-3525

LOCATION: Amsterdam
SPONSOR: CIEE
PROGRAM NAME: Council Study Center
   at the University of Amsterdam
ACADEMIC FOCUS: Dutch, Economics,
   Geography, History, Humanities,
   Literature, European Studies,
   International Relations, Political
   Science
DURATION: Semester or year
COST: (S)$6,950 (Y)$12,510
PHONE NUMBER: (212) 661-1616

LOCATION: Haarlem
SPONSOR: Northern Arizona University
PROGRAM NAME: Study Abroad
   Netherlands
ACADEMIC FOCUS: International Business
DURATION: Semester
COST: $3,348
PHONE NUMBER: (602) 523-2409

LOCATION: Leiden
SPONSOR: Central University of Iowa
PROGRAM NAME: Central College in
   Leiden
ACADEMIC FOCUS: Dutch, History,
   International Relations, Political
   Science
DURATION: Semester or year
COST: (S)$8,200 (Y)$15,100
PHONE NUMBER: (800) 831-3629

LOCATION: Maastricht
SPONSOR: University of North Carolina/
   Chapel Hill
PROGRAM NAME: European Studies
   Program at CES in Maastricht, the
   Netherlands
ACADEMIC FOCUS: Economics,
International Business, International
   Management
DURATION: Semester
COST: $3,890
PHONE NUMBER: (919) 962-7001

New Zealand

LOCATION: Auckland
SPONSOR: Butler University
PROGRAM NAME: University of Auckland
ACADEMIC FOCUS: Anthropology,
   Engineering, Business, Economics,
   Languages, Pacific Studies, Sociology,
   Theology, Zoology, Science
DURATION: Year
COST: $11,350
PHONE NUMBER: (317) 283-9336

LOCATION: Christchurch
SPONSOR: Colorado State University
PROGRAM NAME: Lincoln University,
   New Zealand
ACADEMIC FOCUS: Agriculture, Business,
   Forestry, Maori Studies, Natural
   Resources, Natural Sciences, Parks,
   Physical Sciences, Tourism and Travel
DURATION: Semester or year
COST: (S)$6,495 (Y)$11,990
PHONE NUMBER: (303) 491-5511

LOCATION: Hamilton
SPONSOR: Colorado State University
PROGRAM NAME: Waikato University
ACADEMIC FOCUS: The Arts, Education,
   Environmental Studies, Marketing,
   New Zealand Studies, Humanities,
   Languages, Political Studies,
   Psychology, Religious Studies,
   Sociology, Women's Studies
DURATION: Semester or year
COST: (S)$6,995 (Y)$13,990
PHONE NUMBER: (303) 491-5511

LOCATION: Wellington
SPONSOR: Butler University, Institute for
   Study Abroad
PROGRAM NAME: Victoria University of
   Wellington
ACADEMIC FOCUS: Anthropology, The
   Arts, Commerce, Maori Studies,

Political Science, Science, Theater and
Film
DURATION: Year
COST: $11,550
PHONE NUMBER: (800) 858-0229

Poland

LOCATION: Krakow
SPONSOR: DePaul University
PROGRAM NAME: Quarter Abroad in
Krakow
ACADEMIC FOCUS: Commerce,
International Studies, Liberal Arts,
Polish
DURATION: Semester
COST: $7,000
PHONE NUMBER: (312) 362-6226

LOCATION: Krakow
SPONSOR: Lexia Exchange International
PROGRAM NAME: Semester in Krakow
ACADEMIC FOCUS: Arts, Anthropology,
Business, Literature, Slavic Studies,
Sociology, Economics, History,
Humanities, Political Science
DURATION: Semester or year
COST: (S)$5,995 (Y)$11,495
PHONE NUMBER: (415) 327-9191

LOCATION: Krakow
SPONSOR: University of Wisconsin-
Stevens Pt.
PROGRAM NAME: Semester in Poland
ACADEMIC FOCUS: Geography, History,
Polish, Polish Culture, Political Science
DURATION: Semester
COST: $4,500
PHONE NUMBER: (715) 346-2717

LOCATION: Lublin
SPONSOR: Lock Haven University of
Pennsylvania
PROGRAM NAME: Semester in Poland
ACADEMIC FOCUS: Culture Studies,
Economics, History, Polish, Polish
Studies
DURATION: Semester
COST: $6,000 (airfare not incl.)
PHONE NUMBER: (717) 893-2140

LOCATION: Poznan
SPONSOR: Brown University
PROGRAM NAME: Brown in Poland
ACADEMIC FOCUS: Drama, Economics,
History, Philosophy, Polish Literature,
Sociology
DURATION: Semester or year
COST: (S)$9,764 (Y)$19,528
PHONE NUMBER: (401) 863-3555

LOCATION: Poznan
SPONSOR: University of Massachusetts,
Amherst
PROGRAM NAME: Study in Poland
ACADEMIC FOCUS: Civilization Studies,
Economics, Literature, Polish, Political
Science
DURATION: Semester or year
COST: (S)$6,300 (Y)$12,600
PHONE NUMBER: (413) 545-2710

LOCATION: Warsaw
SPONSOR: CIEE
PROGRAM NAME: Council Study Center
at the Warsaw School of Economics
ACADEMIC FOCUS: Polish, Fine Arts,
History, Sociology, Economics, Political
Science
DURATION: Semester
COST: $5,300
PHONE NUMBER: (212) 661-1414

Puerto Rico

LOCATION: Mayaguez
SPONSOR: SUNY Oswego
PROGRAM NAME: Business
Administration Program in Puerto Rico
ACADEMIC FOCUS: Accounting, Human
Resources, Business, Economics,
Industrial Management, Marketing
DURATION: Semester or year
COST: (S)$4,800 (Y)$9,600
PHONE NUMBER: (315) 341-2477

LOCATION: Ponce
SPONSOR: Rider University
PROGRAM NAME: Study Abroad in Puerto
Rico

ACADEMIC FOCUS: Bilingual Education, Puerto Rican Culture, Spanish
DURATION: Semester or year
COST: (S)$6,625 (Y)$13,250
PHONE NUMBER: (609) 896-5125

LOCATION: San Juan
SPONSOR: SUNY Oswego
PROGRAM NAME: University of Puerto Rico Exchange
ACADEMIC FOCUS: Education, Humanities, Social Sciences
DURATION: Semester or year
COST: (S)$5,810 (Y)$11,620
PHONE NUMBER: (315) 341-2118

Russia

LOCATION: Nationwide
SPONSOR: Virtus Institute
PROGRAM NAME: Russia as She Is
ACADEMIC FOCUS: Russian Art, Architecture, Area Studies, Geography, History, Culture, Economics, Russian, Political Science, Russian Literature
DURATION: Semester or year
COST: (S)$6,980 (Y)$14,310
PHONE NUMBER: (800) 274-9121

LOCATION: Nationwide
SPONSOR: Boston University
PROGRAM NAME: Moscow Internship Program
ACADEMIC FOCUS: Economics, Russian Drama, Russian Media, International Relations, Political Studies, Russian
DURATION: Semester
COST: $7,900
PHONE NUMBER: (317) 353-9888

LOCATION: Moscow
SPONSOR: American University
PROGRAM NAME: Semester in Moscow
ACADEMIC FOCUS: Political Science, Practicum, Russian, Russian Studies
DURATION: Semester
COST: $10,950
PHONE NUMBER: (202) 895-4900

LOCATION: Moscow
SPONSOR: Pushkin Institute Consortium

PROGRAM NAME: OSU-Purdue-Emory Russian Language Program
ACADEMIC FOCUS: Russian Language
DURATION: Semester
COST: $3,600
PHONE NUMBER: (800) 768-6139

LOCATION: Rostov-on-Don
SPONSOR: University of North Carolina at Chapel Hill
PROGRAM NAME: Program in Rostov, Russia
ACADEMIC FOCUS: Political Science, Russian, Russian Art and Culture
DURATION: Semester or year
COST: (S)$3,164 (Y)$6,328 (airfare not incl.)
PHONE NUMBER: (919) 962-7001

LOCATION: St. Petersburg
SPONSOR: AIFS
PROGRAM NAME: St. Petersburg State Technical University Program
ACADEMIC FOCUS: Art History, History, Literature, Political Science, Russian, Russian Art and Culture
DURATION: Semester or year
COST: (S)$4,785 (Y)$9,100
PHONE NUMBER: (800) 727-2437

LOCATION: St. Petersburg
SPONSOR: Colby College
PROGRAM NAME: Colby in St. Petersburg
ACADEMIC FOCUS: Russian, Russian Studies, Russian Literature
DURATION: Semester
COST: $13,320
PHONE NUMBER: (207) 872-3648

LOCATION: St. Petersburg
SPONSOR: Duke University
PROGRAM NAME: Duke in St. Petersburg
ACADEMIC FOCUS: Russian, Media Studies, Russian Art and Culture
DURATION: Semester
COST: $10,200
PHONE NUMBER: (919) 684-2765

LOCATION: St. Petersburg
SPONSOR: University of Massachusetts, Amherst
PROGRAM NAME: Fall Program in Russia

ACADEMIC FOCUS: Independent Study,
  Russian, Russian Studies
DURATION: Fall semester
COST: $6,500
PHONE NUMBER: (413) 545-2710

LOCATION: St. Petersburg
SPONSOR: University of Minnesota
PROGRAM NAME: Russian in St.
  Petersburg
ACADEMIC FOCUS: Russian Literature,
  Russian Studies, Russian
DURATION: Semester
COST: $3,850
PHONE NUMBER: (612) 625-3379

Scotland

LOCATION: Aberdeen
SPONSOR: Beaver College
PROGRAM NAME: University of Aberdeen
ACADEMIC FOCUS: Art History,
  Humanities, Natural Sciences,
  Religion, Social Sciences
DURATION: Semester or year
COST: (S)$7,750 (Y)$13,575
PHONE NUMBER: (800) 755-5607

LOCATION: Edinburgh
SPONSOR: Colorado State University
PROGRAM NAME: Scotland Program
ACADEMIC FOCUS: Fine Arts, History,
  Literature, Planning, Political Studies,
  Recreation, Scottish Studies, Social
  Sciences, Economics, Geography
DURATION: Semester
COST: $4,995
PHONE NUMBER: (303) 491-5511

LOCATION: Edinburgh
SPONSOR: Queen Margaret College
PROGRAM NAME: Study Abroad
ACADEMIC FOCUS: Business,
  Communication, Heath Studies, Hotel
  Management, Management, Nutrition,
  Psychology, Theater, Tourism and
  Travel, Marketing
DURATION: Semester or year
COST: (S)$4,400 (Y)$9,600
PHONE NUMBER: (44) (31) 317 3000

LOCATION: Edinburgh
SPONSOR: University of Delaware
PROGRAM NAME: Spring Semester in
  Scotland
ACADEMIC FOCUS: Art History,
  Educational Studies, Geography,
  History
DURATION: Spring semester
COST: $8,065
PHONE NUMBER: (302) 831-2852

LOCATION: Edinburgh
SPONSOR: University of North Carolina/
  Chapel Hill
PROGRAM NAME: Year at the University
  of Edinburgh, Scotland
ACADEMIC FOCUS: American Studies,
  Arts, British Studies, Classics,
  Economics, Humanities, International
  Studies
DURATION: Semester or year
COST: (S)$9,840 (Y)$18,265
PHONE NUMBER: (919) 962-7001

LOCATION: Glasgow
SPONSOR: Beaver College
PROGRAM NAME: University of Glasgow
ACADEMIC FOCUS: Arts, Engineering,
  Humanities, Natural Sciences, Social
  Sciences
DURATION: Semester or year
COST: (S)$6,000 (Y)$14,500
PHONE NUMBER: (800) 755-5607

LOCATION: Glasgow
SPONSOR: Beloit College
PROGRAM NAME: Glasgow Seminar
ACADEMIC FOCUS: Science, Scottish
  Studies
DURATION: Semester
COST: $10,592
PHONE NUMBER: (608) 363-2269

LOCATION: Glasgow
SPONSOR: Butler University
PROGRAM NAME: University of Glasgow
ACADEMIC FOCUS: Archaeology,
  Business, English, Film and Television,
  History, Law, Russian Studies,
  Sciences, Scottish Studies, Social
  Sciences, Theater Arts
DURATION: Semester or year

COST: (S)$8,575 (Y)$13,450
PHONE NUMBER: (317) 283-9336

LOCATION: Glasgow
SPONSOR: Partnership for Service-
Learning
PROGRAM NAME: Scotland Service-
Learning
ACADEMIC FOCUS: Humanities,
International Studies, Liberal Arts,
Social Sciences
DURATION: Semester or year
COST: (S)$7,100
PHONE NUMBER: (212) 986-0989

LOCATION: Glasgow
SPONSOR: University of North Carolina/
Chapel Hill
PROGRAM NAME: Glasgow, Scotland
ACADEMIC FOCUS: Business, Economics,
International Relations, Liberal Arts,
Political Science, Science, Scottish
History
DURATION: Semester or year
COST: (S)$9,586 (Y)$17,856
PHONE NUMBER: (919) 962-7001

Spain

LOCATION: Alicante
SPONSOR: Council on International
Educational Exchange
PROGRAM NAME: Council Study Center
at the University of Alicante
ACADEMIC FOCUS: Business, Art History,
Economics, History, Political Science,
Spanish, Sociology
DURATION: Semester or year
COST: (S)$6,950 (Y)$11,950
PHONE NUMBER: (212) 661-1414

LOCATION: Barcelona
SPONSOR: SUNY-Oswego
PROGRAM NAME: Barcelona Program
ACADEMIC FOCUS: Spanish, Spanish
Studies, European History
DURATION: Spring semester or year
COST: (S)$7,000 (Y)$14,000 (RT air incl.)
PHONE NUMBER: (315) 341-2118

LOCATION: Granada
SPONSOR: Northern Arizona University

PROGRAM NAME: Study Abroad in Spain
ACADEMIC FOCUS: History, Spanish
grammar, Spanish Literature, Art
DURATION: Semester
COST: $5,200
PHONE NUMBER: (602) 523-2409

LOCATION: Granada
SPONSOR: University of Connecticut
PROGRAM NAME: Spanish Language and
Society in Granada
ACADEMIC FOCUS: Spanish, Liberal Arts,
Literature
DURATION: Semester or year
COST: (S)$6,300 (Y)$12,600
PHONE NUMBER: (203) 486-5022

LOCATION: Madrid
SPONSOR: St. Lawrence University
PROGRAM NAME: Spain Program
ACADEMIC FOCUS: Art and Architecture,
Economics, Environmental Studies,
History, International Business,
Political Science, Sociology
DURATION: Semester or year
COST: (S)$12,225 (Y)$24,450
PHONE NUMBER: (315) 379-5991

LOCATION: Madrid
SPONSOR: Skidmore College
PROGRAM NAME: Study Abroad Madrid
ACADEMIC FOCUS: Art, Business,
Economics, Government, Literature,
Psychology, Women's Studies
DURATION: Semester or year
COST: (S)$10,850 (Y)$21,700
PHONE NUMBER: (518) 584-5000

LOCATION: Madrid
SPONSOR: American University
PROGRAM NAME: Semester in Madrid
ACADEMIC FOCUS: Foreign Policy,
History, Spanish, Spanish Studies,
History, Politics
DURATION: Semester
COST: $12,445
PHONE NUMBER: (202) 958-4900

LOCATION: Madrid
SPONSOR: DePaul University
PROGRAM NAME: Quarter Abroad in
Madrid

ACADEMIC FOCUS: Spanish, Spanish
Literature
DURATION: Semester
COST: $8,000
PHONE NUMBER: (312) 362-6226

LOCATION: Madrid
SPONSOR: Middlebury College
PROGRAM NAME: Program in Spain
ACADEMIC FOCUS: Spanish, Spanish
Culture, Spanish Literature
DURATION: Semester or year
COST: (S)$11,430 (Y)$21,100
PHONE NUMBER: (802) 388-3711, x 5538

LOCATION: Madrid
SPONSOR: Syracuse University
PROGRAM NAME: Semester/Year in Spain
ACADEMIC FOCUS: Anthropology,
Communications, Economics, Fine
Arts, Geography, Political Science,
Women's Studies
DURATION: Semester or year
COST: (S)$11,155 (Y)$21,060
PHONE NUMBER: (800) 235-3472

LOCATION: Malaga
SPONSOR: Dickinson College
PROGRAM NAME: Dickinson in Spain
ACADEMIC FOCUS: Literature, Spanish,
Spanish Culture
DURATION: Semester or year
COST: (S)$11,970 (Y)$23,800
PHONE NUMBER: (315) 437-5605

LOCATION: Oviedo
SPONSOR: University of Massachusetts,
Amherst
PROGRAM NAME: Semester in Spain
ACADEMIC FOCUS: Culture, Spanish,
Spanish Literature
DURATION: Semester
COST: $4,500
PHONE NUMBER: (413) 545-2887

LOCATION: Salamanca
SPONSOR: International Studies Abroad
PROGRAM NAME: Salamanca, Spain
ACADEMIC FOCUS: Cultural Studies,
Literature, Spanish
DURATION: Semester or year

COST: (S)$4,950 (Y)$11,000
PHONE NUMBER: (800) 580-8826

LOCATION: Salamanca
SPONSOR: Ohio Wesleyan University
PROGRAM NAME: Semester at Salamanca
ACADEMIC FOCUS: Spanish, Spanish
Architecture, Spanish Art, Spanish
Culture, Spanish History, Spanish
Literature, Spanish Society
DURATION: Semester
COST: $10,500
PHONE NUMBER: (614) 368-3680

LOCATION: Salamanca
SPONSOR: AIFS
PROGRAM NAME: University of
Salamanca
ACADEMIC FOCUS: Art History,
Economics, History, Languages,
Spanish
DURATION: Semester or year
COST: (S)$7,585 (Y)$13,400
PHONE NUMBER: (800) 727-2437

LOCATION: Salamanca
SPONSOR: IEAS
PROGRAM NAME: Salamanca
ACADEMIC FOCUS: Art History,
Economics, History, International
Relations, Political Science, Religious
Studies, Sociology, Spanish, Spanish
Literature
DURATION: Semester or year
COST: (S)$8,300 (Y)$14,000
PHONE NUMBER: (312) 944-1750

LOCATION: Seville
SPONSOR: International Studies Abroad
PROGRAM NAME: Program in Sevilla,
Spain
ACADEMIC FOCUS: Art History, Cultural
Studies, Geography, History, Spanish,
Spanish Cinema
DURATION: Semester or year
COST: (S)$5,650 (Y)$11,000 (airfare not
incl.)
PHONE NUMBER: (800) 580-8826

LOCATION: Seville
SPONSOR: CIEE
PROGRAM NAME: Council Study Center:

Liberal Arts Program at the University of Seville
ACADEMIC FOCUS: Anthropology, Art History, Language, Geography, History, Linguistics, Literature, Political Science, Spanish, Teaching English as a Second Language
DURATION: Year
COST: $13,365
PHONE NUMBER: (212) 661-1414

LOCATION: Seville
SPONSOR: Sweet Briar College
PROGRAM NAME: Junior Year in Spain
ACADEMIC FOCUS: Arabic, Arabic Studies, Art History, European History, Geography, International Relations, Latin American Studies, Romance Languages, Spanish, Spanish Literature
DURATION: Semester or year
COST: (S)$9,650 (Y)$16,120
PHONE NUMBER: (804) 381-6295

LOCATION: Valencia
SPONSOR: Rutgers, The State University of New Jersey
PROGRAM NAME: Study Abroad in Spain
ACADEMIC FOCUS: Art History, History, Political Science, Spanish, Spanish Literature, Sociology
DURATION: Year
COST: $15,830
PHONE NUMBER: (908) 932-7787

Sweden

LOCATION: Karlstad
SPONSOR: University of Karlstad
PROGRAM NAME: Study in English
ACADEMIC FOCUS: Computer Science, Scandinavian Literature, Swedish Politics, Economics, Geography, Immigration and Ethnicity, International Marketing, Regional Studies, Service Management
DURATION: Semester or year
COST: (S)$4,000 (Y)$8,000
PHONE NUMBER: (54) 838000

LOCATION: Linkoping
SPONSOR: University of Wisconsin–Madison

PROGRAM NAME: Linkoping, Sweden Exchange
ACADEMIC FOCUS: Scandinavian History, Languages, Literature, Politics, Business, Engineering, Natural Sciences, Social Sciences
DURATION: Year
COST: $8,829
PHONE NUMBER: (608) 262-2851

LOCATION: Lund
SPONSOR: Lund University
PROGRAM NAME: Study in Sweden
ACADEMIC FOCUS: Ecology, Environmental Studies, International Economics, International Affairs, Scandinavian Studies, Social Welfare and Services, Swedish Studies, Swedish
DURATION: Semester
COST: (S)$5,930
PHONE NUMBER: (208) 523-1039

LOCATION: Stockholm
SPONSOR: Swedish Program Consortium
PROGRAM NAME: The Swedish Program
ACADEMIC FOCUS: Economics, Education, Environmental Studies, Film and Media Studies, Health Studies, International Relations, Literature, Public Policy, Sociology, Women's Studies
DURATION: Semester or year
COST: (S)$11,575 (Y)$21,400
PHONE NUMBER: (315) 737-0123

LOCATION: Växjö
SPONSOR: University of Wisconsin-Eau Claire
PROGRAM NAME: Växjö Exchange
ACADEMIC FOCUS: Business, Intercultural Studies
DURATION: Semester or year
COST: (S)$3,691 (Y)$7,382
PHONE NUMBER: (715) 836-4411

Switzerland

LOCATION: Engelberg
SPONSOR: Schiller International University
PROGRAM NAME: Study Abroad—SIU Engelberg Campus

ACADEMIC FOCUS: Hotel Management,
   International Business
DURATION: Semester or year
COST: (S)$5,570 (Y)$11,140
PHONE NUMBER: (800) 336-4133

———

LOCATION: Fribourg
SPONSOR: La Salle University
PROGRAM NAME: La Salle in Europe
ACADEMIC FOCUS: French, German,
   International Studies, Liberal Arts
DURATION: Year
COST: $15,220
PHONE NUMBER: (215) 951-1200

———

LOCATION: Geneva
SPONSOR: Cornell University
PROGRAM NAME: Cornell in Geneva
ACADEMIC FOCUS: Education, History,
   International Studies, Languages,
   Literature, Mathematics, Science,
   Social Sciences
DURATION: Year

COST: $23,790
PHONE NUMBER: (607) 255-6224

———

LOCATION: Geneva
SPONSOR: Smith College
PROGRAM NAME: Junior Year in Geneva
ACADEMIC FOCUS: Development Studies,
   Economics, European Studies, French,
   French Literature, French Studies,
   International Relations, Political
   Science, Psychology
DURATION: Year
COST: $24,080
PHONE NUMBER: (413) 585-4905

———

LOCATION: Lausanne
SPONSOR: University of Miami
PROGRAM NAME: University of Lausanne,
   Switzerland
ACADEMIC FOCUS: Business, French,
   Law, Liberal Arts, Public
   Administration, Science
DURATION: Semester or year
COST: (S)$12,600 (Y)$25,200
PHONE NUMBER: (800) 557-5421

We'd like to continue to update and improve this book, and would appreciate any feedback or information you wish to give. Doubtless there are also programs out there that we did not review that many people think deserve to be in our next edition. We'd love to hear about them. Please send any information, brochures, or comments to: Walkabout Publications, 530 Walton Ave., Mamaroneck, NY 10543. Or you can E-mail us at: Walkabout 6@aol.com